A Call to Excellence

An essential guide to practical Christian leadership

Paul Beasley-Murray

Hodder & Stoughton
LONDON SYDNEY AUCKLAND

British Library Cataloguing in Publication Data
A record for this book is available from the British Library.

ISBN 0 340 63037 X

Typeset by Hewer Text Composition Services, Edinburgh
Printed and bound in Great Britain by
Cox & Wyman Ltd, Reading, Berks

Hodder & Stoughton Ltd
A division of Hodder Headline PLC
338 Euston Road
London NW1 3BH

To Caroline
my loyal companion in ministry

'Many women have done excellently,
but you surpass them all!'
(Proverbs 31:29)

A CALL TO EXCELLENCE

Contents

Acknowledgements

In this 25th year of my ordination to the Christian ministry, I wish in the first place to acknowledge the debt I owe to my father, George Raymond Beasley-Murray, who in his ministry of preaching, teaching and writing, has consistently set an inspiring model of excellence to me.

Secondly, I wish to thank those many friends who have stood by me in all the ups and downs of ministry, and in the process have helped me to grow as a person and thereby develop as a Christian leader.

Thirdly, I wish to thank publicly the members of Victoria Road South Baptist Church, Chelmsford, for so generously giving me time to write. Their active encouragement of my ministry beyond Chelmsford is much appreciated.

Fourthly, I am grateful for the facilities afforded me by the libraries of South Western Baptist Theological Seminary, Dallas, Texas, and of Tyndale House, Cambridge.

Finally, I wish to acknowledge all the practical help given to me in the production of this book, both by James Catford and Elspeth Taylor and the team at Hodders, and also by Carol Bulkeley and Helen Marr here in Chelmsford.

Introduction

Ministry in crisis

In many parts of the world Christian ministry is in crisis. And yet, strangely, God's people seem to be oblivious to it.

In Australia, for instance, there are 10,000 ex-pastors; about the same number as those serving in parishes of all denominations. The mind boggles at such a massive haemorrhaging. Rowland Croucher has made a detailed survey of many of these pastors and reports that only 'a quarter left without the hurt, conflict, loss of health, or boredom that characterized the majority'.[1] For most, the pain involved in leaving pastoral ministry was immense.

In the USA the situation is not much better. David McKenna, in a perceptive article written some years ago, wrote:

> Sometimes the ministerial profession looks like a desert over which a cowboy has ridden and moved on, leaving the debris of burned-out pastors on the trail behind. Broken-down, burned-out and cast-off former pastors sit on the sidelines in our churches, sell real estate for a livelihood, and serve as guidance counselors in the public schools. If they could be renewed rather than rejected, there would be no shortage of pastors.[2]

The British scene may not be so dire. And yet as far as some of the main-line denominations are concerned, the figures are still

[1] Rowland Croucher, 'Why Clergy are leaving the church', *Ministry Today* 1 (1994), p. 41.
[2] David L. McKenna, 'Recycling Pastors', *Leadership* I (Fall 1980), pp. 18–19.

disconcerting. For example, a few years ago I went through the names of all those who had been trained for the Baptist ministry at Spurgeon's College, London, in the period 1955–85. During those 30 years 406 students left Spurgeon's to serve in Baptist churches: but of this number only 268 stayed the course. Of the remaining 138, 38 moved into some other form of Christian ministry – whether in a parachurch organisation or in some other denomination – but 100 left Christian ministry altogether. In other words, 25% of those trained at Spurgeon's and subsequently ordained left the Christian ministry altogether. Indeed, the final fall-out figure will almost certainly be higher: there is still plenty of time for a good number of those trained in the 1970s and early 1980s to leave Baptist ministry. It could well be that ultimately almost one third of those trained at Spurgeon's will not remain in Christian ministry. What is more, Spurgeon's is not exceptional – indeed, some theological colleges may have an even higher percentage of their graduates no longer in Christian ministry. Certainly there is no reason to believe that ministerial fall-out is substantially lessening.[3]

Post-ordination perils

Roy Oswald of the Alban Institute has graphically spelt out the perils of ministry.[4]

> The following are some of the things we should anticipate will happen to the clergy we ordain and send into the ministry:
> 1. Some will be unable to endure the stress of ministry and will experience physical and emotional breakdown.
> 2. Approximately a quarter of these clergy will experience a failed marriage.
> 3. Within the first ten years of parish ministry, roughly half will either be fired by their congregations or forced to move.

[3] *Taking Stock (the report of the Committee of Enquiry into the state of the Ministry among Scottish Baptists)* (Baptist Union of Scotland, Glasgow 1986) 3 reported that 'the number of resignations annually has doubled since 1981'.
[4] Roy Oswald in a foreword to *Caring For The Caregiver* by Gary L. Harbaugh, (The Alban Institute, Bethesda, 1992), pp. vi–vii.

Another 15% will be forced out of their parishes during the last ten years of ministry.

4. Some will lose their sense of call and begin placing money and status above the goals of the kingdom.
5. Some will lose all sense of physical stewardship and allow their bodies to balloon to double their normal weight – making them far less credible healers in their members' eyes.
6. Some will get so caught up in ministry successes and workaholic behaviour that they will cease being good models of Grace.
7. Some will enter new parishes and 'shoot themselves in the foot' in the first six months through serious mistakes in judgment.
8. Some will burn out and become exhausted, cynical, disillusioned, self-deprecating clergy.
9. Some are simply not suited for parish ministry and will need a way to exit gracefully.
10. Some will experience personal tragedy and be unable to function for a number of months.
11. Some are going to be caught in sexual malfeasance.
12. Some are simply going to die trying to be effective clergy.

Ministry may be a high calling – but it certainly seems to involve high risk!

Mid-ministry blues

As one ordained into the Christian ministry some 25 years ago, it is perhaps not unnatural that one of my concerns relates to how pastors cope with the 'mid-ministry blues'. The fact is that most, if not all pastors either consciously or unconsciously experience the mid-ministry blues. The mid-ministry blues is the ministerial form of the mid-life crisis to which everybody is subject. These 'blues' may take various forms. For some it involves a crisis of identity: 'Who am I?' For others it may involve a crisis of theology: 'What do I believe?' For yet others there may well be a crisis of meaning: 'What is ministry all about?'

Mid-life is a time when idealism meets realism. The former is well characterised by Ray Ragsdale: 'Most ministers begin their careers with lofty ideals and high expectations. Their commitment is to serve God and humankind, and there is just enough of the *messiah complex* in the young to believe they are going to change the world before they are done.'[5] But with the passing of the years such idealism normally fails to deliver the goods. Mega-status is not for most of us.

The mid-ministry blues, however, do not simply spring from failing to make it to the 'Big Church'. It is often also linked with seeing one's peers, some of whom are apparently less gifted than ourselves, receiving the call to larger churches. To quote one cynical minister: 'Thirst for career status, measured in terms of membership, staff size, and church location, makes for a subtle rat race in which ministers vie with one another under a smoke screen of piosity.'[6] It can prove spiritually and emotionally debilitating when one fails to make it in this ministerial rat race.

Part of the crisis in Christian ministry is to be found in the fact that there are a good number of pastors who have succumbed to the mid-ministry blues. Although they may not have physically left the ministry, in their hearts they have opted out. Burnt-out and disillusioned, their earlier joy and enthusiasm for pastoral ministry has long since gone. Satisfaction, if gained at all, is found outside the normal routines of ministerial life – whether it be in some special involvement in the community, or in sitting on some denominational board, or engaging in some theological research project . . . Clearly there is nothing wrong with any such interest. Indeed, there is a lot to be said for pastors pursuing an interest beyond the local church. But if such interests dominate and become the all-consuming passion, then there is cause for concern. The health of the ministry is in jeopardy where pastors are no longer in love with their calling.

Unwanted grey hairs
There is yet another aspect to this crisis in ministry: ageism. Churches are rejecting older men (and women). For many churches

[5] Ray W. Ragsdale, *The Midlife Crisis Of A Minister* (Word Books, Waco, 1978), p. 40.
[6] Quoted by Ragsdale, *The Midlife Crisis Of A Minister*, p. 41.

the ideal pastor is in his early thirties, married with two children, and with 20 years of experience under his belt! The result is that by and large there is no demand for the older pastor. In a denomination like the Baptists, it is a general rule of thumb that after 53 one is 'on the shelf' and that for the most part one is unlikely to receive a fresh call to another church. To make matters worse, not only are some of these older pastors stuck; they are also in danger of being pushed out by their churches in favour of a younger person.

Correspondence in the *Baptist Times* has reflected something of the difficulties experienced by pastors within at least one major main-line denomination. For example, one anonymous correspondent wrote:

> At a time when we are being told the harvest is ripe but the workers are few the obstacles that are put in front of those (over 50) who are seeking positions of full-time service are enormous. Speaking personally they bring a sense of failure, rejection and the scrap heap.[7]

The 'ministry crisis' is perhaps best summed up by a tongue-in-cheek letter from Michael Docker:

> Possible solutions to the problem of ministry fall-out are being offered from various directions, most of them helpful, to my ears at least. But if you add to fall-out – burn-out, and bear in mind the students having trouble finding pastorates – miss-out; not forgetting the older ministers clinging on because of not being able to move – push-out; and the smaller number of ministers who stay whilst wishing they could leave – want-out; to say nothing of the rest of us wondering how long before we are clapped-out, you are reminded of the standard advice of area superintendents to prospective candidates for ministry – 'Stay out, if you can'.[8]

A call to excellence
It is in such a context that this book is being written. For while *A Call to Excellence* does not pretend to be the universal panacea to

[7] *Baptist Times*, 4 August 1994.
[8] *Baptist Times*, 7 January 1993.

all the problems of Christian ministry, it does seek to offer a way forward. For where excellence is a constant pursuit in the practice of ministry, there growth and development amongst pastors take place. It is my conviction that this is the key to coping with the inevitable challenges of ministry.

This book is written with more than one audience in view. In the first place, it is written with the young pastor in mind: there is much to be said for adopting the pursuit of excellence right from the beginning of one's ministry. However, *A Call to Excellence* is also written to help older pastors cope with the inevitable mid-ministry blues; hopefully it will give them opportunity to reflect theologically on their ministry and to update their skills through the gaining of new ideas.

A personal note

On a more personal note, I am writing this book in the 25th year of my ordination to the Christian ministry. I have *survived*, and God willing, I shall stay the course for another 15 years or more. I began my ministry with the Baptist Missionary Society, teaching New Testament and Greek in the new Protestant Theological Faculty of the National University of Zaire. Uncomfortable with training pastors when I had never been a pastor myself, I returned home and for 13 years was the minister of Altrincham Baptist Church, Cheshire. The next six years were spent as Principal of Spurgeon's College, a Baptist theological college in South London. Since 1993 I have been senior minister of Victoria Road South Baptist Church in Chelmsford, Essex.

I am writing this book too not just as one who has survived a quarter of a century of ministry, but also as one still very much committed to *pastoral* ministry. Interestingly, at the point when I was seeking to return to pastoral ministry from my period as a college principal, some of my friends who had left the pastorate for denominational positions actively sought to dissuade me from returning to a local church. The clear assumption was that it may be fine to cut your ministerial teeth in a local church, but if you've got any pretensions to be a high-flyer, then you'll certainly not want to return. One friend, for instance, felt very strongly that, after having experienced the heady world of 'translocal' ministry, I would soon feel bored with the pastorate. To such a friend I would reply that after two years back in pastoral ministry the last thing I am is bored. For me the local church is at the cutting edge of the kingdom – this is where 'the rubber hits the road'. Yes, it can be tough, yes it can be frustrating, yes it can be painful – but at the end of the day, there is no place where I would sooner be.[9]

Let me add one other personal comment: I am writing this book as one who has experienced both the ups *and downs* – and ups again! – of ministry. I have known what it is like to see a church quadruple in size; I have also known what it is like to see my world appear to collapse around me. I dare to believe that it is precisely because I have experienced much pain in ministry – as well as ecstasy – that a special dimension is added to this book. My own experience of the darker side of ministry has caused me to reflect deeply and to ask many questions. For instance, what do we mean by the terms 'success' and 'failure'? In whose eyes do we measure success and failure, and against what yardstick? It has been said that there is no such thing as failure, only lessons to be learnt – about God, about life, about others, and about oneself. I prefer to talk in terms of apparent success and apparent failure, and within that framework I have experienced both. Inevitably, our humanity will always limit a total over-view of any given situation. God alone sees the full picture and the true dynamics involved. In a very real sense this book is the product of my experience of ministry. I trust that the challenge which is present in this book will never be threatening, but always encouraging.

[9] See further, Paul Beasley-Murray, 'From College to Church: Reflections on Returning to the Pastorate', *Mainstream Newsletter* 48 (Nov. 1993), pp. 4–6.

Chapter 1

The professional pastor

The call to excel

The call to excel is in the first place a call to be professional.

As I write these words, I sense immediate disapprobation. Indeed, my mind goes back to a ministers' conference where I dared to suggest that ministers should seek to be more professional. I was howled down. Almost without exception this group of ministers – drawn from a number of denominations – made it clear that for them 'professionalism' was a dirty word.

As I reflected on that incident I came to see that for this group of ministers the term 'professional' carried two unhelpful connotations. In the first place, it implied unspirituality – a 'professional' minister in their terms was someone paid to do a job, as distinct from someone who sought to live out a calling. In the second place, it implied 'one-man' ministry – a 'professional' minister in their terms was someone who blocked the 'laity' from using the gifts God had given them.[1]

No doubt there are historical reasons for these twin associations of unspirituality and 'one-man' ministry. As far as the former is concerned, the historical roots are to be found in the Old Testament, where the 'true' prophet has received a special calling from God and is contrasted with the institutional prophet and priest, who

[1] See also J. T. Miller, H. Robinson & P. L. Sampson, *So You Want To Be a Baptist Minister* (Baptist Union of Scotland, Glasgow, no date), p. 9: 'A very real danger in the Christian ministry is that of wearing the cloak of professionalism. It is possible for familiarity with sacred things to breed contempt for them in the heart . . . The warmth of a close walk with God will ward off the frosts of professionalism.'

prophesy falsely and act unworthily. This contrast, for instance, is found in Amos' reply to Amaziah: 'I am no prophet, nor a prophet's son; but I am a herdsman, and a dresser of sycamore trees, and the LORD took me from following the flock, and the LORD said to me, "Go, prophesy to my people Israel!" (Amos 7:14–15). Similarly Jeremiah inveighed against the false prophets who had not 'stood in the council of the LORD so as to see and to hear his word' (Jer. 23:18); '"Both prophet and priest are ungodly; even in my house I have found their wickedness," says the LORD' (Jer. 23:11; see also 5:13; 6:13–14). Throughout the history of the Church there have been many heirs to this tradition: one thinks, for example, of some of the 18th-century Anglican vicars, who seem to have been more interested in the gentlemanly pursuits of fishing and hunting than in fulfilling their divine calling.

However, the fact that pastors are remunerated does not necessarily mean that they have been corrupted. There is nothing unspiritual about being paid for services rendered. As Jesus himself said, 'the worker deserves to be paid' (Luke 10:7). Indeed, one could argue that a true professional is a labourer who is genuinely worthy of his hire. Professionals are people who do not neglect or leave undone what they are being paid to do while they do something else.[2]

With regard to the unhelpful associations of 'one-man' ministry, it is true that the 'professional' ministry has often thought itself omnicompetent and in consequence has left little for the 'laity' to do other than tolling the bell and taking up the collection. In this sense George Bernard Shaw was right when he somewhat drily commented, 'All professions are conspiracies against the laity.' However, rightly understood, professionalism has nothing to do with restrictive practices, but rather simply seeks to encourage the practice of excellence. Professionalism in the ministry does not deny the fact that God has gifted all his people for ministry, but rather seeks to encourage ministers to fulfil their particular role to the best of their ability. In so far as one essential aspect of pastoral ministry is enabling all God's people to fulfil their particular ministry (Eph.

[2] See Wayne E. Oates, *New Dimensions In Pastoral Care* (Fortress Press, Philadelphia, 1970), p. 47.

4:11–12), professionalism in ministry should ultimately boost rather than frustrate the ministry of the 'laity'.

Perhaps at this stage a definition of the word 'professional' is called for. The actual word 'profession' stems from the medieval Latin *professio*, which was used of the taking of vows upon entering a religious order. Gradually the word broadened in its usage and came to indicate 'a vocation in which a professed knowledge of some department of learning or science is used in its application to the affairs of others or in the practice of an art founded upon it'.[3] Here the emphasis is very much upon the term 'knowledge' – not so much knowledge for its own sake, but rather knowledge applied in the service of others.

As far as the sociologists are concerned, there do not seem to be any universally accepted criteria for a profession. One approach developed by Wilensky and Hall is employed by Peter Jarvis in his analysis of ministry:

> Wilensky suggested that every profession should have four structural attributes. It should: (a) be a full-time occupation, (b) have its own training school to transmit knowledge and skill, (c) have a professional association, and (d) have a code of ethical practice. Hall added five attitudinal characteristics, which were a sense (a) of autonomy, (b) of self-regulation, (c) of vocation, (d) of service ethic, and (e) of having a colleague reference group.[4]

Similarly James Glasse defined professionalism in the following terms:

> A professional is identified by five characteristics. (1) He is an *educated man*, master of some body of knowledge. This knowledge is not arcane and esoteric, but accessible to students in accredited educational institutions. (2) He is an *expert man*, master of some specific cluster of skills. These skills, while requiring some talent, can be learned and sharpened by practice under supervision. (3) He is an *institutional man*, relating himself to society and rendering his service through a historical social

---

[3] *Oxford English Dictionary*.
[4] Peter Jarvis, 'The Ministry: Occupation, Profession or Status', *Expository Times* 86 (1975), p. 264.

institution of which he is partly servant, partly master. Even
when he has a 'private practice', he is a member of a professional
association which has some control over his activities. (4) He is a
responsible man, who professes to be able to act competently in
situations which require his services. He is committed to practise
his profession according to high standards of competence and
ethics. Finally, (5) he is a *dedicated man*. The professional
characteristically 'professes' something, some value for society.
His dedication to the values of the profession is the ultimate
basis of evaluation for his service.[5]

Anthony Russell offers a third model and describes 'the ideal type
of profession' as

> an occupational group that has specialist functions; a prolonged
> training; a monopoly of legitimate performance; self-regulating
> mechanisms with regard to entry and expulsion; colleague-group
> solidarity; autonomy of role performance; a fiduciary relation-
> ship between practitioner and client; a distinctive professional
> ethic stressing altruistic service; a reward structure and career
> pattern; and a research orientation and control of the institution
> within which the professional role is legitimated.[6]

All these definitions throw helpful light upon our subject of
pastoral ministry. It may be that in some respects pastoral ministry
does not fully fit into a professional ministry – not least because
Christian ministry is more than simply meeting people's needs:
in the first place Christian ministry is about serving God. Yet,
as Joe Trull and James Carter have rightly argued, 'there is more
to be gained than lost by the minister assuming the designation
of a professional'.[7] In particular the designation 'professional' is
to be welcomed because it encourages a more rigorous approach

[5] James D. Glasse, *Profession: Minister* (Abingdon, New York, 1968), p.
38. See also Owen Brandon, *The Pastor And His Ministry* (SPCK, London,
1972), pp. 99–105.
[6] Anthony Russell, *The Clerical Profession* (SPCK, London, 1984), p.
13.
[7] Joe E. Trull and James F. Carter, *Ministerial Ethics: Being A Good
Minister In A Not-So-Good World* (Broadman and Holman, Nashville,
1993), p. 37. Used by permission.

to ministry. And this is right and proper. For only the highest of standards – only excellence – is worthy of our God.

The consequences of a professional approach to ministry include the following five positive benefits. In the first place, the concept of professional ministry encourages pastors to develop a clearer sense of their own identity. 'Full-time service' is not an adequate definition of ministry. Within the overall context of the ministry of the whole people of God, the professional minister is called to exercise a specialist role as the pastor of the flock. This role includes leadership, teaching (preaching), caring, and enabling.

In the second place, the concept of professional ministry encourages people to take training more seriously. A 'call' to ministry is not sufficient for ministry to be exercised. Gifts for ministry need to be developed and trained. Education – including continuing education – is vital if the minister is to have expertise to offer. This expertise will clearly include an ability to handle the Scriptures knowledgeably – but it needs to include much more than biblical and theological competence. Sadly, courses in theological education and ministerial formation do not always match the realities of pastoral ministry, with the result that many ministers perform roles for which they have had no real training.

In the third place, the concept of professional ministry necessitates an occasion when those who have been trained for ministry enter into the ranks of the professionals. Whatever else ordination may signify today, it denotes that the candidate has acquired the necessary skills and qualifications to exercise pastoral ministry as a 'recognised' or 'accredited' minister. Ordination in this sense is a professional rite of passage.

In the fourth place, the concept of professional ministry involves an acceptance of professional standards. Professional standards are standards of excellence. There is no place for an amateurish approach to ministry. Nor is there a place for the second rate. Here is the context for such practices as supervision and appraisal, as also for the development and acceptance of a professional code of ethics.

In the fifth place, the concept of professional ministry implies some kind of independent professional association of ministers.[8] While it is true that all main-line denominations contain some body

---

[8] Glasse, *Profession*, p. 144, for instance, recommended the founding of an American Academy of Parish Clergy.

responsible for overseeing standards in ministry, such bodies are normally so closely tied into the denominational structures, that at times there is little room for true independence. There is much to be said for a body specifically set up to advocate and defend the interests of ministers.[9]

But to return to our main theme. The pursuit of professionalism first and foremost is the pursuit of excellence.[10] Such excellence does not come automatically, but rather is achieved through effort and hard work. In the words of John Gardner, 'Some people have greatness thrust upon them. Very few have excellence thrust upon them ... They achieve it. They do not achieve it unwittingly by "doing what comes naturally" and they don't stumble into it in the course of amusing themselves. All excellence involves discipline and tenacity of purpose.'[11]

Professionalism in this sense inevitably involves offering to God our very best – both of mind and of heart. There is nothing cold or hypocritical about professionalism. Professionalism involves whole-hearted commitment to Christ and his Church. If the truth be told, a lack of professionalism in ministry is more often than not a mark of laziness rather than of unspirituality. 'I will not offer burnt offerings to the Lord my God that cost me nothing', said David (2 Sam. 24:24) – such a spirit is the spirit of the true professional.

Precisely because professionalism in ministry springs from a deep commitment to God, it can never limit itself to the institution of the Church. True professionalism has at its heart not the furtherance of self, but rather the furtherance of the Gospel. In this respect I

[9] An obvious example of the advantage of an independent body is the matter of the pay and conditions of service. Another example is the situation where there is a conflict between a church and its minister: there is an inherent tendency for ecclesiastical hierarchies to come down on the side of the institution rather than of the individual. Interestingly, although such an idea of a 'professional association' was floated amongst English Baptists, it was overwhelmingly rejected on the ground that it 'would tend to divide churches from ministers in a kind of "them-and-us" confrontation': see *The Fraternal* 176 (June 1976), p. 30.

[10] If a scriptural base is required, see 1 Cor. 14:12, NIV: 'try to excel in gifts that build up the church'; also Sirach 33:23: 'Excel in all that you do'.

[11] John Gardner, *Excellence*, quoted by Ted W. Engstrom, *The Pursuit of Excellence* (Zondervan, Grand Rapids, Michigan, 1982), p. 24.

disagree with Kennon Callahan when he declares: 'The day of the professional minister is over. The day of the missionary pastor has come.'[12] As we shall later argue, the professional pastor is at one and the same time the missionary strategist.

The fact is that the term 'professional' is a worthy term. The Church of England was right to entitle one of its recent guides to selection and training for priesthood *Professional Ministry*.[13] Pastors are called to be professional – for they are called to excellence.[14]

How might this excellence display itself? Daniel Biles in his book, *Pursuing Excellence In Ministry*, lists two sets of principles as 'the foundations and the expressions of ministry':[15]

> *The foundations of ministry*
> *Mission:* 'If a parish does not know what it exists to be and do, no amount of "busyness" and "quick-fix" ideas will substitute.'
> *Leadership:* 'The creation and articulation of, the focusing attention on, and the developing commitment to a vision of what God is calling the congregation to be and to do' (i.e. making concrete the mission of the Church).
> *Lay commitment and ownership:* 'The laity "own", take responsibility for and are trusted with carrying out the work of the people of God.'
>
> *The expressions of ministry*
> *Quality worship*, which results in worship becoming 'a driving desire to speak and to do the Gospel'.

[12] Kennon L. Callahan, *Effective Church Leadership* (Harper, San Francisco, 1990), p. 1. Callahan caricatures professional ministers when he writes: 'They maintain a sense of presence, dignity, decorum and decency – with a quietly sad regret – much like the thoughtful undertaker who sees to keeping things in good order throughout the funeral' (p. 4). If Callahan were right, then I would be arguing for a new breed of professionalism!

[13] *Professional Ministry* (Advisory Board of Ministry, Church House, London, no date).

[14] My one regret with the term 'professional' as over against the term 'amateur' lies in the original meaning of the latter. I would like to believe that professional ministers are also 'amateurs' in the sense that 'they do the work of their vocation for the sheer love of it' (Kevin Eastell, *Appointed For Growth* [Mowbray, 1994], p. 30).

[15] Daniel V. Biles, *Pursuing Excellence In Ministry* (The Alban Institute, Bethesda, 1988), pp. 8–9.

Quality education, which involves members becoming 'biblically and theologically literate'.
Quality care and outreach.

Clearly, in all this pursuit of excellence the pastor has a central role to play.

A very different approach is offered by David Jesset, who tackled the related theme of 'quality' by advocating the setting and monitoring of certain measurable 'standards' in the Church.[16] His suggestions for minimum standards offered to all actual or potential church-goers (a Parishioner's Charter!) include the following:

Worship: 'All worship services will be clearly publicised and will start on time.'
Administration: 'All letters to the vicar should receive at least an acknowledgement within one week.'
Pastoral care: 'All relatives of bereaved people will receive at least one visit from a church representative before a funeral and one follow up visit within three months of the service.'
More spiritual 'quality': 'At least three times a year every home in the parish would receive an attractive leaflet setting out some aspect of the Christian gospel and inviting people to come along.'

Here is certainly room for thought – and development! Again, the role of the pastor is central.

My own suggestions for encouraging professionalism are four-fold: (a) annual appraisals; (b) pastoral supervision; (c) a code of ethics; (d) continuing education.

Benefiting from appraisal

In many – if not most – work situations in Britain, annual appraisals have become a way of life. Once a year employees have an opportunity on an individual basis to sit down with their immediate superior and review their past performance with a view to setting fresh goals for the following year.

This formal exercise, amongst other things, gives an opportunity for managers to affirm the person and to say 'well done'; to

[16] David Jesset, 'Towards a "Parishioner's Charter"? – Quality in the Church', *Ministry* 20 (Summer 1993), pp. 1–2.

review previously set objectives and set future goals; to provide a safe environment for discussing problems and, where necessary, to express dissatisfaction; to identify training needs; to rewrite the job description with new emphases; and to determine career prospects. It is important to emphasise that first and foremost appraisal is intended to be a positive process. If appraisal involves criticism, then it is constructive criticism with the well-being of the individual as well as the well-being of the organisation in mind.

It is my conviction that appraisals should also be a way of life for pastors. A mark of a professional pastor is a willingness to undergo annual appraisal, with a view to developing excellence in ministry.[17] Appraisal is in the interests of the pastor. Appraisal is also in the interests of the church.[18]

A theological foundation for appraisal is provided by the United Methodist Church of America:

> Evaluation is natural to the human experience. Evaluation is one of God's ways of bringing the history of the past into dialogue with the hope for the future. Without confession of sin there is

[17] Within the context of ministry, the purpose of appraisal has been defined by the Methodist Church Division of Ministries in their 1992 Conference Report, *Accompanied Self-Appraisal*, as follows:
1. to affirm their gifts, achievements and personality;
2. to step back and take stock (especially with reference to previous goals and unexpected happenings);
3. to reflect on
   (a) their personal aspirations and needs;
   (b) their effectiveness in their daily work;
4. to check out their performance
   (a) in their immediate work context;
   (b) in relationship to the institution within which they operate;
5. to improve skills, insights and gifts;
6. to identify areas for professional and personal development;
7. to recognise challenges, identify achievable goals and determine appropriate strategies for future action.

[18] See William D. Horton, 'Assessment of Ministry', *Expository Times* 95 (March 1984), p. 165: 'The lack of any regular assessment of ministry affects both the church and the pastor. No right-minded church allows its central heating system to deteriorate through failure to renew the annual service contract'!

no reconciliation; without the counting of blessings there is no thanksgiving; without the acknowledgement of accomplishments there is no celebration; without awareness of potential there is no hope; without hope there is no desire for growth; without desire for growth the past will dwarf the future. We are called into new growth and new ministries by taking a realistic and hopeful look at what we have been and what we can still become. Surrounded by God's grace and the crowd of witnesses in the faith, we can look at our past unafraid and from its insights eagerly face the future with new possibilities.[19]

Unfortunately, many ministers feel threatened by the prospect of appraisal. Believing themselves to be primarily accountable to God, they do not want to have to give account of their ministry to another. But if the word 'love' in 1 John 4:20 is changed to 'accountable', we find 'We cannot be accountable to God whom we have not seen, if we are not willing to be accountable to our brother and sister, whom we have seen'![20] If only ministers were to appreciate that appraisal, properly handled, is a positive experience with their welfare in mind, they would welcome the opportunity for appraisal with open arms.

Ministerial appraisals are not an unhelpful bureaucratic invasion into ministry. In one sense they are simply a development of the traditional practice of spiritual direction.[21] From within the British scene David Sheppard, who as the Anglican Bishop of Liverpool has had considerable experience of ministerial appraisals, writes:

> Today's clergy ... are under increasing pressure ... Expectations whether appropriate or not, are high and it is all too easy to

[19] From a pamphlet prepared by the Division of Ordained Ministry of the United Methodist Church, quoted by Jill M. Hudson, *Evaluating Ministry: Principles & Processes for Clergy & Congregations* (The Alban Institute, Bethesda, 1992), p. 7.
[20] Likewise from the Division of Ordained Ministry of the United Methodist Church.
[21] See Michael Jacobs, *Holding In Trust: The Appraisal Of Ministry* (SPCK, London, 1989), p. 7: 'Although [spiritual direction] may historically have concentrated upon the minister's prayer life, inevitably spiritual life is affected by, and in turn affects, the whole of ministry. Spiritual direction at its best is also concerned with the whole person and the whole ministry.'

be lured into an attitude of uncritical and unreflective 'activism'.

I believe all who exercise an ordained ministry in the Church of God need, somehow, to keep alive and foster the vision, excitement and challenge that fuelled their vocation; ministerial review and appraisal ought to be a non-threatening, yet supportive and creative way of doing just this, ensuring that we remain effective disciples all our lives.[22]

In many ways appraisal is more helpful to ministers than almost any other group of workers. For ministry is by and large a lonely profession. Unlike other professionals, ministers for the most part do not work together in teams. They are on their own. True, they are part of a local church, but not even the lay leaders of that local church have any real idea of what is involved in the day-to-day ministry of their pastor. In such a context annual appraisal can break down some of the isolationism and in so doing prove to be extremely supportive.

Annual appraisals also provide an opportunity for any difficulties to be picked up at an early stage and dealt with appropriately. In this sense appraisals may be likened to a form of preventative medicine. Within the context of reviewing a person's ministry, a skilled appraiser can discern areas which, without attention, might lead to subsequent disaster. Appraisals provide an opportunity for early diagnosis of problems. They also provide a safe place for the kind of straight talking which is not otherwise normally possible.

There are, however, particular difficulties with regard to the appraisal of ministers. One difficulty, for instance, is to be found in the fact that very rarely is there a written job description. It is assumed that everyone knows what ministers do and what is required of them. But the reality is that there are a variety of approaches to ministry. There are a variety of ways in which ministers may organise their time and determine their priorities.

Another difficulty in ministerial appraisal is that ministers for the most part are their own bosses. Technically employed by the

[22] David Sheppard in the Foreword to *Appointed For Growth: A Handbook Of Ministry Development And Appraisal* (Mowbray, London, 1994), edited by Kevin Eastell.

church, in reality they act as leaders of the church. To whom are they accountable when it comes to appraisal?

A third difficulty is that the 'performance' of the minister is intimately bound up with the 'performance' of the church. It is difficult to appraise the one without the other. 'To separate the ministry of one Christian, namely the pastor, for evaluation,' writes Jill Hudson, 'without considering the ministry of those with whom he or she shares the work of a particular congregation is not only unjust but theologically unsound.'[23] Ideally the work of the church as a whole should be appraised on an annual basis.

None of these difficulties is insuperable. For example, there is no reason why ministers should not be encouraged to produce their own job descriptions, which might form the basis for review. An alternative approach adopted by one church was to use Lyle Schaller's oft-quoted list of 14 activities of the pastor as a basis for evaluation: viz. administration, community leadership, continuing education, counselling, denominational and ecumenical responsibilities, evangelism, personal and family life, preaching, social ministry, stewardship, teaching, theology, bereavement and crisis visitation, and worship.[24]

This second difficulty is a little more problematic. In one sense, for the local church to evaluate its own minister is a little like patients evaluating their doctor. Although there is a place for such evaluation, the professional is not actually being appraised by a fellow professional. For this reason, in some of the more hierarchical denominations 'line' appraisal is the norm, in which the appraisal is conducted by the archdeacon or equivalent functionary. The drawback here, however, is that in so far as this involves an 'outsider', the appraisal is inevitably based on second-hand knowledge. An alternative is to engage in 'peer' review with another minister or a group of ministers.[25] To my mind the least

23 Hudson, *Evaluating Ministry*, p. 3.
24 Bethlehem Evangelical Lutheran Church, DeKalb, Illinois, cited by Hudson, *Evaluating Ministry*, pp. 39–42. Interestingly, the appraisal process also involved meeting with the pastor's spouse and family 'to show pastoral care'.
25 See Kevin Eastell, 'Survey of Current Use', in *Appointed For Growth*, p. 30: 'Whereas I think that most clergy in the Church of England would find peer group assessment acceptable, they would not respond warmly to external evaluation.'

satisfactory form of appraisal is 'self-assessment', for time and again we fail to see ourselves as we truly are.[26] My own preference is for the appraisal to be conducted by the local church with a ministerial facilitator drawn from outside the fellowship.

Likewise, this third difficulty is not insuperable. A review of the church's ministry as a whole could be conducted at the same time as a review of the ministry of its pastor. Jill Hudson gives an example of Ashby First Parish Church, where not only does every member of the congregation evaluate the minister by way of a questionnaire, but also where every member is asked to look back on goals established at the last annual meeting of the parish and to rate them as accomplished, partly accomplished, or not accomplished. In addition, using a scale of 1 (exceptional) to 5 (needs a lot of work), members are asked to rate the effectiveness of the congregation in 16 areas.[27] The drawback here is the amount of work involved, particularly if this were done on an annual basis. The danger would be that for a significant period of the year the church could be distracted from its task of ministry as a result of this internal auditing process. On the other hand, one could perhaps envisage such a general evaluation taking place once every five years.

For what it is worth, let me share my own experience of appraisal within a local church setting. Having experienced the benefits of appraisal within the context of a theological college, when I came to my present church I was determined to continue to enjoy the benefits of the appraisal system. However, I requested that an external ministerial facilitator be involved. I was mindful of the fact that two Baptist churches had sought to appraise their ministers without the benefit of an experienced outside facilitator, and as a

[26] See Stephen Pattison, *A Critique of Pastoral Care* (SPCK, London, 2nd edition, 1993), p. 148, who underlines the fact that 'people's own evaluation of their success or failure may be wildly at odds with the evaluation of others; hence the phenomenon of people condemning themselves as failures while being celebrated by others for the very thing they think they have failed at'.

[27] Ashby First Parish Church, Unitarian Universalist, Massachusetts, cited by Hudson, *Evaluating Ministry*, pp. 13–18.

consequence both ministers involved had been obliged to leave their churches. I felt that with a fellow professional in place, I would, if necessary, have an 'advocate' who understood my position from within the profession.

In the light of my request for annual appraisal, my deacons set up the following process:

1. A small 'design' group was set up to meet with me with a view to designing not only an appropriate appraisal questionnaire but also the appraisal process.[28] All four members of this 'design' group had considerable experience of conducting appraisals in the secular world, although none of them had ever been previously involved in a ministerial appraisal.

2. Although all 15 of my deacons were asked to fill in the section of the review and appraisal form applicable to them, it was felt it would not be right for my appraisal to be conducted with too large a number of deacons. With my blessing, three 'representative' deacons were chosen for this task: two men from the 'design' group and a woman with expertise in the area of personal and group psycho-dynamics.

3. I filled in my form (it amounted to 14 single-spaced sides!) and the deacons filled in theirs. My completed form – together with a copy of my proposed goals for the next year – were sent to the facilitator and the three representative deacons. At my request – and for the sake of my emotional health! – I did not see all 15 copies, but instead was given a seven-page summary document drawn up by the three representative deacons.

4. The facilitator, however, received all 15 copies, and also the seven-page summary. In addition he was sent a considerable amount of material relating to the life of the church over the past year.

5. The church as a whole was not involved in the appraisal process. They were, however, kept informed.

6. For various reasons none of the other paid church staff were involved in the appraisal process. However, in future not only

---

[28] See Hudson, *Evaluating Ministry*, p. 66: 'A design that is tailor-made to fit the particular situation is often better than a packaged process.'

will they themselves be appraised – they also will be given the opportunity to give input into my appraisal!

7. The actual appraisal took place over the whole of a Saturday:
(i) The appraisal began with a breakfast meeting (8 a.m.–10.30 a.m.) at which the facilitator met with the three representative deacons to explore any areas of doubt or confusion regarding the input of the deacons.
(ii) The facilitator then met with me (11 a.m.–1 p.m.) not only to explore my submission to the appraisal process, but also to discuss some of the feelings my deacons were expressing.
(iii) After lunch the three representative deacons and I came together with the facilitator. In the light of the two earlier meetings in the morning he had drawn up an agenda, which then formed the basis for our discussions. Although our meeting ended at 6 p.m., we all felt that the time had been too short!

8. The following week the facilitator sent a three-page document for the consideration of all the deacons and myself. It was entitled 'Issues on which an interim progress report will be made in six months'. We discovered that he felt that the three representative deacons should meet with me to assess developments, rather than wait for the next formal appraisal in a year's time.[29] He also sent to me a private two-page letter spelling out more personal matters.

This experience, along with previous experiences of appraisal, has been extremely positive. Appraisals should not be viewed as threatening – but rather as challenging and stimulating. Hence the title of this sub-section: 'Benefiting from appraisal'.

Working under supervision

In the helping professions supervision is the norm. Yet while no professional counsellor would operate without giving account on a regular basis to a trained supervisor, ministers for the most part feel free to operate totally independently. The thrust of this section is that this is not right. If ministers are to be professional and are

---

[29] See Michael Jacobs, *Holding in Trust*, p. 75: 'Twice-yearly meetings are, to my mind, the necessary minimum to make effective use of an appraisal procedure.'

to pursue excellence, then they need to reform and discover the benefits of supervision.

Supervision is defined by the British Association for Counselling (BAC) in the following terms:

> Supervision is a formal arrangement for counsellors to discuss their work regularly with someone who is experienced in counselling and supervision. The task is to work together to ensure and develop the efficacy of the counsellor/client relationship, the agenda will be the counselling work and feeling about that work, together with the supervisor's reactions, comments and confrontations. Thus supervision is a process of consultancy to widen the horizons of an experienced practitioner.[30]

In the counselling world supervision is not an optional extra. It is an essential part of the counselling process. Without supervision there can be no accreditation.

There are in fact three main functions or roles to supervision. These three have been well described by Peter Hawkins and Robin Shohet:

1. The *educative* or *formative* function is about developing skills, understanding and abilities of the supervisees. This is done through the reflection on and exploration of the supervisees' work with their clients. In this exploration they may be helped by the supervisor to:
   * understand the client better
   * become more aware of their own reactions and responses to the client
   * look at how they intervened and the consequences of their own interventions
   * explore other ways of working with this and other similar client situations.
2. The *supportive* or *restorative* function is a way of responding to how any workers who are engaged in intimate therapeutic work with clients are necessarily allowing themselves to be affected by the distress, pain and fragmentation of the client and how they need time to become aware of how this has

[30] Information Sheet 8, British Association for Counselling, Rugby.

affected them and to deal with any reactions. These emotions may have been produced through empathy with the client or restimulated by the client, or be a reaction to the client. Not attending to these emotions soon leads to less than effective workers, who become either over-identified with their clients or defended against being further affected by them. This in turn leads to stress and what is now commonly called 'burn-out'.[31]

3. The *managerial* or *formative* aspect of supervision provides the quality-control function in work with people. It is not only lack of training or experience that necessitates the need in us, as workers, to have someone look with us at our work, but our inevitable human failings, blind spots, areas of vulnerability from our own woundedness and our own prejudices.

Supervision in these terms is a very positive process. The 'oversight' offered is not intended to be threatening, but rather is intended to be supportive to both the supervisee and the supervisee's clients. It offers possibilities of personal growth and development. It enables counsellors to gain fresh insights both into their clients and also into themselves. It acts as a safeguard to staleness and serves as a spur to a more creative approach to counselling.

Unfortunately, not everybody sees supervision in such a positive light. Many ministers, in particular, do feel threatened by supervision, in spite of all the benefits it has to offer. In spite of their calling, ministers often display remarkable insecurity. Thus Derek Blows, reflecting on his attempts to introduce supervision to pastoral training, wrote:

The experience of receiving help, and the openness, vulnerability and trust which must accompany it has profound learning value. Indeed, one may ask if anyone can give help who has not also learned to receive it . . . Helpers, however, are notoriously reluctant to receive help. The need to be the strong, self-giving 'man for others', buttressed by a very lopsided development of the

---

[31] Hawkins and Shohet, p. 42, draw a parallel with the British miners in the 1920s, who fought for what was termed 'pit-head time' – the right to wash off the grime of the work in the boss's time rather than take it home with them. Supervision is the equivalent for those that work at the 'coal-face' of personal distress, disease and fragmentation.

Christian tradition which exalts giving help far above receiving it, can make the need to seek help seem shameful and frightening, and only to be followed in dire extremity, preferably of physical illness. This attitude can lead to an emotional impoverishment and isolation that can put the helper and perhaps his marriage and family life at risk.[32]

What precisely can one do to overcome the insecurity of many pastors who find the thought of supervision threatening? Doubtless the sharing by others of their own positive experiences of supervision would be helpful. However, perhaps the key lies in the kind of training given at the stage when ministers receive their primary theological education. It is here that the work of John Foskett and David Lyall is helpful, for in their book *Helping the Helpers* they demonstrate how supervision and pastoral care can be helpfully combined in the initial training period.[33] Once people have had good experience of supervision at theological college, they are likely to ensure that their later ministry is characterised by the good practice of supervision.

It may, however, be objected that the difference between pastoral counselling and pastoral care is such that there is less need of supervision. In the counselling situation it is the norm for counsellors to see their clients for a minimum of six sessions; not infrequently counselling may go on for a year or more. By contrast in a situation of pastoral care the pastoral encounter may be a 'one-off' occasioned by a pastoral visit. Furthermore, whereas the client usually takes the initiative in setting up the counselling

---

[32] Derek Blows, *Help For The Helpers* (1977), quoted by Ronald Smythe, '"Oversight" Or Supervision', *Contact* 77 (1982:4), p. 3.
[33] John Foskett and David Lyall, *Helping the Helpers. Supervision And Pastoral Care* (SPCK, London, 1988). Foskett and Lyall define pastoral supervision as 'a method of doing and reflecting on ministry' (p. 8). They advocate the integrating of theological understanding with pastoral practice by the 'narrative approach': 'In this approach it is assumed that theological reflection upon the practice of ministry draws on material from three sources: (a) the historic beliefs of the community of faith contained in Scripture and the theological tradition; (b) the realities of the pastoral situation; (c) the life experience of the one who offers pastoral care' (p. 43).

situation, in pastoral care the initiative is usually taken by the pastor or carer. This results in somewhat different dynamics. Thus Foskett and Lyall point out that 'in pastoral counselling there is likely to be a greater emphasis upon the unconscious processes. By contrast, pastoral care will tend to focus more upon the conscious forces at work in the pastoral relationship.'[34] This in turn means that, initially at least, the pastoral encounter is less likely to be as deep and demanding as the encounter between counsellor and client.

Yet do such distinctions between pastoral care and pastoral counselling make the supervision of pastoral care less needful? Surely not. If anything, on the contrary, pastors face a greater challenge to break through the superficiality of many pastoral encounters, so that their pastoral care can prove to be a more effective catalyst for personal growth.

How often should a pastor receive such supervision? The minimum requirement for supervision for BAC accreditation purposes is one and a half hours a month. Maybe for pastors the minimum requirement might be lowered to a session of one hour a month – but certainly it should not be less.

There is no doubt that if, overnight, all pastors were to seek supervision, the need could not be met. Currently there are just not sufficient supervisors around. Certainly experienced ministers skilled in psycho-dynamics are relatively few in number. Here then is a challenge for denominational bodies to encourage suitably gifted pastors to offer themselves for training. From a denominational perspective, a spin-off resulting from giving proper professional support to pastors would be that less resources would have to be used to deal with crises in the lives of pastors!

However, supervision does not have to take place on a one-to-one basis. Group supervision is also possible: on such a model the supervisor would meet with a number of ministers, who would take turns in sharing and reflecting on their case-load. Another possibility for those who have benefited from individual supervision over a period of time is peer group supervision: on this

---

[34] Foskett and Lyall, _Helping the Helpers_, p. 110.

model three or more pastors would share the responsibility for providing each other's supervision within the context of a group meeting.

So far we have been thinking of supervision of pastoral care and counselling. However, there is a good case for extending supervision beyond the confines of actual pastoral care, so as to include the work of pastoral ministry as a whole. Here the supervisor would become a 'work consultant', with a watching brief for all aspects of ministry. It does not need much imagination to see how beneficial such an over-view could prove. It would certainly help pastors to become more effective in the use of their time.

One side-effect of such supervision/work consultancy might be the lowering of the number of ministerial sexual indiscretions, which all too often find their beginning in a pastor's over-zealous attention to the apparently spiritual needs of certain members of the opposite sex. To take an extreme example, the supervisor, in asking to see the whole of a pastor's diary, might discover that the minister had seen the same person four or five times in the week! Such a discovery might be revealed only as the supervisor probed and through questioning established that the apparently unfulfilled time-slots were, in fact, used. In such a scenario – and in other less extreme examples too – supervision could prove a form of preventative pastoral care.

Supervision could be given even broader dimensions, and relate not only to the work of the ministry, but also to the spiritual health of the ministry. In other words, supervision could include spiritual direction, and hold ministers accountable for their spiritual as well as their personal and professional development.

Certainly some form of spiritual direction is essential for every pastor seeking excellence in ministry. For the sake of our own pastoral integrity, each of us must have someone who can hold us accountable for our spiritual growth and development. In this respect the words of John Henry Newman are still as relevant as ever:

Perhaps the reason why the standard of holiness among us is

so low, why our attainments are so poor, our view of the truth
so dim, our belief so unreal . . . is this: we dare not trust each
other with the secrets of our hearts . . . we keep it to ourselves
and we fear, as a cause of estrangement, that which really would
be a bond of union. We do not probe the wounds of our nature
thoroughly, we do not lay the foundation of our religion in the
ground of our heart.[35]

For some such 'probing' of the heart might be entrusted to
a 'supervisor/work consultant'; others might prefer to separate
their spiritual lives from their professional lives and be separately
accountable both to a supervisor and to a 'spiritual director'.
Whatever, in the pursuit of excellence the need for supervision
is unquestionable.

Developing a code of ethics

Any profession worthy of the name has a code of ethics. Rena
Gordelin in her book *Codes of Professional Responsibility* has
drawn together 37 'codes of professional responsibility' – accountancy, advertising, architecture, banking, business management,
engineering and many more professions are represented, but significantly, not pastoral ministry.[36] The fact is that, by and large,
most ministers do not operate with a formal code of ethics.
Certainly this is true in England: none of the main-line denominations has produced a binding code by which ministers should
operate.

According to Bishop Nolan Harmon such a lack of a code is
unsurprising: 'In the very nature of things, nothing like a binding
code of conduct can be drawn up, for it would be impossible to
get general agreement among ministers . . . The whole system of
Protestantism is bound up with the individual's rights.'[37] But is
this true? Or, if it is true, is it an acceptable state of affairs?

[35] John Henry Newman, 'Sermon on Christian Sympathy', Works V, No.
IX (1857).
[36] Rena A. Gordelin, *Codes of Professional Responsibility* (Bureau of
National Affairs Inc., Washington D.C., 2nd edition, 1990).
[37] Nolan B. Harmon, *Ministerial Ethics And Etiquette* (Abingdon Press,
Nashville, 2nd revised edition, 1987), p. 12.

Surely it would be helpful to develop some basic guidelines for the practice of ministry. As it is, for the most part no such guidance is given. In my own denomination, for instance, it is possible for a person to be removed from the ministerial list on grounds of 'conduct unbecoming a minister', but surprisingly the nature of such unbecoming conduct is not spelled out in advance to ministers entering on the accredited list. Such knowledge seems to be assumed!

True, ministers are not left totally without guidance in the area of moral conduct. In the first place we have as our basic textbook the Bible, which is our primary guide for all matters of faith and practice. In the second place, at their ordination ministers make vows, which likewise set some very basic guidelines for the practice of ministry. And yet although the Bible and the ordination vows have much to say about the importance of right relationships both with God and with one another, there are a host of consequences which need to be worked out with the practical realities of day-to-day pastoral ministry in mind.

Let me illustrate some of these consequences by examining the ethical implications of some of the relationships involved:

Relationship to God
It almost goes without saying that for a minister this relationship is the most fundamental. We shall explore something of the nature of this relationship in Chapter 7. Our effectiveness as ministers rises or falls according to the extent we seek to root our life and ministry in God. Any code of ministry must begin by recognising the importance of our setting aside 'time intentionally directed to God'.[38] Activism is no substitute for a disciplined life of prayer.

Relationship to the family
A healthy marriage for a married minister is another precondition for effective ministry. In spite of all the pressures of ministry, ministers need to make time to maintain a healthy relationship

[38] Gaylord Noyce, *Pastoral Ethics* (Abingdon Press, Nashville, 1988), p. 31.

with their spouses and children. Indeed, for those of us who are married with families, then part of our service to God is making space for quality family life. If this means the end to the traditional 70-hour and 80-hour work-weeks of a former generation of pastors, then so be it – indeed such a workload is 'questionable even on moral grounds'. For, as Gaylord Noyce amusingly puts it, 'Love in marriage demands time and care considerably beyond a Dagwood-to-Blondie peck on the cheek between church meetings and pastoral appointments.'[39] It is precisely because many ministers do not make their spouses a priority, that time and again ministerial casualties take place in counselling relationships. A secure marriage is always the best antidote to infidelity. Furthermore, in a world where Martin Luther's question 'How can I find a gracious God?' has been supplanted by the question 'How can I make my marriage work?', it is vital that ministers by their very lifestyle show that there is an answer.

Relationship to the church

Ministers have a responsibility toward their churches in ensuring that they remain competent in their job. This in turn means that they will make study a priority. John Wesley used to tell his ministers to devote five hours a day to reading![40] In the first place this means that they will be men and women of the Word. But it also will involve more general commitment to on-going professional growth and development.

Closely related to study is the preparation of sermons. In terms of ministerial ethics, ministers have a responsibility to ensure that they are faithful to Scripture, that they do not abuse Scripture in order to make their point. The words of the old cliche come to mind: 'A text without a context is a pretext.' Interestingly, in their writing on the ethics of preaching American authors tend to make much of the error of plagiarism. By all means read other people's sermons and see how they have sought to apply God's Word, but

---

[39] Ibid., p. 189.
[40] 'Read the most useful books, and that regularly and constantly. Steadily spend all the morning in this employ, and at least five hours in four-and-twenty' (John Wesley, *Minutes of Several Conversations Between The Rev Mr Wesley And Others, From The Year 1744 To 1789*, Question 32).

let such sermons be a springboard for your own creativity rather than a template for imitation.

A minister's leadership style within the church has ethical overtones. As ministers of Christ we are called to be servant-leaders: on the one hand this involves not abusing our power by exploiting our position; but on the other hand it also involves not vacating our calling by running away from our leadership role.

So far we have been speaking of a pastor's relationship to the church as a whole. But clearly there are also ethical implications in the way in which we relate to individual church members. One area in particular which is a potential minefield is the counselling relationship. The very fact that secular counselling agencies have their own detailed codes of conduct indicates the need for extreme care in this area. Compassion must always be combined with distance.[41] Yet here the minister faces particular difficulties: for example, unlike the professional counsellor, the pastor will probably be a friend of the person concerned; nor will the pastor's interaction with the 'client'-member be restricted to a predetermined appointment time.

Relationship to former churches

According to Noyce, this is 'probably the issue most in need of commonly enforced rules in ministry'.[42] Far too many ministers find it difficult to cut the pastoral umbilical cord as they move away. In this regard the quaintly worded advice of the veteran American ethicist Nolan Harmon is worth attention:

> Above all, when a man leaves a charge, let him leave it. No minister should be constantly going back to gossip with the brethren or hear comments on the work of his successor. Great harm has been done in this way by some ministers. The outgoing pastor should get all his supplies, trunks, boxes, barrels, the piano, the typewriter, the bread box, the garden hose and Willie's

---

41 See W. E. Wiest and E. A. Smith, *Ethics In Ministry* (Augsburg Fortress, Minneapolis, 1990), p. 185: 'Ministers, like physicians, must find ways to protect themselves from the powerful emotion often associated with their ministries.'

42 Gaylord Noyce, *Pastoral Ethics*, p. 135.

shotgun – everything loaded at one time, should give a good-by, making it as tearful as desired, but having started the truck, look not back! . . . 'Get out and stay out' is the injunction here![43]

It is painful to cut the deep ties of friendship built up maybe over a long and happy pastorate. And yet for the sake of the future ministry, it is vital. If invitations to take funerals and weddings come to the former pastor, then the former pastor should insist that any such invitation to return be extended only through the present minister – indeed, should make it clear that there would be an expectation for the present minister to share in the service.

Needless to say, not only are there obligations on the part of predecessors; there are also obligations on the part of successors to honour the ministers who have gone before them. As one ministerial code of ethics puts it: 'I will refrain from speaking disparagingly about the work of either my predecessor or my successor.'[44]

Relationship to other ministers and churches

The fact that the body of Christ is far bigger than any local church has a number of consequences. In the first place, there is surely an obligation for a minister to develop relationships with other pastors and churches. Isolationism is contrary to the spirit of the Gospel. Secondly, even where there are deep theological differences, the standing of others in Christ should always be respected. In the words of one ministerial code of ethics: 'I will consider all ministers my co-laborers in the work of Christ and even though I may differ from them, I shall respect their Christian earnestness

---

[43] Nolan Harmon, *Ministerial Ethics*, p. 72.
[44] Christian Church (Disciples of Christ), 'My Ministerial Code of Ethics', quoted by Noyce, *Pastoral Ethics*, p. 137. See also Charles Bugg, 'Professional Ethics Among Ministers', *Review and Expositor* 86 (1989), p. 570, who suggests several ways in which a former minister's contributions to the church can be recognised: e.g., 'Your predecessor can be invited back periodically to lead in some way in the life of the church. Never to invite a pastor back reveals more about our insecurities than anything else. The former pastor has been a part of the life of that church. The pastor has invested in the joys and struggles of that congregation and to treat a former pastor as *persona non grata* is to fail to recognize these contributions to the church.'

and sincerity.'[45] Thirdly, there is no place for competition between ministers and churches. This means that it is not ethical to actively encourage people to transfer from one church to another. Furthermore, if people do wish to transfer from a neighbouring church, then they should be encouraged as a matter of courtesy in the first place to go and talk their feelings through with their minister!

The above are just some of the issues which might be included in a code of ministerial ethics. The list is certainly not exhaustive. Other areas of concern which would benefit from inclusion relate, for instance, to finance,[46] evangelism,[47] and to community relationships.[48]

Two examples

There is no one universal code of ministerial ethics which is right for each and every situation. Rather, what I am seeking to encourage in this chapter is the development of codes of ethics appropriate to particular denominations and situations.

In this respect let me give two examples: the first is a very simple code of ethics which has been developed by the Baptist Union of New Zealand; the second is a more detailed American 'sample' code of ethics proposed by Joe Trull and James Carter.

A New Zealand code of ethics

1. I will love God with my body, mind and spirit.
2. I will seek to minister rather than be ministered unto, placing service above salary and personal recognition; and the unity and welfare of the church above my own.
3. I will model my caring for others on a professional level

---

[45] Christian Church (Disciples of Christ), 'My Ministerial Code of Ethics', cited by Noyce, *Pastoral Ethics*, p. 138.

[46] Noyce, *Pastoral Ethics*, pp. 113–31 devotes a whole chapter to 'Financing Ministry'. He includes matters such as moonlighting and tent-making, and also fees and honoraria. His comments on 'the simple life' repay thought: 'Those clergy who see the church more as an arena of self-employment and self-aggrandizement than a body whose witness can be strengthened through economic humility have missed part of the marrow of good pastoral ethics' (p. 130).

[47] See Noyce, *Pastoral Ethics*, pp. 171–81, and in particular his 'four affirmations': (i) the goal of evangelism – increase in faith – is not to be confused with means; (ii) persons are ends, not means; (iii) in personal evangelism, our goal is a person's ultimate well-being; (iv) evangelism must go hand in hand with witness for justice.

[48] See Trull and Carter, *Ministerial Ethics*, pp. 155–81.

with skill and wisdom so that others can experience my integrity, and be drawn towards exercising the same care for others.

4. I will hold as sacred, all confidences shared with me.

5. I will not violate another person's body, mind or spirit; and will not participate in the oppression of any person or community. I will not misuse the faith and resources entrusted to me.

6. I will try and live a balanced life: working responsibly and hard; caring for and nurturing family relationships; and not neglecting playfulness, humour and rest.

7. Before any action, I will think how it will appear to God, to my congregation and to my fellow pastors.

8. I will endeavour to lead my congregation without discrediting other churches, soliciting members from them or criticizing other pastors.

9. I will, with my resignation, sever my pastoral relations with my former church members, and will not make pastoral contacts among those relating to another church without the other pastor's knowledge and consent.

10. Having accepted a pastorate, I will not use my influence to alienate the church or any of its members from its denominational loyalty and support. Rather I will do all within my power to strengthen the bonds. If my convictions change, I will withdraw from the church.

A sample American code
The following code is a generic example of numerous American ministerial codes.[49]

Preamble
As a minister of Jesus Christ, called by God to proclaim the gospel and gifted by the Spirit to pastor the church, I dedicate myself to conduct my ministry according to the ethical guidelines and principles set forth in this code of ethics, in order that my

[49] Trull and Carter, *Ministerial Ethics*, pp. 253–5.

ministry be acceptable to God, my service be beneficial to the Christian community, and my life be a witness to the world.

Responsibilities to self
1. I will maintain my physical and emotional health through regular exercise, good eating habits, and the proper care of my body.
2. I will nurture my devotional life through a regular time of prayer, reading of the Scriptures and meditation.
3. I will continue to grow intellectually through personal study, comprehensive reading, and attending growth conferences.
4. I will manage my time well by properly balancing personal obligations, church duties, and family responsibilities, and by observing a weekly day off and an annual vacation.
5. I will be honest and responsible in my finances by paying all debts on time, never seeking special gratuities or privileges, giving generously to worthwhile causes, and living a Christian lifestyle.
6. I will be truthful in my speech, never plagiarizing another's work, exaggerating the facts, misusing personal experiences, or communicating gossip.
7. I will seek to be Christlike in attitude and action toward all persons regardless of race, social class, religious beliefs, or position of influence within the church and community.

Responsibilities to family
1. I will be fair to every member of my family, giving them the time, love, and consideration they need.
2. I will understand the unique role of my spouse, recognizing his or her primary responsibility is as marital partner and parent to the children, and secondarily as church worker and assistant to the pastor.
3. I will regard my children as a gift from God and seek to meet their individual needs without imposing undue expectations upon them.

Responsibilities to the congregation
1. I will seek to be a servant-minister of the church by following the example of Christ in faith, love, wisdom, courage and integrity.
2. I will faithfully discharge my time and energies as pastor, teacher, preacher, and administrator through proper work habits and reasonable work schedules.
3. In my administrative and pastoral duties, I will be impartial and fair to all members.
4. In my preaching responsibilities, I will give adequate time to prayer and preparation, so that my presentation will be biblically based, theologically correct, and clearly communicated.
5. In my pastoral counselling, I will maintain strict confidentiality, except in cases where disclosure is necessary to prevent harm to persons and/or is required by law.
6. In my evangelistic responsibilities, I will seek to lead persons to salvation and to church membership without manipulating converts, proselytizing members of other churches, or demeaning other religious faiths.
7. In my visitation and counselling practices, I will never be alone with a person of another sex unless another church member is present nearby.
8. I will not charge fees to church members for weddings or funerals; for nonmembers I will establish policies based on ministry opportunities, time constraints, and theological beliefs.
9. As a full-time minister, I will not accept any other remunerative work without the expressed consent of the church.
10. In leaving a congregation, I will seek to strengthen the church through proper timing, verbal affirmation, and an appropriate closure of ministry.

Responsibilities to colleagues
1. I will endeavour to relate to all ministers, especially those with whom I serve in my church, as partners in the work of God, respecting their ministry and co-operating with them.

2. I will seek to serve my minister colleagues and their families with counsel, support, and personal assistance.
3. I will refuse to treat other ministers as competition in order to gain a church, receive an honour, or achieve statistical success.
4. I will refrain from speaking disparagingly about the person or work of any other minister, especially my predecessor or my successor.
5. I will enhance the ministry of my successor by refusing to interfere in any way with the church I formerly served.
6. I will return to a former church field for professional services, such as weddings and funerals, only if invited by the resident pastor.
7. I will treat with respect and courtesy any predecessor who returns to my church field.
8. I will be thoughtful and respectful to all retired ministers and, upon my retirement, I will support and love my pastor.
9. I will be honest and kind in my recommendations of other ministers to church positions or other inquiries.
10. If aware of serious misconduct by a minister, I will contact responsible officials of that minister's church body and inform them of the incident.

Responsibilities to the community

1. I will consider my primary responsibility is to be pastor of my congregation and will never neglect ministerial duties in order to serve in the community.
2. I will accept reasonable responsibilities for community service, recognizing the minister has a public ministry.
3. I will support public morality in the community through responsible prophetic witness and social action.
4. I will obey the laws of my government unless they require my disobedience to the law of God.
5. I will practise Christian citizenship without engaging in partisan politics or political activities that are unethical, unbiblical, or unwise.

Responsibilities to my denomination

1. I will love, support and co-operate with the faith community of which I am a part, recognizing the debt I owe to my denomination for its contribution to my life, my ministry, and my church.
2. I will work to improve my denomination in its efforts to expand and extend the kingdom of God.

Advantages outweigh disadvantages

Clearly, with any code of ethics there are dangers. Any code runs the risk of legalism; it also runs the risk of missing out on the heart of ministry.

In this respect a powerful exposure of the limitations of all such codes has been made by Walter Wiest and Elwyn Smith: 'The figure of the Pharisee warns us: the person who knows how to pray expertly is the Pharisee. Only if there is something of the hopelessly unprofessional publican within can one hope for authenticity in the clergy life ... Responsible professional behaviour is the product of a prolonged and continuing process of personal formation.'[50] A few pages later on Wiest and Smith hammer home the same point: 'The professional character is profoundly formed "in Christ", not forced into the straitjacket of an approved code of ethics. In this world the comfort of knowing oneself to be right is denied to all but the Pharisees among us.'[51]   The positive point that Wiest and Smith make is undeniable. The key to ministerial integrity lies in the individual minister's walk with the Lord. Yet this fact does not do away with the desirability of a code of ethics. Rather than leave individuals to do their own hermeneutical work and reinvent the equivalent of the ministerial wheel, it surely is helpful to have a code of ethics which develops some of the practical implications for a minister of going the way of Christ. To avoid the charge of legalism, there might be something to be said for drawing up a simple code of ethics and then accompanying it with a more detailed commentary – somewhat akin to the Jewish *haggadah* – illustrating the way in which the code might be applied.

[50] Wiest & Smith, *Ethics In Ministry*, p. 181.
[51] Ibid., p. 190.

Learning for life

Professional pastors never finish learning. There is no such person as a 'fully trained' pastor. The three or so years at theological college are only a springboard for a life devoted to learning. Theological college marks only the primary stage of theological education. There are many more stages yet to come, as pastors review and reflect on their ministry and discover fresh resources for ministry. In this process continuing education for ministry is a 'must'.

Continuing education is a mark of professionalism. Christian ministry apart, in almost all professions in-service training is a necessity of life. For example, in order to be able to continue to practise as an accountant, it is necessary to do a predetermined minimum number of hours of further training a year. It doesn't matter how far one may have reached in the profession – one could be the senior partner in the largest accountancy firm in the country – one could not continue to practise without annual professional updating.

Likewise, in a fast-changing world ministers need regular in-service training. Continual updating of personal and professional skills is a 'must', if ministers are not to be 'happy amateurs'. And yet many ministers have received very little training since they left college. Roy Oswald quotes some American statistics to the effect that 'only 20% of clergy in the US engage in regular continuing education events of five days or more each year'.[52] Would that we could maintain that the statistics for the UK were any higher!

My own perception of the continuing education in which ministers engage tends often to be more related to traditional theological disciplines rather than to the needs of the ministry itself. However, my concern is not for education *per se*, but rather for education which relates directly to the needs and challenges of pastoral ministry.

What are these needs and challenges? A report to the Anglican House of Bishops set out five broad areas for guidance and reflection:[53]

[52] Roy Oswald, *Clergy Self-Care* (The Alban Institute, Bethesda, 1991), p. 12.
[53] *The Continuing Education Of The Church's Ministers* (Advisory Council For The Church's Ministry, London, 1980).

1. Pastoral care and spiritual direction

In his ministry to individuals the minister is expected to provide guidance in each member's spiritual journey towards Christian maturity, as well as pastoral care and counselling for those experiencing stress. This ministry requires a deep awareness of self, of other people, and of God.

2. The ministry of the laity in the world

The minister also acts as part of the support system which encourages, stimulates and strengthens the laity in the attitudes they adopt and the decisions they take with regard to their occupational, political, social and other responsibilities. This requires some understanding of the issues which confront lay people in their various spheres, an understanding which can best be obtained by listening to the laity and learning from them.

3. The ministry of the laity in the Church

One role of the accredited leader is to minister to the ministers, to help them identify and use their gifts of ministry. This requires understanding the ways in which the life of a congregation may be affected by the operation of unconsciously held assumptions.

4. Preaching, teaching and leading of worship

The traditional functions of the ordained minister . . . call for skills of communication and presentation.

5. Church management

For example, handling letters, agendas and accounts.

This is certainly not an exhaustive list of possible areas for continuing education. A sixth broad area should surely focus on evangelism, which strangely does not receive a mention at all! Nonetheless, with the addition of evangelism, we have here a useful multi-stranded basis for continuing education.

All of the main-line denominations in one way or another are now currently seeking to encourage continuing education. The Baptist denomination recommends its constituent churches to grant its ministers not only five weeks of holiday every year, but also a study week each year. The Methodist Church in Britain has an excellent system of offering further ministerial training at key periods in a minister's life: for example, there are courses for those who have been in ministry for five years, ten years, twenty years and thirty years. Sabbaticals are becoming an increasing feature of the ministerial scene: for example, English Baptist ministers are encouraged to take a three-month sabbatical every seventh year after ordination.

Over the last few years an increasing number of British theological colleges have been setting up degree courses in practical theology, somewhat along the lines of the long-established American 'Doctor of Ministry' programmes. This is an excellent development. However, such degree courses, welcome as they are, are not the final solution to the need for continuing education within the ministry. For these degree courses are inevitably limited in time – some can be completed in a year on a full-time basis, others take up to five years on a part-time basis. But a professional approach to ministry involves learning for life. It means that at every stage of ministry – even right up to and including the sixties – ministers are expected to be engaged in in-service training on an annual basis.

Yet in spite of all that is on offer, many ministers do not avail themselves of any of these opportunities to stretch their minds, to reflect on their ministry, and to discover new resources for the task in hand. Such a claim may sound somewhat extravagant. Sadly, a perusal of ministers' libraries reveals that with the exception of a few paperbacks, their personal library has not been substantially expanded since college days.

The ideal would be for continuing education to be compulsory, and for every minister to register for a minimum of five study days a year. However, if compulsory continuing education is not a practical possibility, then maybe the main-line denominations should find some way of indicating within their ministerial handbooks those ministers who are committed to pursuing excellence in ministry by regular in-service training as distinct from those who are not. Admittedly, attendance at such courses does not necessarily guarantee excellence. To that extent the idea of awarding ministers 'stars' along the lines of hotels being awarded stars might not be helpful. Nonetheless, there must be some way of indicating that ministers have met certain minimal standards relating to continuing education.

To return to our overall theme: if pastors are to be effective in the mission to which Christ has called them, then a professional approach to ministry is necessary. The professional pastor is the pastor who refuses to be content with the second best, but rather for the sake of the Church and indeed for the sake of the wider world constantly seeks excellence in ministry.

Chapter 2

The effective leader

The call to lead

Leadership is the key pastoral task

'Leadership,' declares George Barna, is 'the indispensable quality' for a pastor.[1] Leadership is indispensable, because without it churches engage in maintenance rather than in mission. Without leadership churches die.

Peter Wagner's first vital sign of a healthy, growing church is leadership[2] – and rightly so. Without leadership, all the other vital signs are of no effect. True, at the end of the day it is God who gives the growth – but it is the task of the leader to ensure that the sails of the church are set to catch the wind of God's Spirit. Leadership is the essence of the pastoral task. A call to excellence in ministry inevitably involves a call to leadership.

In similar vein, Lyle Schaller defines leadership as the key role of pastors who want to see their churches grow: 'The pastor must have a strong future-orientation. The pastor must be able to see opportunities where others see problems and conflicts. The pastor must be willing to accept and fill a strong leadership role and serve as the number-one leader in the congregation.'[3]

[1] George Barna, *Today's Pastors* (Regal Books, Ventura, California, 1993), p. 117.
[2] C. Peter Wagner, *Your Church Can Grow* (Regal Books, Glendale, California, 1976), pp. 55–68.
[3] Lyle E. Schaller, *Growing Plans* (Abingdon Press, Nashville, 1983). Although Schaller was here writing specifically about larger churches, he later makes the same point more generally in *44 Steps Up Off the Plateau* (Abingdon, Nashville, 1993), p. 61, as he talks of the need for 'visionary initiating leadership'.

The concept of leadership, of course, is not a modern discovery. The Bible has much to say about leadership.[4] It is, for instance, highly significant that in all three lists of spiritual gifts in Paul's writings the gift of leadership is to be found: Romans 12:8, 1 Corinthians 12:8 and Ephesians 4:11. Indeed, with such scriptural precedent in mind, I have argued elsewhere that 'this concept of leadership is the distinguishing concept between the ordained ministry of the church and the general ministry of the church'.[5]

Leadership defined

Leadership has been defined in a variety of ways.[6] Robert Dale, for instance, writes: 'In essence, leadership involves vision and initiative. More comprehensively, pastoral leaders see visions of ministry, communicate our dreams clearly, gain consensus and commitment to common objectives, and multiply our influence by transforming followers into new leaders.'[7] In other words, leadership is first and foremost pro-active. It begins with the dreaming of dreams and the seeing of visions, and then moves on to share those dreams and visions with the church with a view to implementing them in the life of the church and of the wider community.

George Barna in a survey of over 1,000 senior American pastors (i.e. leaders of pastoral teams) found that 'fewer than 4% of all senior pastors were able to communicate a clear vision for their ministry'.[8] It is important to state that by 'vision' Barna does not mean some general mission statement, such as 'to evangelize the lost' or 'to be God's agents of change in a world that needs to be transformed by his love, compassion and grace'.[9] Rather Barna is

[4] A most imaginative approach to leadership in the Bible is provided by Robert D. Dale in *Good News From Great Leaders* (Alban, Bethesda, 1992), which involves an overview of 20 key leadership incidents in the Bible in the light of modern leadership theory.
[5] Paul Beasley-Murray, *Anyone for Ordination?* (Monarch, Tunbridge Wells, 1993), p. 161.
[6] See Paul Beasley-Murray, *Dynamic Leadership* (Marc, Eastbourne, 1990), pp. 13–14.
[7] Robert W. Dale, *Pastoral Leadership* (Abingdon Press, Nashville, 1986), p. 14.
[8] Barna, *Today's Pastors*, p. 118.
[9] Ibid., pp. 117–18.

referring to 'a detailed sense of why God wants a church to exist in the community and how it is unique in comparison'.[10] In this sense 'vision' is equivalent to *God's particular plan for a church*. Barna goes on: 'Why is the Church struggling in America? Because we do not have visionary leaders championing the cause. Is the problem that pastors today are incapable of being visionary leaders or that they have not invested themselves sufficiently in the process to grasp God's vision for their church?'[11]

I believe that Barna is saying something very significant. If pastors wish to excel, then it is not sufficient for them to be leaders, but to be leaders with a purpose. It is not sufficient for a pastor to have a general philosophy of ministry, but rather time needs to be taken to gain a clear sense of God's direction for one's particular church. In this respect I am reminded of John Wimber, whom I heard in his pre-charismatic days speaking of how every Friday morning he used to lie down by his swimming pool, with a glass of Coke in one hand and a Bible in another, and dream dreams! We may not all have our own swimming pool, but this is no reason why we cannot make time to dream dreams and discover God's vision for our church. I confess that a weekly dreaming session seems to me a bit of a luxury – but the principle of taking time out for prayerfully thinking and planning is vital. One reason why churches in England do not prosper is that many pastors are so busy chasing their tails in their pastoral duties that they never make time to find the 'vision'.

Dreaming, of course, is not the monopoly of the pastor. The pastor has no exclusive rights on the Holy Spirit. Indeed, leadership within any given church is always called to be a corporate affair: the leadership is to be shared with other suitably gifted people, be they deacons, elders, or whatever. I for one have benefited greatly from the insights and ideas of my deacons. However, ultimately it is the pastor who has the task – and the privilege – to share the vision with the congregation and then lead the church in implementing the vision.

[10] Ibid., p. 119.
[11] Ibid., p. 120.

Models of leadership

A model of leadership developed by Ernest Mosley[12] and popularised by Robert Dale[13] revolves around three interlocking circles: proclaim, lead and care:

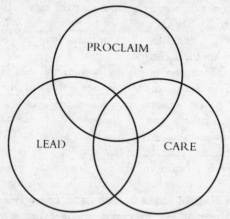

Christian ministry calls on us to (1) proclaim the gospel to believers and unbelievers by means of preaching and worship as well as evangelism and nurture, (2) care for the church's members and other persons in the community through pastoral counselling and visitation as well as through family ministries and grief support, and (3) lead the church in the achievement of its mission.

Undoubtedly the Christian ministry involves all these three activities. However, in the way in which this model is presented, leadership seems to assume a secondary role to preaching and caring. Certainly in the way in which the three circles are drawn 'proclaim' is set above 'lead' and 'care', whereas in our estimation 'lead' should be set above 'proclaim' and 'care'.

A similar point is made by John Finney in a highly perceptive article on 'Patterns of Ministry', where he explores the same three aspects of ministry under three separate categories: pastor, evangelist

[12] Ernest E. Mosley, *Called To Joy: Design For Pastoral Ministries* (Convention Press, Nashville, 1973), pp. 12–28.
[13] Dale, *Pastoral Leadership*, pp. 17–23.

and leader.[14] He gives for each category a description. As far as the pastor and evangelist are concerned, they are a mirror image of one another:

The pastor: centre of interest inside church; adaptor of other's ideas; interested in ongoing relationships; routine is a necessary framework for life; probably introvert; abhors conflict; steady, reliable; limited ambition; happy to live within structures; works well in a team.

The evangelist: centre of interest outside church, creative innovator; interested in the stranger; routine is irksome; probably extrovert; not frightened of conflict; mercurial, unpredictable; ambitious for Christ; impatient of structures; individualistic.

The leader: analytical and strategic thinker who can convey vision; administrator; team builder who gets the best out of others; deep personal spirituality; able to face conflict and enable change; warm personality with a heart for mission.

Of these three, Finney rightly maintains that what a modern congregation most needs is '*leaders*':

A pastor will give them a sense of well-being and of being cared for. A pastor's church is like a warm bath, but it can be enervating for the personal growth of the members of the congregation. It feels as though it is not going anywhere and those who see the church as serving the community feel frustrated ... An evangelist's church will be so orientated towards the outside that those inside feel unloved. The fish are being brought in but then left to flap on the deck until they expire.

On the other hand, a church run by a leader will have a sense of vision and cohesion. It will be truly 'collaborative' for the gifts of everyone will be being honoured and developed. It will balance the need to move outwards in mission with the need to care for the personal needs of the congregation.[15]

In the light of this emphasis on leadership, my own preferred

[14] John Finney, 'Patterns of Ministry' in *Treasure In The Field*, edited by David Gillett & Michael Scott-Joynt (Fount, London, 1993), pp. 88–90.
[15] Finney, 'Patterns of Ministry', pp. 90–91.

model is based on three interlocking circles relating to the three functions of achieving the task, building and maintaining the team, and developing the individual:

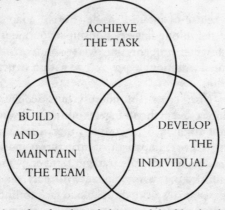

John Adair, who developed this model of leadership, defined the good leader as one who 'works as a senior partner with other members to achieve the task, build the team, and meet individual needs'.[16] In *Dynamic Leadership* I further developed this model in terms of the church, and showed how the good pastor – in the context of this book, the pastor striving for excellence – works as a senior partner with members of the church's leadership team to achieve the 'mission' or 'vision' of the church, to build the church together as a team with a view to it becoming more effective in its mission, and to meet the varied needs of the individual members (such as the need to be led in worship, to be taught, to receive pastoral care, to experience fellowship, to find avenues of service).

Leadership is more than management

Much has been written about the distinction between leadership and management. It is often said, for instance, that leadership is about solving problems, while management is about containing problems. Leadership 'thrives on finding new opportunities', while management 'thrives on accomplishing goals'. Personally I believe that any effective leader of an organisation needs to have certain

[16] John Adair, *Effective Leadership* (Pan, London, 1983), p. 51.

basic management gifts. The most basic of these gifts are to be found in this anonymous 'short course on effective leadership in management':

The *six* most important words:
I admit I made a mistake.

The *five* most important words:
I am proud of you.

The *four* most important words:
What is your opinion?

The *three* most important words:
If you please.

The *two* most important words:
Thank you.

The *one* most important word:
We.

The *least* important word:
I.

Mastering change

In their book *In Search of Excellence* Peters and Waterman analysed 43 of America's best-run companies like IBM and 3M.[17]

But two years after the publication of that best-seller, 14 of these businesses were in financial trouble. *Business Week* magazine explained the reason why: 'failure to react and respond to change'. Leith Anderson, who gives this example, commented: 'One of the realities of the emerging 21st century is that yesterday's successes are no guarantee for tomorrow's survival.'[18] Yes, neither for businesses nor for churches is there room for leaders to sit on their laurels. No institution has ever 'arrived': we are always *en route* to our goal.

[17] Thomas J. Peters & Robert H. Waterman, *In Search Of Excellence* (Harper & Row, New York, 1982).
[18] Leith Anderson, *A Church For The 21st Century* (Bethany House, Minneapolis, 1992), p. 17.

What is more, although the overall goal may not change, the tactics we use to achieve that overall goal will have to vary, if we are to be successful. In this respect there is no magic formula, which once found need not be changed. Some churches appear to think of themselves as jumbo jets, and set themselves on 'auto-pilot'. The reality is that the church is more like a sailing ship, which needs to tack first in one direction and then in another direction if it is to catch the wind of the Spirit.

Change masters

Several years ago my attention was drawn to *The Change Masters* by Rosabeth Moss Kanter, Professor of Business Administration at the Harvard Business School.[19] It made a fascinating read. Although Rosabeth Moss Kanter was writing about 'the need for an American corporate renaissance', the parallels for church life abound. For churches, like businesses, are in the market-place, and if they fail to adapt to a changing world, they too wither and die.

The very title of the book is significant: *The Change Masters*. How many pastors see themselves as 'change masters'? According to Professor Kanter, change masters are 'those people and organizations adept at the art of anticipating the need for, and of leading, productive change'.[20] In this regard I am reminded of the poster which read, 'Plan ahead. It wasn't raining when Noah built the ark.' Or in the words of Samuel Johnson's dictum, 'The future is purchased by the present.' Pastors striving after excellence will want to anticipate the future, in order to master change, rather than be mastered by change.

Change and the past

This best-seller abounds with quotable quotes. For example: 'The change master is partly a historian who knows what pieces of the past to honour and preserve while moving toward a different future,

---

[19] *The Change Masters: Corporate Entrepreneurs At Work* (British edition: Unwin Paperbacks, London, 1984). This formed the subsequent basis of a lengthy review article I wrote for *Church Growth Digest* XIV.2 (Winter 1992/3), pp. 2–3, much of which I have reproduced.
[20] Kanter, *The Change Masters*, p. 13.

but that is not at all the same as letting the past define the future.'[21]
How true that is. A church's history needs to be understood and
honoured, but to allow itself to be bound by its past tradition is
tantamount to receiving the kiss of death.

The activity of change

According to Professor Kanter, 'a prototypical innovation has three
identifiable waves of activity':

firstly, *problem definition* – the acquisition and application of
information to shape a feasible, focused project;

secondly, *coalition building* – the development of a network of
backers who agree to provide resources and/or support;

thirdly, *mobilization* – the investment of the acquired resources,
information and support in the project itself, including activation
of the project's working team to bring the innovation from idea
to use.[22]

Again, what is true of the world is true of the church. If change
is to be successfully managed in a church, the same process must be
followed. True, we may use somewhat different terminology, but
the general thrust is the same.

The tactics of change

I found somewhat amusing Professor Kanter's list of eight 'tactics
that innovators used to disarm opponents':[23]

1. *waiting it out* (when the entrepreneurs had no tools with
   which to counter the opposition directly);
2. *wearing them down* (continuing to repeat the same arguments
   and not giving ground);
3. *appealing to larger principles* (tying the innovation to an
   unassailable value or person);
4. *inviting them in* (finding a way that opponents could share
   the 'spoils' of the innovation);

[21] Ibid., p. 33.
[22] Ibid., p. 217.
[23] Ibid., p. 231.

5. *sending emissaries to smooth the way and plead the case* (picking diplomats on the project team to visit critics periodically and present them with information);
6. *displaying support* (asking sponsors for a visible demonstration of backing);
7. *reducing the stakes* (de-escalating the number of losses or changes implied by the innovation);
8. *warning the critics* (letting them know they would be challenged at an important meeting – with top management, for example).

It doesn't take much imagination to see that all of these tactics could be profitably applied to a local church. I particularly appreciated the book's stress on the need for change masters to be 'masters of the use of participation'.[24] Autocracy doesn't work – either inside or outside the church.

Change is costly
Change is costly in two respects. Firstly, change is costly in terms of hard work and effort. This cost of change is admirably brought out by Leith Anderson in the form of an equation:

$$(D + Pr)HW + PG = \text{changed church}$$

In this equation D = diagnosis; Pr = prescription; HW = hard work; and PG = the power of God. Anderson writes:

Correct diagnosis and right prescription usually need to be *multiplied* by hard work. Change within a church is seldom easy. It takes enormous amounts of prayer, time, money and ministry. There are few shortcuts. Effective churches are most often the product of years of zealous labour rightly deployed.[25]

In other words, excellence in ministry involves 'blood, sweat and tears'. It involves hard work – not least the hard work of thinking through how to manage the process of change within the church.

Secondly, change is costly, for most of us are creatures of habit,

[24] Ibid., p. 241.
[25] Anderson, *A Church For The 21st Century*, pp. 12–13.

who do not like having to adapt to a different way of 'doing church'. To quote Anderson again:

> There is a basic principle of church growth: 'For a church to grow, it must want to grow and be willing to pay the price'. The price is least counted in dollars. It comes in the more costly currency of change. It is doing church in new ways, incorporating new people, moving out of comfort zones, and existing for others rather than for self.[26]

How true that is – and how blind people can be. Time and again people resist change, and in resisting fail to see that they are motivated by concern for self, rather than concern for others.

Change takes time

Change is a process which takes time. How often we learn this to our cost. As Nick Mercer delightfully put it, sudden change

> is a bit like having a baby without being pregnant for nine months. The leaders have spent many hours and days in discussion, in the gestation of the idea. Then the 'baby' is suddenly presented at a Church Meeting which has forty-five minutes to make up its mind! No wonder there are so many unhappy births. The congregation must share in the pregnancy if it is to be a healthy baby.[27]

Certainly, if a major change is to be introduced, plenty of time must be given for the church to absorb its implications. Let me give an illustration from my experience in my present church at Chelmsford to make the point.

In our deacons' meeting of September 1993 we began to talk about the need to draw up a strategy for the church. A sub-group was set up to formulate an appropriate strategy. From then on at every succeeding monthly meeting strategy was on the deacons' agenda. In January 1994 we were ready to bring the strategy to the church. Recognising, however, the importance of the decision, we realised that the church needed time to think the proposals through

[26] Ibid., p. 192
[27] Nick Mercer, 'Coping with Change', *The Fraternal* 234 (April 1991), p. 5.

before having to make a decision. So the strategy was outlined at the January Church Meeting – but with no discussion allowed. Instead it formed the basis for three weeks of discussion in our home groups. In February we then came together for a Sunday afternoon church conference and discussed the proposals in larger groups – but still did not have a plenary debate. It wasn't until the March Church Meeting that we brought the proposals to the vote – by that stage sufficient time had elapsed for most of the church to come behind the leadership, with the result that at a well-attended meeting well over 90% voted in favour. But had the vote been taken in January, the odds are that a very different decision would have been taken.

Change and generations

Many changes which take place in the church have nothing to do with theology, but everything to do with culture. Cultures can be many and varied, but one set of cultures relates purely to age. The period during which people were children has often a lasting impact on the way in which they see the world later as adults.

American church growth pundits see the church as made up of three generations: the *pre-boomers* (born before 1946), the *boomers* or *baby-boomers* (born 1946–64) and the *post-boomers* or *baby-busters*. Each of these generations sees church differently.[28] For example:

Pre-boomers	Boomers	Post-boomers
	Religious factors	
Commitment to Christ = commitment to church	Commitment to Christ = commitment to relationships	Commitment to Christ = commitment to community
Program-oriented	People-oriented	Community-oriented
Money to missions	Money to people	Money to causes
In-depth Bible study & prayer	Practical Bible study, prayer/share	Issue-oriented Bible study, prayer/share
Loyalty to denomination	Loyalty to people	Loyalty to causes
Minister out of duty	Minister for personal satisfaction	Minister to confront issues

[28] This set of generational categories has been variously credited. Leith Anderson, *A Church For The 21st Century* (Bethany House, Minneapolis, 1992), p. 159, attributes it to Gary L. McIntosh. It has also been attributed to Win & Charles Arn, 'Paradigm Shifts', *Church Growth Digest* 13 (Winter 1991/2), pp. 3–5, & 14 (Spring 1992), pp. 14–15.

Programme

Relate to missions	Relate to people	Relate to causes
Stress in-depth Bible study & prayer	Stress fellowship & support groups	Stress Bible studies on issues
Maintain stability	Use variety	Use variety
Focus on marriage & retirement	Focus on marriage & family	Focus on marriage & singles
Be formal	Be relational	Be spontaneous
Encourage contact with post-boomers	Encourage involvement in small groups	Encourage involvement in community issues

Worship

Quietness	Talking	Talking
Hymns	Praise songs	Praise songs
Expository sermons	'How to' sermons	Issue-sermons
Pastoral prayer	Various people pray	Various people pray
Guests recognised	Guests anonymous	Guests anonymous
Organ/piano	Guitars/drums	Jazz ensemble
Low audience participation	Higher audience participation	Lower audience participation

Implications for the future

Ability to carry on programs & projects will wane	Support of people-oriented projects will continue	More involvement with issue-oriented projects
Giving will continue until retirement	Giving will be related to people projects	Giving will be related to issues & causes
Mass evangelism will continue to decline	Friendship evangelism will continue strong	Twelve-step evangelism events will grow
Loyalty to institutions declines	Loyalty to people will continue strong	Loyalty to issues or causes will grow

To what extent some of these categorisations apply to the UK may be debatable. However, the overall thrust of this threefold set of distinctions is undoubtedly right. Different generations see things very differently. Once this basic point is understood by a church, in fact the introduction of change is considerably eased. No longer are proposed changes perceived to be in principle right or wrong, but rather such changes are seen to be age-related. This being so, a lot of the steam is taken out of the debate, and it then becomes easier for a church to consider more calmly the advantages or disadvantages of the proposed change.

Managing conflict

Conflict is a reality in many churches.

On any given day in perhaps three-quarters of all churches the ministry of that congregation is reduced significantly as a result of non-productive conflict. In perhaps one-fourth of all churches that internal conflict is so sufficiently severe that it must be reduced before the parish can redirect its energies and resources towards formulating new goals and expanding its ministry.[29]

Needless to say, any pastor seeking excellence must be able to manage conflict when it arises in the church.

The inevitability of conflict

Conflict management begins by understanding that conflict in the church is inevitable. It is no exaggeration to say that where two or three are gathered in Jesus' name . . . then there is almost bound to be conflict at one time or another. If the truth be told, had someone spoken to me at the beginning of my ministry about the inevitability of conflict, I would have been deeply shocked and would have strongly disagreed. My youthful idealism had no room for conflict in the church. With the passing of 25 years, I have grown wiser!

Much of the conflict that takes place in the Christian Church is rooted in human sinfulness. There is nothing glorifying to God in the statistic that 'involuntary terminations' amongst Southern Baptists have escalated by 31% since 1984.[30] On the other hand, low-level conflict is not necessarily sinful. The presence of low-level conflict, far from indicating breaches in fellowship, may actually indicate depth in fellowship. Churches where differences of opinion never surface may not necessarily be united fellowships; rather, they are probably unreal in their fellowship. Joyce Huggett was indeed right when she wrote: 'Friction in the fellowship need not be feared. Friction, the rubbing together of opposite, sometimes even opposing, viewpoints and personalities, is an integral part of firm relationships. Fellowship breeds friction. You can't have one

[29] Lyle E. Schaller in Foreword to *Leadership And Conflict* by Speed Leas (Abingdon Press, Nashville, 1982).
[30] See also Jerry L. Scruggs, 'The Flexible Leader', *Search* (Winter 1991), p. 30: 'Southern Baptists pastors, according to a recent survey, are being fired by their congregations at the alarming rate of 116 per month.'

without the other.'[31] I find it fascinating how Paul, in a context of unity, urges his fellow-Christians to 'speak the truth in love' to one another (Eph. 4:15): such speaking the truth in love inevitably involves expressions of disagreement and difference. Churches which for 'love's' sake suppress the expression of disagreement and difference, suppress at the same time 'the truth'. For the truth is that the body of Christ is made up of many different kinds of individuals with different experiences and different points of view: it is only as these experiences and points of view are shared that we grow together in maturity in the kind of way that Paul envisages (Eph. 4:16).

This understanding of low-level conflict is surely behind Proverbs 27:17: 'As iron sharpens iron, so one man sharpens another.' It is precisely through the clash of ideas that progress is often made. It is in the powerful exchange of ideas that 'People learn from one another' (Prov. 27:17, GNB). I, for one, would be unhappy to be surrounded by a group of 'yes-men' as my deacons – I learn so much more from people who disagree and have different perspectives on the issue of the day. My church is the stronger precisely because our leadership team is made up of disparate people who are not all in the pastor's mould.

There is therefore a positive side to conflict. Conflict can be beneficial. Indeed, according to Speed Leas, 'unless an organization encourages regular and thorough internal challenge to what it has been doing, it is unlikely to be able to keep up with the changing world'.[32] Similarly Paul Avis states:

> Conflict gives vitality to an institution. It allows internal interest groups to pursue their aims, which may be for the overall benefit of the system. It opens up the system to its environment as fresh energies are drawn in to replace those energies consumed in internal conflicts. It clarifies the true interests of the organization, corrects imbalances and stimulates reform and renewal.

[31] Joyce Huggett, *Conflict: Friend Or Foe* (Kingsway, Eastbourne, 1984), p. 25.
[32] Speed Leas, 'Tension Isn't All Bad', p. 29, in *Mastering Conflict And Controversy* by E. G. Dobson, S. B. Leas & M. Shelley (Multnomah, Portland, Oregon, 1992).

All attempts to create a 'totally homogeneous, unargumentative, no disputations' organization, have tended, as Charles Handy insists, to result in low output and low morale.[33]

For some pastors this kind of thinking may be disturbing. They long for the quiet life – they long for leaders' meetings and church meetings where differences are not expressed, where all is sweetness and light. But such 'rubber stamping' does a disservice to the church. Pastors seeking excellence will encourage diversity of opinion and healthy conflict. Where healthy conflict is present, there issues get more fully explored, better decisions are made, and people become more committed to those decisions.

Encouraging good conflict

How can we encourage our churches to engage in positive debate, without at the same time encouraging anger, bitterness, and resentment? How can we enable our churches to 'fight gracefully'? Speed Leas has some useful suggestions.[34] In summary these are:

1. *Preach about low-level conflict*. Mention in sermons that by articulating differences congregations can grow and mature.
2. *Praise disagreement*. When people disagree with you or others in the congregation, affirm them for raising their concerns. Let them know that, in the long run, such disagreement enhances the church's life.
3. *Mix-up committees*. Encourage chairpersons to put people with different perspective on their committees so that the committee can come to stronger decisions.
4. *Put newcomers on leadership boards*. What old timers have taken for granted, they will question.
5. *Set standards for the work of the church*. Once a year, have committees look at what has happened in the church and ask 'How did we do?' and 'What can we do better?' If not the first year, certainly by the second and third, members will start

---

[33] Paul Avis, *Authority, Leadership And Conflict In The Church* (Mowbray, London, 1992), p. 120.
[34] Speed Leas, 'Tension Isn't All Bad', p. 39 in *Mastering Conflict And Controversy*.

getting the idea that disagreement and challenge is genuinely being sought.

6. *Make clear the rules of healthy conflict.* No hitting! No personal attacks! No talking about people behind their backs!

Conflict, of course, is not always beneficial. All too often conflict can get out of hand and have disastrous effects on the life of the church for years to come. Richard Rusbuldt, for instance, reckons that

> any conflict beyond the simplest levels will cost the church at least ten years before ever recovering its scope and level of ministry at the time the conflict emerged – if it ever does. Pastors (and sometimes their families even more so) suffer significant damage, as well, and some will not be able (or will not want to) continue in pastoral ministry.[35]

Such conflict is clearly to be avoided!

The various levels of conflict

At this stage it may be useful to distinguish between the various levels of conflict. Not all conflicts are all-out war! The various levels of conflict have been helpfully mapped out by Speed Leas:[36]

I. *Predicaments.* The major objective of the parties is to solve the problem. Level-I disputants don't accuse people.

II. *Disagreement.* Parties are still concerned about solving the problem but they are especially concerned about coming out of the situation looking good.

III. *Contest.* The 'players' are less concerned about the problem or looking good: now they want to win and get their way.

IV. *Fight/flight.* The major objective of parties is to break the relationship, either by leaving or getting the other to withdraw. No longer is victory palatable; now the very relationship is a problem.

V. *Intractable.* People believe the opposition is so evil and

[35] Richard E. Rusbuldt, 'When Differences Tear Apart The Body Of Christ', *Ministry Today* 1 (1994), p. 24.
[36] 'The varieties of religious strife', pp. 83–94 in *Mastering Conflict And Controversy.*

virulent that simply getting rid of them will not do. The opposition must be punished and destroyed.

Church conflicts can, alas, become bloody affairs. Indeed, church conflicts can become even bloodier than many a conflict in the world. For church people invoke God and declare him to be on their side, with the result that the conflict becomes even more intense – winning (and beating the living daylights out of the opposition) becomes a tenet of faith. Charles Westermann says: 'How easy to forget that it was the Devil whose tactic in Genesis 3 was getting two people to believe, "You will be like God, knowing good and evil". How tempting even today to mistake our will for God's; how devilish to believe that disagreeing with me is disagreeing with God.'[37] These are sobering words. Sadly, in the heat of the battle, reason goes out of the window and emotion, in the form of religious fanaticism, prevails.

Causes of conflict

The causes of conflict are seldom simple, and often emerge from more than one root. At their simplest, church conflicts may be divided into two types: conflict over facts and conflict involving feelings. Robert Dale writes: 'Fact-based conflicts revolve around role-conflict, philosophical differences, lack of co-operation or competition for leadership. Feeling-orientated differences centre around incompatible personalities, blocked personal or interpersonal needs, and differences or similarities over leader style.'[38] Clearly, feelings and facts impinge on one another, but in low-level conflict normally one or the other predominates. In high-level conflict feelings always predominate!

A more complex categorisation divides conflict into eight types:[39]

    1. *Values Conflict:* e.g. Liberals v. Conservatives, Charismatics v. Non-Charismatics.

---

[37] Quoted by Marshall Shelley, 'Surviving A Power Play', p. 78 in *Mastering Conflict And Controversy.*
[38] Robert Dale, *Pastoral Leadership*, p. 160.
[39] See George Parsons, *Intervening In A Church Fight: A Manual For Internal Consultants* (Alban, Bethesda, 1989), pp. 29–32, following the pioneering work of Speed Leas.

2. *Incompetent pastor or lay-leaders:* e.g. interpersonal or professional incompetence.
3. *Conflict over goals or methods:* e.g. changes to worship.
4. *Interpersonal difficulty:* e.g. unmet needs for inclusion, power, affection as with an 'old guard' and a 'new guard'.
5. *Lack of success, inability to achieve, frustration, blaming:* e.g. decreasing numbers, inability to pay bills.
6. *Bored, apathetic, frightened:* e.g. after a major conflict, suppressed anger may come to the surface.
7. *Breach of organization's trust (usually by clergy):* e.g. theft, sexual misdemeanour.
8. *Structural conflict:* e.g. lack of clear communication between groups.

My own conviction is that a major cause of conflict is change – or the threat of change. 'Probably no other phenomenon in the life of the church today is more disruptive than that of change . . . Older generations, long holding the power reins in churches, will quickly pit themselves against younger generations.'[40] Although theological justification is often given for positions adopted, time and again the underlying reason is not theological at all, but has much more to do with feelings of personal insecurity or the need to be wanted.

Another major cause of conflict, interestingly not mentioned by name in either of the two sets of analyses, is plain old-fashioned 'sin'! Personal jealousies are often at the root of many a church fight.[41]

Handling conflict

The first step to handling negative conflict is to become aware of conflict, before it has time to gestate and devour the church.

[40] Rusbuldt, 'When Differences Tear Apart The Body Of Christ', p. 28.
[41] Sometimes these jealousies hook into the sin of former generations which have never been properly dealt with. Institutions seem to breed 'institutional viruses', which, if unresolved, dog one generation after another. For example, Brian Thorne and Kathleen Baker, reporting on conflict at Lincoln Cathedral, spoke of 'powerful unconscious forces at work . . . These basic assumptions have probably permeated the Lincoln environment for centuries and they operate in complete opposition to the spirit of the cathedral statutes, which require collegiality and co-operation based on an atmosphere of trust' (*The Times*, 30 November 1991).

Rusbuldt is so alarmed by the increase in conflict in today's churches that he even advocates pastors 'at least once a week' spending an hour alone in introspection regarding the life of their church:

> Get off alone by yourself and identify and examine every relationship you have with leaders, groups, or the congregation itself. What about relationships between individual leaders, groups etc.? . . . Don't become another *Titanic*! Remember every major conflict began as the tip of an ice cube.[42]

The advice may sound somewhat over-dramatic: on the other hand, there is nothing worse than waking up and finding you have a major fire on your hands, which is threatening to go out of control.

Having checked out one's feelings and assumptions, the second step is to bring the concerns out into the open. The differences need to be owned and acknowledged. Speed Leas emphasises the need for the leader to 'empower' the apparently 'weaker' party by giving them a voice, for 'the weaker the people perceive themselves to be, the more likely they will fight dirty or use violence'.[43]

The third step is to establish boundaries by setting up ground rules for solving the problem at hand. For example:

1. No one is allowed to define the situation for the other. Each person expresses *only* his or her viewpoint.
2. Space is always given for an alternative point of view.
3. Respond to the statement of the other before expressing your own view.
4. It is OK to disagree. You can enjoy a conversation without coming to agreement. You only need to hear, understand and accept what the other has said as his or her point of view.[44]

Particularly where feelings are involved, it is important to be able to ventilate those feelings in a safe way. Where facts are involved, it is vital for each side to be able to listen to the other – a non-structured

---

[42] Rusbuldt, 'When Differences Tear Apart The Body Of Christ', pp. 22–3.
[43] Speed Leas, *Leadership And Conflict*, p. 29.
[44] David Luecke, *The Relationship Manual*, quoted by Speed Leas, *Leadership And Conflict*, pp. 70–71.

process encourages intensity of debate, which only serves to obstruct the truth.

The fourth step is to seek to negotiate a way forward together. This may involve identifying and building on common points of agreement. It may involve brainstorming for new solutions. It may involve give and take on both sides. It may involve agreeing to disagree, and accepting the will of the majority.

Sadly, there are times when conflict gets out of control. However, even when truth seems to have gone out of the window, it is vital that pastors should retain their composure and integrity. In this regard Jonathan Edwards had wise words to say: 'Resolved: that all men should live for the glory of God. Resolved second: that whether others do or not, I will.' Needless to say, this is sometimes easier said than done. In a conflict situation where ministers find themselves struggling to keep their cool, there is much to be said for 'supervision', which can provide not only a safe outlet for emotions to be expressed, but also an understanding of the aetiology of these emotions. Supervision can help ministers gain perspective, balance and self-control. Supervision can be a channel of healing for pastors in pain.

Maximising time

Maximising time? It doesn't make sense – there are only 168 hours a week! Although there are times when I wish the French Revolution had succeeded in establishing a ten-day week – it would, for instance, mean that I would have fewer sermons to prepare! – I do not mean adding extra hours to the week, but rather making the most of those God has given us.

Ministers for the most part are notorious workaholics.[45] Yes, there are exceptions. There are lazy ministers, but in my experience they are rare. Speed Leas reports on two studies of what an average work-week is for ministers.[46] In one study of 913 clergy of the

45 Robert Banks, *The Tyranny Of Time* (Paternoster, Exeter, 1993), p. 33: 'It would probably be true to say that the clergyman or clergywoman is the busy person par excellence of our times; his or her life more than anyone else's exhibits the desperate shortage of time and accelerating pace of life that have become characteristic of our age.'
46 Speed Leas, *Time Management* (Abingdon, Nashville, 1978), pp. 22–4.

American Episcopal Church, the average clergy work-week was 66.7 hours. Another study by *Minister's Life* revealed an average work-week of 53.7 hours. Leas puts the two together, which average out at ten hours per day. Bearing in mind that this is only an average, half the ministers in the survey were working well over ten hours per day, six days per week – which puts most other groups of workers in the shade.[47]

It is true, of course, that ministers are not the only people working long hours. If one includes commuting time, the hours which many members of my church work in London are frightening. Yet, unlike the average minister, most have two days off at the weekend!

Furthermore, many lay-people not only work long hours, they also give extra time to the church. Some will, for instance, attend church morning and evening on a Sunday, and they will go along to a mid-week home group, and they may give up another evening for church purposes as well. All that could add up to another six or even ten hours a week. Should that not be put into the equation when making comparisons? I am not convinced. The time that lay-people give is discretionary time – it is freely given. Even more importantly, their work for the church is different from their paid employment – it actually is a break from their other routines. Not so for the minister!

Why is it that ministers are such compulsive workers? Eugene Peterson gives two suggestions. First, 'I am busy because I am vain. I want to appear important. Significant. What better way than to be busy?'[48] But why this desire to appear important? Is this desire linked to low self-esteem? This certainly is the verdict of Dianne Fassel: 'Because they judge themselves by their accomplishments, they have the illusion they must always be doing something worthwhile, in order to feel good about themselves ... [Their] sense of self is not separated from their achievements; rather it actually depends upon their achievements. Much

---

[47] British figures appear to be roughly similar. Peter Bates, 'Time – Servant or Master', *Ministry* 22 (Spring 1994), p. 5: 'Studies that I have carried out over many years of the use of their time by clergy show that the average priest in parochial ministry "works" for about 61 hours a week.'
[48] Eugene H. Peterson, 'The Unbusy Pastor', *Leadership* II (Summer 1981), p. 71.

of [their] frantic activity is an attempt to suppress or deny low self-esteem.'[49]

The second reason which Peterson advances for busyness is laziness. 'I indolently let other people decide what I will do instead of resolutely deciding myself. I let people who do not understand the work of the pastor write the agenda for my day's work because I am too slipshod to write it myself.'[50] Here too there is much truth. Many ministers may work long hours, but whether they have got their priorities right is debatable. Part of the trouble is that, in the past at least, by and large most churches have not held their ministers accountable for the use of their time.

Speed Leas adds four other reasons for ministerial workaholism:[51]

Fear of death. Leas quotes Wayne Oates, the distinguished American pastoral consultant: 'I have never met a work addict that I did not think was preoccupied subconsciously with the imminence of his own death. He works intensely, as if there is only a very little time left in which to accomplish his tasks.' Presumably this is linked with low self-esteem.

Fear of failure. This arises from the fact that it is very difficult to measure the results of one's work in ministry. We never really know how we are doing. So we work a little harder, in case we are failing to measure up. Again, this too is linked with lack of self-esteem.

Fear of intimacy. 'Hard work is a wonderful way to avoid getting close to people.' The truth is that some ministers find it very hard to make meaningful relationships – they can be lonely even in the midst of people.

Fear of being alone with yourself. Some ministers are such activists, that they don't know how to be still – either with themselves, or, even more tragically, with God.

Determining priorities

The 19th-century Italian economist, Alfredo Pareto, established

---

49 Dianne Fassel, *Working Ourselves To Death*, quoted in *The Time Crunch* (Multnomah, Sisters, Oregon, 1993), p. 20, by G. Asimakoupoulos, J. Maxwell & S. McKinley.
50 Eugene H. Peterson, 'The Unbusy Pastor', *Leadership* II (Summer 1981), p. 71.
51 Speed Leas, *Time Management*, pp. 26–30.

the 80/20 principle regarding effectiveness of time: 80% of our productivity comes from doing the top 20% of our priorities, while only 20% of productivity comes from the bottom 80% of our priorities.[52] All the more reason to get our priorities straight!

From his perspective as senior pastor of a large Californian church, John Maxwell lists his five priorities:

1. To cast the vision;
2. to be the primary preaching pastor;
3. to take responsibility for the progress of the church;
4. to live a life of integrity as senior pastor;
5. to teach leadership to the pastoral staff.[53]

Others express their priorities differently. Eugene Peterson, for instance, says he has three priorities:

1. I want to be a pastor who prays.
2. I want to be a pastor who preaches.
3. I want to be a pastor who listens.[54]

Priorities vary from minister to minister. The important thing is that we establish our priorities and then stick to them. Instead of being blown hither and thither by every whim of our church members, we will instead be able to develop an 'intentional ministry'.[55]

Determining priorities will involve delegation – and remember that delegation does not involve 'dumping'. Accountability must be built into the process.[56]

Determining priorities may mean not turning up to every session of a conference I'm booked into. Instead, if I regard a session as not of immediate relevance, I'll retire to my room and stimulate my mind with one of a pile of books I have brought along.

[52] Peter Brierley, *Priorities, Planning And Paperwork* (MARC/Monarch, Tunbridge Wells, 1992), pp. 54–5.
[53] John Maxwell, 'Overcoming Procrastination', p. 42 in *The Time Crunch* (Multnomah, Sisters, Oregon, 1993), by G. Asimakoupoulos, J. Maxwell & S. McKinley.
[54] Peterson, 'The Unbusy Pastor', *Leadership* II (Summer 1981), pp. 72–3.
[55] See Glenn Farquhar-Nicol, 'Developing An Intentional Ministry', *Congregations* (Jan./Feb. 1994), pp. 10–11.
[56] See Paul Beasley-Murray, *Dynamic Leadership*, pp. 139–40.

Determining priorities may mean recycling material. It is, for instance, not a good stewardship of time to prepare a new address for every occasion. Thus, in the run-up to Christmas, with all the many carol services a minister may be called to speak at, there is no reason why one's theme in any given year may not for the most part be the same at each.

Once priorities have been set, we have great freedom in being able to say 'no'. The fact is that every time the phone rings, it is not always God on the line![57]

Clearing the clutter

Steve McKinley lists seven 'time bandits':

1. disorganisation
2. chasing rabbits
3. perfectionism
4. poor use of secretary
5. not calling ahead
6. not setting limits
7. reading useless mail[58]

Let me comment on them:

Disorganisation becomes a time bandit when office disciplines are not observed.

Chasing rabbits becomes a time bandit whenever priorities are not observed. It has been said that 'You waste your time, whenever you spend it on something less important when you could be spending it on something more important. Importance is determined by measuring your activities against your objectives.'[59]

Perfectionism becomes a time bandit when we waste time by trying to improve on secondary issues: e.g. my secretary always gives me a draft of the minutes of deacons' and church meetings

[57] See Douglas J. Rumford, 'How To Say No Graciously', *Leadership* III (Fall 1982), pp. 93–8.
[58] Steve McKinley, 'Time Bandits', pp. 65–74 in *The Time Crunch* (Multnomah, Sisters, Oregon, 1993), by G. Asimakoupoulos, J. Maxwell & S. McKinley.
[59] Merrill & Donna Douglass, *Manage Your Time, Manage Your Work, Manage Yourself*, quoted by McKinley, 'Time Bandits', p. 65.

– I am only concerned to ensure that they are a correct record; I am not interested in the quality of the prose.

Poor use of one's secretary becomes a time bandit when I have not prepared the work I need to give her. Incidentally, in my book those ministers who do not have a secretary are not let off the hook – there is no reason why they cannot find themselves a part-time secretary, even if she/he has to work for love rather than for money.

Not calling ahead becomes a time bandit when we do not plan our visiting programme. With almost no exception, I always phone ahead and book my visits. Otherwise, one never knows when a person might be out or when company is expected.

Not setting limits becomes a time bandit when we allow pastoral visits or counselling sessions to go beyond a certain time. An hour should be the absolute maximum length of any visit or session. Indeed, when I hold my weekly pastoral surgery, I allow no more than 30 minutes per person.

Reading useless mail becomes a time bandit when I fail to throw into the waste-paper basket the latest circular. May I make a confession? There are many letters from various worthy charities which I never trouble to open.

Setting a reasonable work-load

What is a reasonable work-load for pastors? Opinions vary greatly. Roy Oswald of the Alban Institute wrote: 'I believe each of us can learn to do our ministries in a fifty-hour work week. That is still ten hours more per week than many persons work.'[60]

The English Methodist Church does not give any detailed guidelines. Nonetheless it exhorts its ministers to take:

> 35 days of holiday a year;
> a break of three consecutive weekdays each quarter;
> a minimum break of 24 hours without structured work each week;
> an hour's break each day for relaxation and exercise![61]

[60] Roy M. Oswald, *Clergy Self-Care: Finding A Balance For Effective Ministry* (The Alban Institute, Bethesda, 1991), p. 123.
[61] Quoted by Ann Bird, *Great Expectations* (Methodist Church Division of Ministries, London, 1990), p. 5.

A different approach to determining a minister's workload is not to count hours, but rather time blocks. Each week has 21 time blocks: i.e. each week consists of seven days of three sessions a day. An employed person in a secular job normally works five days and two sessions per day – i.e. ten sessions a week. Therefore a minister should at the very least work ten sessions a week.

Greg Asimakoupoulos tells of one American pastor who on this basis of time blocks works twelve units a week: a typical week finds him putting in three units each on Mondays and Wednesday; he takes Tuesday off and works mornings and afternoons on Thursday and Friday – two units each day; and he works two more units on a Sunday.[62]

On the same basis of time blocks one friend of mine reckons to work 15 sessions a week. His reasoning is as follows: if, in addition to the ten sessions per week taken up by his normal employment, a member attends church twice on Sunday, the total becomes twelve sessions; a deacon or other church officer might spend two evenings a week on church business; the minister should pave the way and do three – hence 15 sessions. This leaves six sessions (two days) clear. My friend reckons that this is 'quite generous'.

Structuring time

Most books on time management recommend the practice of regularly recording time, then analysing the use of one's time, with a view to becoming a better manager of it.[63] Much as this may prove helpful to some, I have to confess to never having had much success with it. Life is so varied, I am not sure that I am any wiser at the end of it.

I do, however, find it helpful to map out a plan for each day, and to have an overarching structure for each week. For example, I know that I will spend every morning in my office, unless there

62 *The Time Crunch*, p. 91. See also Roger Helland, 'Necessity: Mother Of Invention', *Faith And Renewal* xvii: 6 (May/June 1993), p. 14, who advocates a working week of no more than 13 time blocks: 'It limits us to three (and sometimes four) nights out, and safeguards about one-and-a-half to two days off per week.'
63 For example, Peter Brierley, *Priorities, Planning And Paperwork* (MARC/ Monarch, Tunbridge Wells, 1992).

is a compelling reason for me not to be there. Monday mornings I meet with my staff and sort out a lot of the administration trivia. Friday is my day off. Since whatever else I do on a Saturday, I never prepare my sermons, this means that Tuesday, Wednesday and Thursday mornings are devoted to my sermons. In the afternoons I am flexible: sometimes I continue to work in my office, sometimes I am out visiting. Four evenings a week – Monday to Thursday – are generally devoted to meetings or to visiting.

Note that I work from my office in the church. I find it so much more business-like to be able to go to work. What a relief, too, to be able to go back home and forget work for an hour or two – yes, the telephone still rings, but at least my word processor and all my papers are back at the church. Furthermore, in our particular situation it makes sense all the more, since all our church staff work from the church.

Coping with pressure

One clergyman has said:

> I am appalled at what is required of me. I am supposed to move from sick-bed to administrative meeting, to planning, to supervising, to counselling, to praying, to trouble-shooting, to budgeting, to audio systems, to meditation, to worship preparation, to newsletter, to staff problems, to mission projects, to conflict management, to community leadership, to study, to funerals, to weddings, to preaching. I am supposed to be 'in charge' but not *too* in charge, administrative, executive, sensitive pastor, skilful counselor, public speaker, spiritual guide, politically savvy, intellectually sophisticated. And I am not supposed to be depressed, discouraged, cynical, angry, hurt. I am supposed to be up-beat, positive, strong, willing, available. Right now I am not filling any of those expectations very well. And I am tired.[64]

Stress appears to be the order of the day in Christian ministry. Books abound with such titles as *At Cross Purposes: Stress & Support*

---

[64] Quoted by Barbara Gilbert, *Who Ministers To Ministers? A Study Of Support Systems For Clergy And Spouses* (The Alban Institute, Bethesda, 1987), p. 5.

For The Wounded Healer;[65] Clergy And Laity Burnout;[66] Clergy Stress: The Hidden Conflicts In Ministry;[67] High Calling, High Stress;[68] Honourably Wounded: Stress Among Christian Leaders;[69] Living With Stress – A Guide For Christian Ministers;[70] Ministry Burnout;[71] and Pastors Under Pressure[72] – all of them written with the pastor in mind!

No stage in Christian ministry appears to be exempt. Every phase appears to have its challenge. One survey of ministers, doctors and psychiatrists experienced in counselling ministers in Victoria, Australia, asked the question: 'Do particular periods of stress relate to the age cycle?' The respondents identified, in order of importance, the following 'decades of distress' in the ministry:

30s – career changes, family pressures
40s – mid-life crises, coming to terms with expectations and relationships
50s – approaching retirement
60s – retirement phase.[73]

A different study of ministers in the same state of Victoria revealed a different ordering.[74] In response to the question, 'In your experience, do particular periods of negative stress relate to events along your vocational/career path? In order of importance for you personally, rank the following periods from highest to least stress', the mid-career period won hands down:

65 Robin Pryor, At Cross Purposes (Uniting Church in Australia, Synod of Victoria, Australia), 1986.
66 William H. Willimon, Clergy And Laity Burnout (Abingdon, Nashville, 1989).
67 Mary Anne Coate, Clergy Stress (SPCK, London, 1989).
68 Robin Pryor, High Calling, High Stress (Uniting Church in Australia, Synod of Victoria, Australia), 1982.
69 Marjorie Foyle, Honourably Wounded (MARC Europe, London, 1987).
70 Sarah Horsman, Living With Stress (Society of Mary & Martha, Sheldon, Exeter, 1987).
71 John Sandford, Ministry Burnout (British edition: Arthur James, London, 1984).
72 Paul Beasley-Murray, Pastors Under Pressure (Kingsway, Eastbourne, 1989).
73 Pryor, At Cross Purposes, p. 74.
74 Ibid., pp. 75–6.

Mid-career	1
Second settlement	2
Training for ministry	3
Later in first settlement	4
Ministerial selection process	5
Arrival in first settlement	6
Approaching retirement	7

In response to why they had ranked a particular period as the stage of highest stress, the respondents' answers fell into four categories:

Pressures: 48% (e.g. work, study, family, marital, synod/presbytery, health, age, to leave ministry, financial, mid-life crisis, lack of support, selection procedures).

Unresolved problems: 23% (career choice, theological clash, parish problems, working with colleague).

Changes, readjustments: 17% (work, family, study, city-country, adjusting to role of minister).

Expectations: 12% (expectations of ministry unfulfilled, rejection by colleague/church, training not relevant, poor self-image).

If nothing else, these results reveal the complexity of the stress suffered by ministers. It's hard being a pastor!

My own conviction is that, in the UK at least, the pressures upon ministers are even more broad-ranging. It seems to me that we can divide pressures experienced by ministers into two groups. The first group is *long-standing pressures* which have long been with us: image, visibility, the scapegoat, time, finance, loneliness, powerlessness, few quantifiable results, the endless task, differing if not contradictory expectations.

The second group is *more recent pressures* which are relatively new to ministry: the current theological whirlpool, the numerical decline of the mainline churches, the numerical growth of some churches, the democratisation of education, the influence of the competitive society, the complexity of moral issues, the development of the welfare state, the slowing down of mobility, the uncertainty of the pastor's role.[75]

[75] See Paul Beasley-Murray, *Pastors Under Pressure*, pp. 17–34.

Pressures abound! However, our concern is not so much to analyse the pressures of ministry, but to find ways and means of coping with pressure.

The strategies generally suggested relate for the most part to changing the person. For example, Mary Coates suggests that stress can be managed through:

Support networks (e.g. family, friends, religious superiors, peer support, spiritual direction).

Medical & psychiatric care (where more specialist and focused help is needed).

Self-help preventative activities (e.g. time off, hobbies, time with family and non-work friends, in-service training).

Counselling and therapy.[76]

Roy Oswald's self-care strategies are much more detailed:

Spiritual uplift (e.g. the spiritual disciplines of meditation, journaling, having a spiritual director, chanting, fasting, somatic spirituality, retreats).

Letting go techniques (e.g. biofeed back, autogenic training, hatha yoga).

Time out (e.g. daily, weekly, quarterly and annual breaks; sabbaticals).

Support systems that work (e.g. support networks).

Getting the body moving (e.g. exercise and workouts).

Monitoring our intake (e.g. limiting certain foods, choosing a weight-loss programme).

The psychotherapy tune-up.

Getting control of our time (e.g. role clarity, working to a plan).

The value of assertiveness.

The power of laughter.

Monitoring our ambitions.

Routes to detachment (e.g. hobbies, sports, arts, reflective/expressive work).[77]

[76] Mary Coate, *Clergy Stress*, pp. 192–205.
[77] Roy Oswald, *Clergy Self-Care*, pp. 91–188.

All these strategies have their uses. Of course ministers need to manage their time, of course they need to develop support networks,[78] of course they need to cultivate the spiritual disciplines. But equally – if not more – important is to remove the actual causes of stress, which tend to centre around a wrong understanding of ministry. In this respect Roy Oswald is on the right track when in the category of 'Getting control of our time' he refers to the need for 'role clarity'. If ministers believe that they need to be their church's ever-present omnicompetent dogsbody, then the stress is bound to be overwhelming.

My own definition of pastoral ministry is threefold:

Pastoral ministry is God's ministry. Pastors in the first place are called to be ministers of Christ and not ministers of his Church. True, God calls pastors to serve his Church, and therefore they have an accountability towards those who pay their salaries – but ultimately they are accountable to God. This, although at times a fearful thought, is a liberating thought. It means that ultimately pastors are not dependent upon what others may think of them – it is not other people's judgment which counts, but God's. This theological conviction gives inner security and confidence.

Pastoral ministry is shared ministry. Rightly understood, a church's membership roll is its ministry roll, for every member has a ministry to exercise. This means that it is not all down to the pastor. The work-load is to be shared. What is more, in any given church God has gifted not only the pastor but also a number of others with leadership gifts: these leaders (deacons, elders, members of the

---

[78] I like the six functions of a support group as developed by Barbara Gilbert, *Who Ministers To Ministers?*, p. 22: Comfort, Clarification, Confrontation, Collaboration, Clowning, and Celebration: 'We need people who we can trust with our pain and uncertainty who will *comfort* us, often by just being good listeners. We need people who will help us *clarify* by asking the right questions and pointing us to significant resources. We need people who are about us enough to lovingly *confront* us with that which we don't see or have been avoiding ... We need people to work with who have some of the same goals, visions and problems we do, and who therefore can be *collaborators* (or colleagues) and help us avoid isolation and stagnation in ministry. *Clowns* are persons who can add perspective and support through humor or a light touch at an appropriate moment ... We need people who will *celebrate* our triumphs, large or small, and affirm us as persons.'

PCC, or whoever) are there to share the burden of leadership with the pastor.

Where the ministry of all God's people is taken seriously, pastors are freed to step down from their pedestals and to be liberated from all the false expectations associated with one-man ministry.

Pastoral ministry is specialist ministry. Within this general context of shared ministry, the pastor has a particular ministry to perform. He is not called to be Jack-of-all-trades, but rather he has a particular role to fulfil. According to William Willimon, 'people appear to burn out in the church not necessarily because they are overworked, but because they are overburdened with the trivial and the unimportant'.[79]

The way in which that role is defined varies according to one's philosophy of ministry. In the first place, I see myself called to fulfil four particular roles which cannot be delegated to anyone else: to be a man of God, to be a leader, to be a preacher-teacher, and to be an enabler. In the second place, I see myself caring for those within the fellowship, and also for those outside the church, but many aspects of these tasks of pastoral care, evangelism and social action can be shared and delegated with others.

Where the specialist ministry of the pastor is taken seriously, there the pastor is free to say 'no' to those tasks which rightly belong to others. It is precisely because there is confusion about the pastoral role, that so many pastors find it difficult to say 'no': 'We say yes to everything out of fear that we may say no to the thing we truly ought to be doing.'[80] There is, for instance, no good reason why the pastor needs to be present at every meeting of the church: what pastoral skills, for instance, does the pastor have to offer to the meetings of the fabric and finance committees?

None of this, however, just happens. Few, if any, churches take the initiative into their own hands and redefine the role of the pastor. Rather pastors – as effective leaders – must take the initiative themselves and redefine their role for their people.

Needless to say, at the end of the day we cannot remove all stress – but then, life without stress would be turgid and lacking

[79] Willimon, *Clergy and Laity Burnout*, p. 25.
[80] Ibid., pp. 62–3.

in stimulus. Indeed, a certain amount of stress is necessary to get us motivated and moving. Excellence in ministry disappears when stresses are overwhelming; but it can come to the fore where stress levels are moderate. As Richard Baxter wrote:

> What have we our time and strength for, but to lay them out for God? What is a candle made for but to burn? Burned and wasted we must be; but is it not fitter it should be in lighting men to heaven and in working for God than in living to the flesh?[81]

In conclusion

As the very shepherd imagery inherent in the word 'pastor' implies, pastors are called to be leaders. This is part of their God-given calling. And along with their calling, God provides gifts for leadership. These gifts vary – and no doubt are dependent upon personality. The task of pastors seeking excellence is to develop their God-given gifts. For leaders are not just born – they also are made. In other words, when it comes to leading God's people, it is not sufficient for us to fall back upon our natural ability. Rather, there is much to be gained by applying our minds and learning from others about such vital issues as the management of change or the handling of conflict. The pursuit of excellence involves the constant pursuit of self-improvement. Needless to say, for any pastors worth their salt, this pursuit is never an end in itself, but rather always has the life, health and growth of the church in view.

[81] Richard Baxter, *The Reformed Pastor* (Banner of Truth, London, 1974 edition), p. 218.

Chapter 3

The charismatic preacher

The call to preach

Has preaching had its day?

If there is one area in which pastors should excel, it is preaching. Preaching – for Protestantism at least – lies at the heart of ministry. In North America, for instance, the pastor is often known as 'the preacher'. Not surprisingly, in Barna's survey of more than 1,000 senior American pastors, preaching tops the list as far as the primary joys of pastoring are concerned.[1] Preaching for many ministers is their number-one priority.

But all is not well with preaching. For although in some evangelical circles at least, preaching has become the virility test of ministry, the ministry is in a parlous state at the moment. Time and again all too many preachers are boring, long-winded, and irrelevant.

Not that there is anything new in all this. In 1857 Anthony Trollope wrote:

> There is, perhaps, no greater hardship at present inflicted on mankind in civilized and free countries, than the necessity of listening to sermons. No-one but a preaching clergyman has, in these realms, the power of compelling an audience to sit silent and be tormented. No-one but a preaching clergyman can revel in platitudes, truisms and untruisms, and yet receive, as his undisputed privilege, the same respectful demeanour as though

[1] George Barna, *Today's Pastors*, p. 65.

words of impassioned eloquence, or persuasive logic, fell from his lips.[2]

The truth is that in many ways Trollope does not overstate his case. The mind boggles at how unself-aware some ministers must be – otherwise they would have packed up preaching a long time ago!

The question therefore arises: has preaching had its day? Just as churches are rapidly scrapping their pews today, should they scrap their pulpits too?

Preaching, it is said, because it is non-cooperative communication, is no longer suitable for our time. It is like using a paraffin lamp in the age of electric light.[3] The sermon has been described as 'a monstrous monologue by a moron to mutes'. Furthermore, not only is preaching often boring, it is also frequently remarkably ineffective. American research has indicated that immediately following the worship service, fewer than one-third of the persons tested could give a reasonably clear statement of the primary 'question' of the sermon or the 'answer' suggested in the message. In another research project the results were even worse: 21% of the 271 persons (who all felt that the sermon was either 'superior' or 'good') could reflect the preacher's central message clearly and accurately.[4] And, of course, none of this research indicated whether or not those who did remember what the sermon was about, actually changed their minds or behaviour as a result of what they heard!

I'm reminded of the wonderfully perceptive comment of the 19th-century preacher, Henry Ward Beecher, who complained that 'the churches of the land are sprinkled all over with bald-headed old sinners whose hair has been worn off by the friction of countless sermons that have been aimed at them and have glanced off and hit the man in the pew behind'! In other words, it's all too possible to hear what the preacher is saying, and yet fail to apply it personally.

---

[2] Quoted by John R. W. Stott, *I Believe In Preaching* (Hodder & Stoughton, London, 1982), pp. 53–4.
[3] H. D. Bastian, cited by Klaas Runia, *The Sermon Under Attack* (Paternoster, Exeter, 1983), p. 9.
[4] Klaas Runia, *The Sermon Under Attack*, pp. 10–11.

In the light of such criticisms and comments, it is tempting to ditch preaching altogether. Haven't we preachers got better things to do with our time? Just think of all the hours that are put into sermon preparation week by week. Then multiply these hours by the number of sermons preached in the country. It is estimated that in England and Wales alone some 50,000 sermons are delivered each week. Think of all the positive things that could be done with the time currently devoted to preaching!

But, of course, it is not as simple as that. Undoubtedly many sermons are boring. We have all counted the number of pipes in the organ or panes of glass in the window. Indeed, maybe we've been gently anaesthetised and fallen asleep. Edmund Jones tells of a minister who received a query from the Civil Defence Unit asking how many people could be accommodated in his church in the event of an attack. 'I don't rightly know,' he replied, 'but we sleep 300 comfortably every Sunday'![5]

However, the abuse of the medium does not invalidate the medium. Let me illustrate. Many video shops do a flourishing trade in hiring out films glorifying violence and sex. But does the abuse of that medium necessarily invalidate that medium? Of course not! The same argument applies to preaching. The fact that much preaching falls far short of the mark, does not necessarily mean that all preaching should therefore be scrapped. There are times when preaching can be remarkably effective. Many a Christian can testify to a time when, quite unexpectedly, God broke through and addressed them directly by means of a sermon. True, this is not an experience that happens to everybody every Sunday, but even that does not invalidate the ordinary preaching that goes on Sunday by Sunday.

All this is well illustrated in a correspondence that took place a number of years ago in the former *British Weekly*. It began with the publishing of this provocative letter:

Dear Sir,
It seems ministers feel their sermons are very important and spend a great deal of time preparing them. I have been

5 Edmund Jones, *Expository Times* 92 (1980–81), 'Preparing The Weekly Sermon', p. 228.

attending church quite regularly for 30 years and I have probably heard 3,000 of them. To my consternation, I discover I cannot remember a single sermon. I wonder if a minister's time might be more profitably spent on something else?

The *British Weekly* received a storm of responses. The correspondence was finally ended by the following letter:

Dear Sir,

I have been married for 30 years. During that time I have eaten 32,850 meals – mostly my wife's cooking. Suddenly I have discovered I cannot remember the menu of a single meal. And yet . . . I have the distinct impression that without them, I would have starved to death long ago.

I find this argument convincing. Not all preaching has to be remembered to be effective. On the other hand, we must not be fooled into believing that there is no room for improvement. Far from it: there is much room for improvement. But this does not mean that the basic institution of preaching has had its day and is now ready to be scrapped.

For if preaching has had its day, then what else would we put in its place? How else would the Gospel be communicated? For a good number of years, small groups have been very much in vogue in church life. Probably most churches have now switched to home groups in place of the traditional mid-week meeting. A few churches have even experimented with discussion groups instead of the evening service. But are discussion groups the solution for the sermon? Surely not. The discussion group might supplement the sermon, but can never replace it. The Gospel is about news, and not views. The preacher is God's herald and proclaims the great acts of God in Christ. There is a place for 'one-way' communication. The implications of the Good News can no doubt be discussed, but the 'news' itself is beyond dispute and needs to be made known. This is the task of the preacher. In the splendid words of the great Scottish preacher, James Stewart,

The Church needs men [and women!] who, knowing the world around them, and knowing the Christ above them and within, will set the trumpet of the Gospel to their lips, and proclaim His sovereignty and all-sufficiency.[6]

Yes, of course there are other means by which the Gospel can be communicated. There is a very real place for dance, drama, film and video-clip. But none of these will ever take the place of the sermon. At the turn of the century the Scottish theologian, P. T. Forsyth, was not over-bold when he declared: 'with its preaching Christianity stands or falls'.[7]

It is not without significance that the churches that are growing today are, in the vast majority of cases, the churches where preaching and teaching are taken seriously. 'Is it not clear,' asked Martyn Lloyd Jones, 'that the decadent periods and eras in the history of the Church have always been those periods when preaching had declined?'[8]

A defence of preaching, however, does not involve a defence of preachers. The fact is that in many places the Church today is experiencing a dearth of good preaching. Haddon Robinson does not exaggerate: 'Most modern preaching evokes little more than a wide yawn. God is not in it.'[9] We preachers cannot, therefore, afford to sit on our laurels. We need to turn the tide of mediocrity and strive instead for excellence.

Preaching with the Gospel in view

Preaching is essentially the declaration of the Good News of Jesus Christ. Mark's summary account of the ministry of Jesus – 'Jesus went . . . proclaiming the good news of God. "The time has come," he said. "The kingdom of God is near. Repent and believe the good news!"' (Mark 1:14–15) – is a paradigm for all Christian preachers.

[6] J. S. S. Stewart, Preaching (Hodder & Stoughton, London, 2nd edition, 1955), p. 12.
[7] P. T. Forsyth, Positive Preaching And The Modern Mind (Independent Press, London, 1907), p. 1, begins with the words: 'It is, perhaps, an overbold beginning, but I will venture to say that with its preaching Christianity stands or falls.'
[8] D. Martyn Lloyd Jones, Preaching And Preachers (Hodder & Stoughton, London, 1971), p. 24.
[9] Haddon W. Robinson, Expository Preaching: Principles & Practice (British edition: IVP, Leicester, 1986), p. 18.

As far as the Early Church was concerned, that declaration of the Good News was primarily directed toward those outside the Church (see, for instance, Acts 8:15, 25, 40; 10:36; 14:7, 21; 16:10). It has often been pointed out that in the New Testament there is a distinction between preaching or 'proclamation' (*kerygma*) and 'teaching' (*didache*). The former was the public proclamation of the Good News of Jesus to the non-Christian world; the latter was teaching directed toward the Church. Does this mean that there is no room for 'preaching' in the Church? Clearly not.

First of all, every church at the very least has its special occasions when 'outsiders' are present. Whether it be Christmas or Easter, a guest service or a baptismal service, or just an 'ordinary' service, every church has times when people are present who know not the Saviour. On those occasions when non-Christians are present in large numbers, I find it an awesome responsibility to have to preach the Gospel. This may be the one and only occasion that some may darken the door of a church, the one and only opportunity they may have to hear the Gospel. How can I present it in ways which are meaningful and relevant to them? How can I ensure that my preaching – indeed, the service as a whole – is not a stumbling-block to the Gospel?

At the very least the presence of visitors in our midst means that all that is said and done needs to be 'seeker-friendly'. For some, seeker-friendly evangelism means holding 'seeker services' which involve doing away with the normal worship of the church. It is argued that 'only the most determined seekers, or those seekers who have been exposed to a church culture in the past . . . will be able to penetrate the mysteries offered in a worship service intended for believers'.[10] So special services are being designed to enable the visitor to feel comfortable and at home in a church context:

> As you arrive you'll be given a programme and you can sit and listen to live music, which may be classical, jazz or rock. The service will continue the musical theme with either a soloist or a small group singing. You may be asked to join in a particular song of worship (words will be on the

[10] Martin Robinson, *A World Apart: Creating A Church For The Unchurched* (Monarch, Tunbridge Wells, 1992), p. 74.

programme) as you stay seated. If you prefer, please feel free just to observe.

Each service will be different but the basic element of music, drama, contemporary song and audio-visual presentations will be maintained. You may be led in prayer by someone on the stage and a relevant passage from the Bible may be read after a brief introductory explanation. There'll be a talk on the issue of the day – hopefully you'll find that not just easy to listen to, but informative and personally relevant.

Our aim is to give you a totally new experience of church from what you may have had in the past. A church service designed for the 1990s. A church service for the non-religious, non-church attender. A church service that's relevant to you as you cope with the pressures of modern life.[11]

Much as I am impressed by such a presentation, I am not convinced that a 'seeker-friendly' service has to do away with the worship of the church. For Christian worship can be winsome:

When Christians are to be found really worshipping God, loving Him, excited with Him, and when their worship makes them into a caring community of love, then questions will certainly be asked, leading to excellent opportunities for sharing the good news of Christ.[12]

My mind goes to the story of the conversion of the Ukraine, and how the prince of Kiev sent several of his followers out to find the true religion. In their travels, they visited a mosque where they reportedly found 'no joy'. Further searching of various religions and worship practices revealed nothing satisfactory. But in Constantinople they worshipped at a Christian church. Here they experienced a worship that drew them to God and converted them to Christ. 'We knew not whether we were in heaven or on earth,' they wrote. 'We cannot describe it to you: only this we know, that God dwells there among men, and that their service

---

[11] Part of a printed invitation to 'First Sunday', the Seeker Service of Altrincham Baptist Church, Cheshire.
[12] David Watson, *I Believe In Evangelism* (Hodder & Stoughton, London, 1979), p. 166.

surpasses the worship of all other places.'[13] Their experience was indeed the experience envisaged by Paul, where within the context of a worshipping congregation the person would 'fall down and worship God, exclaiming, "God is really among you!"' (1 Cor. 14:25).[14]

But worship apart, one thing is for sure: in a context where non-Christians are present, the Good News needs to be proclaimed in a way which relates to the crucified and risen Lord Jesus to the perceptions and felt needs of its hearers. The language used in such a presentation will hopefully be jargon-free. But in essence there should be no difference in method between preaching to Christians and preaching to non-Christians. There are not 'evangelistic' sermons as over against 'expository' sermons. Rather, some expository sermons are 'evangelistic' in nature, while others may have the 'edification of the saints' in mind. Both, however, need to be rooted in Scripture and rooted in the contemporary world.

Secondly, even when no 'outsiders' are apparently present, God's people still need to hear that God loves them. They may not need to hear 'evangelistic' sermons; but they certainly need to hear 'evangelical' sermons: that is, 'preaching is always the articulation of the *evangelion* of what God has done, is doing, and will do in Jesus Christ'.[15] For life can be tough; behind their masks many Christian people today are hurting. They need constantly to be reminded that whatever their outward circumstances, one thing is for sure: God loves them, and the proof of that is his Son. In the context of the world's suffering we need to preach Christ crucified and risen. In the words of James Stewart:

> Be very clear about this, that what men and women need, face to face with the mystery of pain and trouble and tragedy, is not a solution that will satisfy the intellect, not that primarily at any rate, but a force that will stabilize the soul; not a convincing

---

[13] Robert Webber, 'Evangelism through Worship', *Decision* (July-Aug 1989), p. 23. See also Paul Beasley-Murray, 'Worship and Presence Evangelism', *Global Church Growth* 30 (Jan.–Mar.1993), pp. 11–12.
[14] See also Paul Beasley-Murray, *Faith And Festivity* (Marc/Monarch, Eastbourne, 1991), pp. 117–22.
[15] Richard J. Neuhaus, *Freedom For Ministry*, p. 157.

and coercive argument as to the origins of evil or the reasons why such suffering is permitted on the earth, but a power that will enable them to 'stand in the evil day, and having done all, to stand'; in short, not an explanation, but a victory.[16]

Expounding God's Word for today

Preachers who have excellence in view in the first place must expound God's Word for today. This means, on the one hand, taking God's Word seriously, and, on the other hand, relating God's Word to the real world in which our hearers live.

Taking God's Word seriously

First and foremost, the pursuit of excellence means taking God's Word seriously. In the title of H. H. Farmer's book, the preacher is *The Servant Of The Word*.[17] We are not in the business of sharing our views on the week's news, but rather our business is to expound God's Word. The task of the preacher is not to entertain the congregation, but to enable God's people to hear God speak.

'All true Christian preaching is expository preaching,' declared John Stott, and rightly so.[18] The Bible is the source of the preacher's authority. Our only claim to be heard is that our message is rooted in the Word of God. If as preachers we preach our own opinions, our congregations may listen to them politely, but at the end they have every right to reject them. But if the content of our preaching is Bible-centred and Bible-driven, then our preaching has a God-given authority – we then become God's heralds, his ambassadors, his agents.

Taking God's Word seriously inevitably leads to expository preaching. Haddon Robinson has defined expository preaching as

the communication of a biblical concept, derived from and transmitted through a historical, grammatical and literary study

[16] James Stewart, *Preaching*, p. 67.
[17] Herbert H. Farmer, *The Servant Of The Word* (Nisbet & Co., London, 1941).
[18] John Stott, *I Believe In Preaching*, p. 125.

of a passage in its context, which the Holy Spirit first applies to the personality and experience of the preacher, then through him to his hearers.[19]

More simply put, expository preaching is 'unpacking' God's Word and making it clear for all to see. Expository preaching is truly biblical preaching. Preaching is truly biblical, said Leander Keck, 'when (a) the Bible governs the content of the sermon and when (b) the function of the sermon is analogous to that of the text. In other words, preaching is Biblical when it imparts a Bible-shaped word in a Bible-shaped way.'[20]

Let me hammer this point home. Expository preaching involves expounding God's Word as found in the Bible as distinct from imposing our 'word' upon a biblical text. Biblical preaching involves *exegesis* – a reading out; rather than *eisegesis* – a reading in. Expository preaching wrestles with the message contained within the text; it does not allow the text to become a peg for our ideas and preconceptions.

There is more to expository preaching than having a text. 'Some brethren,' remarked the Victorian prince of preachers, Charles Haddon Spurgeon, 'have done with their text as soon as they have read it. Having paid all due honour to that particular passage by announcing it, they feel no necessity further to refer to it. They touch their hats, as it were, to that part of Scripture, and pass on to fresh fields and pastures new . . . Surely the words of inspiration were never meant to be boothooks to help a Talkative to draw on his seven-leagued boots in which to leap from pole to pole.'[21] As it is, in many churches the text can be likened to the national anthem played at a football game – 'it gets the thing started, but is not heard again during the afternoon'.[22]

Gordon Rupp tells the delightful apocryphal story of three of the disciples who, when Jesus and the fishermen apostles had gone,

[19] Haddon Robinson, *Expository Preaching*, p. 20.
[20] Leander Keck, *The Bible In The Pulpit* (Abingdon, Nashville, 1978), p. 106.
[21] C. H. Spurgeon, *Lectures To My Students* (First Series, Passmore & Alabaster, London, 1897), p. 75.
[22] Haddon Robinson, *Expository Preaching*, p. 20.

decided to try their own hand at preaching from a boat. So they pushed out the little craft and addressed the people standing on the shore. But they had forgotten to tie the mooring rope and so as they spoke they drifted further and further away, became less and less audible, began to shout louder and louder and gesticulate more and more wildly until they fell backwards into the lake. 'As a parable it is perhaps nearer to Monty Python than the NT but it has a point,' commented Gordon Rupp. 'A Biblical text is at least a mooring rope.'[23]

We may also add that expository preaching involves more than citing Scripture texts throughout the sermon. I well remember listening to one elderly minister preach; he peppered his address with more than 50 Scripture quotations. But the quotations added nothing to the preaching. He took proof texts from Scripture to support his thesis; he failed to submit himself and his sermon to the Word of God, in the sense that the Scriptures failed to shape his sermon. The old saying is still true: a text without a context is a pretext.

The benefits of expository preaching have been well set out by John Stott:[24]

1. First, *exposition sets us limits*. It restricts us to the scriptural text, since expository preaching is Biblical preaching.
2. Secondly, *exposition demands integrity* . . . What every Bible student must look for is the plain, natural, obvious meaning of each text, without subtleties.
3. Thirdly, *exposition identifies the pitfalls* we must at all costs avoid. Since the resolve of the expositor is to be faithful to his text, the two main pitfalls may be termed forgetfulness and disloyalty. The forgetful expositor loses sight of his text by going off at a tangent and following his own fancy. The disloyal expositor appears to remain with his text, but strains and stretches it into something quite different from its original and natural meaning.
4. Fourthly, *exposition gives us confidence to preach* . . . Like

[23] Gordon Rupp, *THE WORD and the words* (Diamond Jubilee Lecture of the London Baptist Preachers' Association, London, 1972), p. 10.
[24] John Stott, *I Believe In Preaching*, pp. 126–33.

the ancient Jews we have been 'entrusted with the oracles of God' (Rom. 3:2).

A fifth advantage, not mentioned by John Stott here, is that expository preaching enables the preacher to remain fresh. When we conscientiously expound God's Word Sunday by Sunday, we discover that we are always finding new truths to impart. But left to our own devices, we soon run out of bright ideas. 'The preacher who expounds his own limited stock of ideas becomes deadly wearisome at last. The preacher who expounds the Bible has endless variety at his disposal. For no two texts say exactly the same thing.'[25]

Let it be said loud and clear: orthodoxy is no guarantee of Bible-shaped preaching. There are many preachers who happily subscribe to the authority of the Scriptures, and yet fail to put their high view of Scripture into practical effect. They stand there with an open Bible in their hands, but in fact never open up God's Word to his people.

So what in practical terms does taking God's Word seriously mean? It means that those who aim at excellence must be prepared to study the Scriptures, and to study them in depth. For the sake of our own personal integrity, it means that we must have wrestled with the text, and ensured that we have really understood what the writer was seeking to say in the first place. For those who are able, this will mean reading the passage in its original Hebrew or Greek. It will certainly mean comparing one English version with another to gain the various nuances present in the text. We shall want to see how God has guided his people in the past in understanding the text (2 Pet. 1:20). We shall therefore want to read several commentaries on the passage in question. Not just popular commentaries – although they can be helpful because of the illustrations they may provide – but scholarly commentaries too. We shall consult the concordance. We shall want to use every tool that is at our disposal in getting to grips with the text. We shall not be satisfied until we have plumbed the depths of the passage in question.

Relating God's Word to today
Secondly, excellence in preaching means applying God's Word to our congregations creatively, sensitively and relevantly.

[25] James Stewart, *Preaching*, p. 96.

It is not enough to understand what God said hundreds of years ago. We need to know what God through his Word of old is now saying to us and to our congregation today.[26] God's Word must be brought to bear upon life as it is today. In the words of Jim Packer, 'As preaching is God-centered in its viewpoint, Christ-centered in its substance, so it is life-centered in its focus and life-changing in its thrust. Preaching is the practical communication of truth about God as it bears on our present existence.'[27] In other words, 'preaching must be more than talk about Biblical texts'.[28] Faithful preaching which is not relevant preaching is useless preaching.

The German preacher-theologian Helmut Thielicke told young aspiring preachers:

> As long as I discover no connection between the gospel and the problems of my life, then it has nothing to say to me and I am not interested. And that is precisely why the gospel must be told in new ways to every generation, since every generation has its own unique questions. This is why the gospel must constantly be forwarded to a new address, because the recipient is repeatedly changing his place of residence.[29]

That is why it does no good for us to preach again great sermons from past eras. I have on my shelves a complete set of Spurgeon's sermons; I have too all Alexander Maclaren's sermons. But these sermons are unpreachable. In their day Spurgeon and Maclaren made

[26] For a sermon to be effective, the Word must in the first place speak to the preacher: see John Goldingay, 'The Spirituality of Preaching', *Expository Times* 98 (1976–7), p. 198: 'I doubt whether preaching that searches and nurtures generally results from attempting to discover what the Bible has to say to *them*. It issues from realizing what the Bible has to say to me.' On the other hand, there is also a place for what Goldingay calls 'vicarious listening'.

[27] J. I. Packer, 'Why Preach?' p. 10 in *The Preacher And Preaching* (Presbyterian & Reformed Publishing Co., Phillipsburg, New Jersey, 1986), edited by S. T. Logan.

[28] W. A. Beardslee, J. B. Cobb, D. J. Lull, R. Pregeant, T. J. Weeden & B. A. Woodbridge, *Biblical Preaching On The Death Of Jesus* (Abingdon, Nashville, 1989), p. 17.

[29] Helmut Thielicke, *How Modern Should Theology Be?* (British edition: Collins Fontana, London, 1970), p. 10.

a great impact on their contemporaries: crowds flocked to hear them in London and Manchester respectively. But their sermons, though once highly relevant, are now dated. It is not that the Word of God has become dated; it is, of course, that the situation has changed.

How do we root our sermons in the real world of today? First of all, by keeping abreast of what is happening in the world of today. 'What do you do to prepare your Sunday sermon?' Karl Barth was once asked. He answered: 'I take the Bible in one hand and the daily newspaper in the other.' Similarly, precisely because he wants to speak relevantly to the ordinary unchurched person, Bill Hybels, the senior pastor of Willow Creek Community Church, Chicago, in addition to reading a daily paper, watching the television and listening to the radio, reads *Time, Newsweek, US News & World Report, Forbes* and usually *Business Week*.[30] We may not be a Karl Barth or a Bill Hybels, but this does not discharge us from an obligation to be familiar with the culture of our day. Preachers dare not retreat into a religious ghetto if they wish to preach effectively. I believe it a cause of concern that there are pastors who do not, for instance, take a daily paper. It is not enough to say 'I don't have the time.' We need to make the time to hear what other people are thinking and saying. Ezekiel sat down amongst his contemporaries and experienced something of their pain (Ezek. 3:15); preachers today need to follow his example.

Inevitably this creates a tension within the preacher. Preaching must on the one hand relate to the real world in which our hearers live. But on the other hand, preaching, if it is to be biblical, must be anchored in the Word of God. This tension has been well expressed by Ian Pitt-Watson:

> Every sermon is stretched like a bowstring between the text of the Bible on the one hand and the problems of contemporary human life on the other. If the string is insecurely tethered to either end, the bow is useless.[31]

---

[30] Bill Hybels, 'Speaking to the Secularized Mind', p. 36 in *Mastering Contemporary Preaching* (British edition: IVP, Leicester, 1991), by Bill Hybels, Stuart Briscoe & Haddon Robinson.
[31] Ian Pitt-Watson, *A Kind Of Folly: Toward A Practical Theology Of Preaching* (St Andrew Press, Edinburgh, 1976), p. 57.

In other words, it doesn't matter how 'sound' the sermon might be, how faithful the preacher is to the text: if the sermon fails to connect to the world of today, then the sermon fails. Preaching involves the preacher – and the congregation – living in two worlds, the world of the Bible and the world of the here and now. The two must be inextricably linked if the sermon is to hit its mark.

Preaching, according to Bishop Stephen Neill, may therefore be likened to weaving:

> There are the two factors of the warp and the woof. There is the fixed, unalterable element, which for us is the Word of God, and there is the variable element, which enables the weaver to change and vary the pattern at his will. For us that variable element is the constantly changing pattern of people and situations.[32]

The skill of the preacher lies in combining faithfulness to the Word of God and sensitivity to the world. Preachers of a more conservative theological persuasion tend to be good at being biblical, but less successful at being contemporary; while preachers of a more liberal theological persuasion tend to be good at being contemporary, but less successful at being biblical. Excellence in preaching involves being at one and the same time both biblical and contemporary.

But for the pastor, preaching must not only be rooted in the real world out there, it must also be rooted in the real world as represented in the congregation. The two are not always the same. One of the frustrations of itinerant preaching is that the visiting preacher does not know where the local congregation is at. Preaching in such a context is like firing off a hail of bullets in all directions in the hope that one or two of them will hit the target. The joy of pastoral preaching is discovering that time and again not only does God's Word speak into the general contemporary scene; there is also a specific word for the local church too.

Hence, when it comes to sermon preparation, not only do we need to be listening to voices in the world, we need also to be listening to voices in the congregation. Pastoral preaching is, for instance, always the better for pastoral visiting.

[32] Stephen Neill, *On The Ministry* (SCM, London, 1952), p. 74.

David Schlafer describes what is involved in listening to a congregation:

> Listening to a congregation does not mean that the preacher will try to figure out what the people want to hear. Nor does it mean that members of a congregation will be shocked by (or apprehensive about) the use of personal confessions or life secrets from the pulpit. A preacher does not listen to parishioners in order to seek out foibles against which to rail, anonymously or in the abstract. Rather, in regular parish activities, casual conversations, and formal appointments, preachers listen for the heartbeat of the parish – its fears, hopes, joys, stresses, blind spots; its rough and cutting edges. If this listening is intent and ongoing, a preacher will be able to offer a relevant word in moments of crisis, as well as to draw attention to subtle shifts in parish mood and direction that need to be encouraged or held up to scrutiny.[33]

Preaching relevantly will therefore mean that no sermon can ever be repeated without revision. If preaching is proclaiming God's Word into a particular situation, then inevitably such preaching has a sell-by date. The temptation for busy pastors who move to a new church is to draw upon their stock of old sermons; but to do so without listening afresh to the voices of the day is a recipe for ineffectiveness.

Preparing to preach

Excellence in preaching centres on expounding God's Word to today's people. Such excellence, however, is only achieved as care and effort are given to the creation of the actual sermon itself. Effective preaching involves more than inspiration – it also involves the hard grind of painstaking sermon preparation. And yet, preaching is only truly effective as God himself takes our words and

[33] David J. Schlafer, *Surviving The Sermon: A Guide To Preaching For Those Who Have To Listen* (Cowley Publications, Boston, Massachusetts, 1992), p. 48.

empowers them by his Spirit. Effective preaching therefore demands that our preparation includes a sense of expectancy that God will use us in his service. In other words, we need to preach memorably, with due care, and with a sense of spiritual expectancy.

Preaching memorably

First of all, in our preparation we need to give shape to our preaching, so that God's Word is allowed maximum impact on our hearers. Only so will preaching become fixed in people's minds and hearts; only so will it become, in the best sense of the word, memorable.

Preparing a sermon, therefore, involves three stages: it involves listening to the voice of God in Scripture, listening to the voices in the world of today, and then fixing the listening process in a way which enables people to hear clearly what God would say to them through the preacher. Shaping the sermon involves hard work.

Needless to say, there is no one God-given way in which sermons must be shaped. In some traditions a good sermon has three points together with an introduction and a conclusion. However, there is no reason why a sermon should not have four points or five points, or two main points, each with two sub-points. Sermons assume many forms. The important thing is that the preacher does not engage in a leisurely discursive ramble, but rather that the preacher has a structure which serves to ram home the points that need to be made on the basis of the passage for the day.

Structure gives clarity to preaching. Napoleon is said to have had three commands for his messengers: 'Be clear! Be clear! Be clear!' Preachers too need to be crystal clear. Our congregations need to be able to leave the service under no illusion about what was said.

Structure gives purpose and power to preaching. It enables preachers to develop an argument and apply it so that there is only one conclusion. For preachers, like barristers, are advocates – they are seeking a verdict. Preaching is not about God and about 20 minutes. True preaching, at least, has a very definite purpose in mind. In the words of R. W. Dale, the great Congregational preacher,

'To carry the vote and fire the zeal' of our congregations, this, gentlemen, is our true business. If we are to be successful, there must be vigorous intellectual activity, but it must be directed by a definite intention to produce a definite result.[34]

Preaching is, said H. H. Farmer, 'a knock on the door . . . It is a call for an answer . . . Yet how many sermons I have heard which lack this summoning note almost entirely. They begin, they trickle on, they stop, like the turning on and turning off a tap behind which there is no head of water.'[35] It is only a well-structured sermon which enables preachers to fulfil the maxim of Richard Baxter and 'screw God's truth into their minds'.[36]

Preaching with due care

If excellence in preaching is to be achieved, then priority will have to be given to the sermon in the week leading up to Sunday. It takes time and effort to produce powerful sermons which address the concerns of both the Bible and of the world. Such time and effort are only possible where preaching is the pastor's priority. True, there are many other tasks crowding in upon us. But preaching is at the heart of the pastoral call. This high calling is well expressed by William Sangster:

Called to preach! That is the basic thing at the last . . . Commissioned of God to teach the word! A herald of the great King! A witness of the Eternal Gospel! Could any work be more high and holy? To this supreme task God sent His only begotten Son. In all the frustration and confusion of the times, is it possible to imagine a work comparable in importance with that of proclaiming the will of God to wayward men?[37]

What is more, in sheer numerical terms, it makes sense to give preaching a priority. For when one bears in mind the number of people present, and multiplies that number by the 20 or so

---

[34] R. W. Dale, quoted by James Stewart, *Preaching*, pp. 248–9.
[35] H. H. Farmer, *The Servant Of The Word*, pp. 65–6.
[36] Richard Baxter, *The Reformed Pastor*, p. 160.
[37] William Sangster, *The Craft Of The Sermon* (Epworth Press, London, 1954), pp. 14–15. Used by kind permission.

minutes of the sermon, and then divides the resulting figure by 60 minutes, that then gives the number of hours one would have to spend speaking to one person at a time!

What does this mean in practical terms? Firstly it means that we will not leave the preparation of a sermon until the Saturday, let alone to early Sunday morning, as is the habit of one American pastor. Sermon preparation takes time. Harry Emerson Fosdick reckoned to devote one hour's work to every minute of his Sunday sermon, and he had a staff of researchers. Few, if any of us, are in that fortunate position to devote that amount of time – and even more so those who have to preach twice a Sunday. James Black urged his readers to 'finish a sermon within eight hours'. He added: 'At the beginning, however, for your own future good, you cannot put too much ground into your own preparation.'[38] Black's advice does not seem to me to be excessive. A sermon is more than a mere morning's work.

Secondly it means that we will write out our sermons in full. In saying this I am aware that some preachers only write out headings for their sermons. I am far from convinced of the wisdom of this practice. Preaching is an art and a science in which every word counts. Only the most gifted of extempore preachers can get away with not writing out their sermon. Indeed, my experience is that it is precisely the most gifted preachers who have taken the most trouble in the writing out of their sermons. Writing out the sermon not only helps us to think straight; it also ensures that we do not slip into the same old well-worn phrases and words. Opinion varies about whether or not it is good to take the full manuscript into the pulpit. In my earlier days I used to reduce my manuscript to notes, and take the notes with me into the pulpit. Now, however, I take into the pulpit the full manuscript, suitably highlighted in various colours. This doesn't mean that I have to read the manuscript. It is already part of me. Nor does it stop me from departing from my manuscript if I feel prompted by the Spirit to develop a point in a way which had not previously come to mind. The full manuscript does, however, mean that I am able to do justice to every part of

[38] James Black, *The Mystery Of Preaching* (Marshall, Morgan & Scott, London, revised edition, 1977), p. 47.

the sermon which I have worked at and honed to the best of my ability in the past week.

Thirdly, it means that we will not be over-wordy or over-long in our delivery, but rather preach succinctly and to the point. True, there is no infallible guide to the length of a sermon. In days gone past people were happy with long sermons. 'In my judgement,' maintained P. T. Forsyth, 'the demand for short sermons on the part of Christian people is one of the most fatal influences to destroy preaching in the true sense of the word . . . Brevity may be the soul of wit, but that preacher is not a wit. And those who say they want little sermons because they are there to worship God and not hear man, have not grasped the rudiments of the first idea of Christian worship . . . A Christianity of short sermons is a Christianity of short fibre.'[39] But there is a danger in long sermons, as Charles Simeon long ago perceived: 'Endeavour to rivet their attention on your message for a reasonable time; but remember, that the mind, and especially among the generality of persons, or the uneducated, will only bear a certain amount of tension.'[40] If that was true then, it is even more true today in an age where everything in the media is communicated in limited bite-sizes. The biblical scholar F. F. Bruce used to say that if preachers had anything worthwhile to say, they could say it within 20 minutes; if they had nothing to say, then they would need at least 40 minutes! Maybe we should end with John Stott's rule of thumb: 'ten minutes are too short and forty minutes are too long'.[41]

Yes, if we would aim at excellence, then we need to work at our sermons. We need to give sermon preparation a priority in the week, even if it means that other things then go by the board. No pastor has ever been the poorer for having prepared with due care – no church for that matter, either. We do well to heed the wisdom of James Black, culled from his experience:

Resolve early to make your preaching the big business in your life . . . If only a man gives his best, he will experience from the

[39] P. T. Forsyth, *Positive Preaching*, p. 72.
[40] Charles Simeon quoted by Robert Patterson, *Short, Sharp & Off The Point* (MARC Europe/Kingsway, Eastbourne, 1987), p. 45.
[41] John Stott, *I Believe In Preaching*, p. 294.

hands of any average congregation a loyalty that shames him in his own heart, and a love from simple souls that should make him better than his best.[42]

Preaching expectantly

Excellence in preaching also means recognising our limitations and looking to God to bless our efforts. Having done our best, we can only entrust our work to the Lord who declared that his Word shall not 'return to me empty, but shall accomplish that which I purpose, and succeed in the thing for which I sent it' (Isa. 55:11).

Such trust in God is not to be equated with some kind of fatalistic resignation. If we trust God, then we shall believe that in one way or another he is going to bless our preaching.

The story is told of a young minister who came to C. H. Spurgeon and said with some concern: 'I don't seem to have many converts.' 'Surely you don't look for a convert every time you preach,' replied Spurgeon. 'Oh no, of course not,' the young minister answered. 'That is why you are not having them,' Spurgeon retorted.

True, for a sermon to have its full effect there must also be faith on the part of the hearer. But the preacher too must have faith. The faith of a preacher acts as it were like a catalyst for the Holy Spirit to work in the lives of the congregation. Preachers, as well as their hearers, can hinder God's work by their unbelief (see Matt. 13:58).

Effective preaching is expectant preaching. James Stewart rightly challenges us when he stated:

Every Sunday morning when it comes ought to find you awed and thrilled by the reflection – 'God is to be in action today, through me, for these people: this day may be crucial, this service decisive, for someone now ripe for the vision of Jesus'. Remember that every soul before you has its own story of need, and that if the Gospel of Christ does not meet such need nothing on earth can. Aim at results. Expect mighty works to happen. Realize that, although your congregation may be small, every soul is

[42] James Black, *The Mystery of Preaching*, p. 4.

infinitely precious. Never forget that Christ himself, according to His promise, is in the midst, making the plainest and most ordinary church building into the house of God and the gate of heaven. Hear his voice saying, 'This day is the Scripture fulfilled in your ears. This day is salvation come to this house'. Then preaching, which might otherwise be a dead formality and a barren routine, an implicit denial of its own high claim, will become a power and a passion; and the note of strong, decisive reality, like a trumpet, will awaken the souls of men.[43]

As preachers we need to personalise Ephesians 3:20 and believe that our God, 'according to his power that is at work within us' is able to do 'immeasurably more than all we ask or imagine'. God is able – there is no limit to his divine power. But this power only becomes operational in our preaching when we believe. God's power is released when we open our hearts to him and trust him to truly bless the preaching of his Word. In this context the words of Paul in Ephesians 1:18–19 are significant: 'I ask that your minds may be opened to see his light, so that you will know ... how rich are the wonderful blessings he promises his people, and how very great is his power at work in us who believe' (GNB). Stuart Briscoe tells of how he came to apply the great Pauline doxology of Ephesians 3:20–21 to preaching and comments: 'I will never forget the sense of exhilaration that filled me as I began to preach, expecting the indwelling Spirit to be at work in and through the preaching.'[44]

Again, how does this work out in practical terms? How can we cultivate such a spirit of expectancy? In part the solution is down to us and to the kind of spiritual discipline we exercise on a Sunday morning, as in the quietness of our studies or church offices we seek God's blessing on the day. But in part too the solution is to surround ourselves with our fellow leaders and together look expectantly to God to bless the service in general and the preaching in particular. I find that the meeting together with my deacons prior to the service not only warms my spirit, it also confirms my faith, so that as I step

[43] James Stewart, *Preaching*, p. 42.
[44] D. Stuart Briscoe, *Fresh Air In The Pulpit* (British edition: IVP, Leicester, 1994), p. 23.

out into the church, I step out confident in the power of the Spirit to preach God's Word.[45]

Receiving feedback

Excellence in preaching is a constant pursuit. The preacher has never truly arrived, but rather is always in the process of developing and becoming. Preachers therefore must be willing to listen and learn from others.

As part of our own weekly discipline at Chelmsford there is always a Monday post-mortem on the Sunday services, in which amongst other things we reflect on our preaching and see how we could have improved in either the content or the delivery of the sermon. But not every pastor has another colleague with whom the Sunday preaching may be evaluated. And even if we all were part of a ministerial team, might there not be a place for our general hearers to give us feedback on their perception of our sermons?

In this respect I was very much challenged by David Schlafer, who suggests the formation of a 'sermon reflection group' with a view to addressing the following set of questions:[46]

1. How does this sermon manifest the preacher's ability to listen?
2. How does this sermon speak for and with the Christian community, even though it is being delivered by a single individual?
3. How does this sermon show us God and the world, rather than simply tell us what we ought to do or be?
4. How does this sermon call forth an awareness of God's already-present grace, rather than merely exhort us to catch up with it?

---

[45] In this one small way perhaps I may dare to draw a parallel with Spurgeon, who used to say to himself as he mounted the steps to his high pulpit, 'I believe in the Holy Ghost, I believe in the Holy Ghost, I believe in the Holy Ghost.'

[46] Schlafer, *Surviving The Sermon*, pp. 128–9.

5. How does this sermon encourage the ongoing process of God's redeeming work in the hearts and lives of hearers?

6. How does this sermon function as a 'performative utterance'? To what extent is it an extension of the enfleshed saving Word, rather than simply a report of what happened 'once upon a time'?

7. If the sermon does not seem to do much of any of these, how is it trying to do so, or how might it do so?

Schlafer then suggests some further questions as catalysts for reflection and insight.[47] For example:

1. How did this sermon connect to
   – the liturgy of the day?
   – events that have been in the news this week?
   – ongoing issues of concern in the culture?
   – joys, problems, and sorrows of those in the parish community?
   – your own raw edges?
   – other sermons that have been preached in previous weeks?
   – the ministry of your church in the world?

2. Describe in as much detail as possible the 'plot' of the sermon. Into what kind of journey did it invite you? What were the different stages of that sermon journey?

3. Are there ways in which the sermon left you feeling
   – confused?
   – angry?
   – grateful?
   – empty?
   – nourished?
   – questioning?
   – in significant disagreement?
   – confirmed and centered?
   – eager to talk about it?
   – alienated?
   – connected to others?

[47] Ibid., pp. 130–32.

4. If you had been preaching on this text, how would you have approached it differently?

5. How did the sermon ground you more fully in God's love?

To sit in a sermon reflection group and listen to members evaluate the sermon in the light of such questions might well not be the most comfortable of experiences. And yet, it could prove to be a most helpful experience. Criticism can be positive and upbuilding.

At the end of the day, of course, we are accountable not to our congregation, but to God. This places an awesome responsibility upon us. For God is the ultimate listener of our sermons. James Stewart related how Bishop Gore used to give his final charge to candidates on the eve of their ordination in these impressive words: 'Tomorrow I shall say to you, "Wilt thou, wilt thou, wilt thou?" But there will come a day to you when Another will say to you, "Hast thou, hast thou, hast thou?" God grant us unwavering fidelity to our high theme, lest we be ashamed to stand at last before the face of the Son of Man.'[48]

Similarly the Danish philosopher, Søren Kierkegaard, expressed the theme of the preacher's accountability when he wrote:

It is a venturesome thing to preach; for when I mount to that sacred place – whether the church be crowded or as good as empty – I have, though I may not be aware of it, one hearer in addition to those visible to me, namely, God in heaven, whom I cannot see, but who verily can see me.

This hearer listens attentively to discover whether what I say is true. He looks also to discern whether my life expresses what I say. And although I possess no authority to impose an obligation upon any other person, yet what I have said in the sermon puts *me* under obligation. God has heard it!

Most people have a notion that it requires courage to step out upon the stage like an actor and to encounter all eyes fixed upon you. And yet this danger is in a sense, like everything else on stage, an illusion.

For personally, the actor is aloof from it all; his part is to deceive, to disguise himself, to represent another. The preacher

48 James Stewart, *Preaching*, p. 87.

of Christian truth, on the other hand, steps out in a place where, even if all eyes are not fixed upon him, the eye of omniscience is.

The preacher's part is to be himself. And he's in an environment, God's house, which requires of him only this: that he be himself, and he be true.[49]

Preaching Sunday by Sunday

'Enough of theory!' some reader may declare. 'How does all this work out Sunday by Sunday?'

For me the key to Sunday preaching is series of sermons. In this regard I know that I differ from many, who prefer to work their way through the lectionary and preach on the passage for the day. But although there is an internal logic to the lectionary, that logic is not always discernible to the hearer. Lectionary preaching tends to appear to be 'bitty', whereas preaching through a book of the Bible or on some biblical theme gives the preaching an overall coherence. Certainly, my experience is that the congregation much prefers to be able to work away at a series, rather than jump from one theme to another.

Congregations also like variety. For this reason there is a lot to be said for limiting the length of a series, and if necessary returning to the book or to the theme at a later date. Taking a year or two to work through a gospel, for instance, can lead to unbalanced preaching. If we are to be true to the example which Paul set in his Ephesian ministry and preach 'the whole will of God' (Acts 20:27), then it seems to me that we need to have a balanced diet, whereby we expose our congregation to Old and New Testament alike, to history and to prophecy, to gospel and to letter. Precisely how that balance is achieved, must be left to the individual preacher to decide.

According to Stephen Neill, 'If you found that of your texts for the year, 40% were drawn from the Gospels, 25% from the rest of the New Testament, 25% from the Old Testament, you might feel that you had been reasonably faithful to your obligation.' Neill goes

---

[49] Søren Kierkegaard, *Training in Christianity*, quoted in *Leadership* XV (Winter 1994), p. 3.

on, 'You will note that leaves you five or six Sundays in the year, but no more, to preach on special topics without necessarily taking a text from the Scriptures.'[50] I confess that with that last point I totally disagree. At no point is there justification for not rooting a message within Scripture. My own rule of thumb is to ensure that along with observing the great festivals of the Church (Christmas, Easter, Whitsunday, and also such seasons as Advent, Lent and Trinity), we observe a tripartite balance between the gospels, the letters and the Old Testament.

How might such sermon series look? Let me illustrate by giving some examples of recent preaching.

On Sunday mornings last autumn I felt it would be helpful to do a series on popular objections to the Christian faith, but to link each objection to one Scripture passage in particular. The series took the following form:

1. 'All religions lead to God' (John 14:6).
2. 'Jesus was just a good man' (Mark 2:1–12).
3. 'Once dead, always dead' (1 Cor. 15:20–28).
4. 'Christians are a bunch of hypocrites' (Mark 2:13–17).
5. 'Church is boring' (Ps. 96).
6. 'No God would allow suffering' (Rom. 5:1–11).
7. 'No God of love would send people to hell' (John 3:16–21).
8. 'You can't believe the Bible' (Luke 1:1–4).
9. 'Virgins don't have babies' (Matt. 1:18–25).
10. 'Christmas? It's a fairy story' (John 1:14).

Running parallel to that autumn series for some of the time was a series on 'Human Basics' in which we looked at the opening chapters of Genesis:

1. In the beginning God (Gen. 1:1–2:4).
2. Between ape and angel (Gen. 1:26–7).
3. Is work a blessing? (Gen. 2:15).
4. Spare rib? (Gen. 2:18–25).
5. Tragedy strikes (Gen. 3).
6. East of Eden (Gen. 4).
7. Captain Noah and his floating zoo (Gen. 6–9).

50 Stephen Neill, *On The Ministry*, p. 67.

Over the summer the Sunday evening series focused on 'Night Scenes in the Old Testament'. For example:

1. Jacob's ladder (Gen. 28).
2. Israel's passover (Exod. 12).
3. Gideon's triumph (Judg. 7).
4. Samuel's call (1 Sam. 3).
5. Nehemiah's inspection (Neh. 2).
6. Belshazzar's feast (Dan. 5).

A previous series had included eight sermons on the Beatitudes (Matt. 5:1–12). Another series had been five sermons on Romans 8:

1. Free to live (verses 1–4).
2. Living as children of God (verses 5–17).
3. Groaning yet rejoicing (verses 18–25).
4. The Spirit our helper (verses 26–30).
5. We shall overcome (verses 31–9).

We began a series on 1 Corinthians, but called a halt after the first six chapters, with a view to resuming it later:

1. To Corinth with love (1:1–9).
2. A crucified God (1:18–23).
3. We boast in God (1:24–31).
4. Can a thinking person be a Christian? (2).
5. God's way to grow a church (3:1–9).
6. Purgatory: fact or fiction? (3:10–15).
7. Is life a picnic? (4).
8. A conspiracy of silence (5).
9. When Christians disagree (6:1–8).
10. Can a Christian be a homosexual? (6:9–11).
11. Sex and the glory of God (6:12–20).

One might imagine that preaching a series of sermons worked out some months in advance might result in sermons which fail to respond to the issues of the day. Yet time and again experience shows that God can speak powerfully and relevantly through passages chosen well ahead. Even within the context of a predetermined preaching plan, God's Word is not bound (see 2 Tim. 2:9!). On the other hand, there is no reason why from time to time pastors may not set aside their preaching plan and address an issue which has arisen in the life of the church or in the life of the wider world. Nor does preaching sermon series mean that one is unable to observe special Sundays connected with the Christian Year. Inevitably there must be flexibility. On the other hand, preaching series gives both the congregation and the preacher a helpful structure within which there is plenty of room for learning and growth on the part of both.

In conclusion

Preaching is at the very heart of Christian ministry. It is not without significance that Paul in Ephesians 4:11 defined the pastoral role as a teaching role: the gifts that the risen Christ gives to his Church include 'pastor-teachers'. Here we have a clear reminder that the prime task of the shepherd is to feed the sheep. All the more need, therefore, for selectors for Christian ministry to ensure that those whom they select have a preaching gift.

However, excellence in preaching is not achieved simply by having gifted preachers. Pastors need constantly to be working at their gift. Gifting needs to be allied to hard work. 'Becoming an effective teacher is simple,' commented Marlene LeFever. 'You just prepare and prepare until drops of blood appear on your forehead.'[51] There are no short-cuts to excellence!

[51] Marlene LeFever, *Leadership* VIII (Summer 1987), p. 19.

Chapter 4

The creative liturgist

The call to worship

Christian worship, declared Karl Barth, is 'the most momentous, the most urgent, the most glorious action that can take place in human life'.[1] In worship we respond with heart, mind and voice to the God who has supremely revealed himself in Jesus Christ. As we focus on all that God has done for us our hearts overflow with wonder, love and praise. In the words of Mark Santer,

> We lose ourselves and find ourselves again as children of God. We come together now in the assembly of the Lord to receive a pledge and a foretaste of what we are promised in the end: heaven and earth made new, with heaven brought down to earth and earth taken up into heaven.[2]

This is worship at its best. And yet all of us have experienced worship that is dull and earth-bound. We have not always been swept up into the presence of Almighty God. Instead we have gone through the motions of an empty ritual.

I believe that one of the reasons why our worship fails to reach its potential is because many worship leaders have lost their way. Certainly this is true in a broad section of the more evangelical wing of Christendom. The old liturgical wineskins were split apart by the new wine of charismatic renewal, but many churches have

---

[1] Karl Barth, quoted by J. J. Von Allmen, *Worship: Its Theology And Practice* (Lutterworth Press, London, 1965), p. 15.
[2] Mark Santer, 'The Praises of God', p. 4 in *Liturgy For A New Century* (SPCK/Alcuin Club, London, 1991), edited by Michael Perham.

yet to find new wineskins to contain the worship of God's people. The result is that in many churches there is no direction or structure to worship. We need today a new sense of liturgical awareness. And here the role of the pastor as the creative liturgist is crucial.

Peter James Flamming has imaginatively likened the role of the pastor to a 'worship composer':

> Consider a worship service with the five movements of praise, nurture, commitment, inspiration and quiet centering [meditation]. As in a symphony, the number of movements may remain the same week after week. It is what happens within those movements that makes every symphony, and every sermon different.
>
> To carry the analogy further, the notes and chords that make up those movements might be Scripture, preaching, music, sharing and prayer. Other harmonies may also appear such as the offering, communion, baptism, baby dedication, a shared witness [testimony], and a call to commitment. It is how these are used that gives the service its life, its stability, and its variety. In a given church the movements of worship are not apt to change much, but the variety within those movements needs to be changed from week to week.[3]

Such richness and variation within the worship symphony do not just happen. Rather, they come about as the result of the skill, dedication and hard work of the worship composer. The demands of Sunday-by-Sunday worship call for excellence and creativity on the part of the pastor.

My prime concern in this section, however, is not to encourage excellence in the leading of Sunday worship services – I have already sought to deal with this in *Faith And Festivity*[4] – but rather to encourage a more creative approach to what I have termed the 'new' rites of passage. To quote Mark Santer again,

[3] Peter James Flamming, *The Pastor as Worship Composer* (Baptist World Alliance, McLean, Virginia, 1992), p. 4.
[4] Paul Beasley-Murray, *Faith And Festivity* (MARC/Monarch, Eastbourne, 1991).

The ministry of the liturgist is one of helping people to bring their real lives, their real world, our world, to God – with its pains and sorrows and its failures as well as its joys and thanksgivings. It is to help them to bring their world to God and find it transformed by his grace into a foretaste of heaven; to help them to receive the divine life in such a way that they can go back into their daily lives renewed – so that, having gone out into the world, they can bring it back again.[5]

My concern is that we should develop 'liturgy' for the 'new' rites of passage in order to enable people to bring more meaningfully the 'real world' to God. This, surely, is no optional extra. Where excellence in pastoral ministry is in view, then a creative approach to liturgy is inevitable.

Pioneering new rites of passage

Rites of passage old and new

The three major events of life – birth, marriage and death – are marked by the three traditional Christian rites of passage: viz. the christening, the wedding and the funeral. Within the context of a nominal Christian society, these three occasions are often the only times some people may darken the door of a church. Indeed, such people may be referred to as 'four-wheeler Christians' – the four wheels being provided first by the pram, secondly by the wedding car, and thirdly by the funeral hearse!

A fourth major rite of passage may be found in the rite of 'believer's baptism' (or, in churches practising infant baptism, 'confirmation'). Although such a rite may take place at any time of life, very often it is the Christian equivalent of a rite of puberty, marking the end of childhood and the entering into at least some of the responsibilities of adulthood.

For all these four rites of passage much guidance and help is afforded to the pastor in a wide variety of service books.

[5] Santer, 'The Praises of God', p. 7.

There patterns of worship may be found together with additional appropriate scriptures and prayers. Although there is always room for imagination and creativity, for the most part pastors are content to follow the suggested order.

But life today is far more complex than the traditional rites of the Church would suggest. Most of us have to pass through many more than four major life transitions. Indeed, in one sense life is a continuous process of transition; for change is part of the warp and woof of life. Change – transition – is in fact the norm.[6]

Yet even if transition is a permanent way of life, it is true to say that there are specific experiences or stages of transition through which we go. Such experiences or stages serve as boundaries to situations of 'relative' stability – 'relative because in reality there are no situations of complete stability and lack of movement in human life'.[7] The thrust of this chapter is that many of these less-recognised transitions would benefit from a rite of passage, in which at the very least prayer and Scripture were combined to mark the passing over into a new phase of life.

Yet important though these transitions are, little guidance is offered to pastors on how to mark these profound changes in people's lives. It is left to the pastor's own imagination and creativity to find worship resources appropriate for the occasion. Here is a gap which surely needs to be filled. In the meantime this chapter is offered as small contribution to the future production of an appropriate manual.[8]

With respect to this chapter let me emphasise two things. First of all, any rite of passage always has to be individually tailored. There is no one set of words appropriate to each and every occasion. This does not, however, mean that every pastor has

---

6 See Philip Sheldrake, *Befriending Our Desires* (Darton, Longman & Todd, London, 1994), p. 94: 'Movement, change, and a lack of final clarity are what we live with most of the time. The other moments are occasional resting places.'
7 So Sheldrake, *Befriending Our Desires*, p. 97.
8 Certainly, within the UK there would be a ready market for a collection of resource material for the busy pastor, providing prayers, Scripture readings, liturgies – even possibly hymns and songs.

to start from scratch and, as it were, re-invent the wheel. A collection of worship resource material would provide a foundation upon which pastors could build an appropriate rite of passage.

Secondly, it would not be right for every transition to be marked by a public rite of passage. Unlike a baptism or a wedding which are conducted in public before a congregation, some of these other transitions would of necessity be recognised within the context of a private pastoral visit. But the privacy of a home or of the pastor's office does not rule out the helpfulness of an appropriate form of words (a 'liturgy') which enables, for instance, the people concerned to give thanks for the past – and where appropriate to ask God's forgiveness for where they have failed him and others; to seek God's strength for the present and his blessing for the future. True, such a rite of passage need not always be formalised within a set 'liturgy' – it might simply take the form of an extempore prayer. And yet there are occasions when a set form of words may reinforce confession or blessing.

The family and rites of passage

Many of the rites of passage may seem to involve only one or two individuals – and yet indirectly it is the whole family which is involved. In a divorce, for instance, the two major players are the husband and wife – and yet where there are children and parents, they too are affected. The birth of the first child not only creates parents, it also creates grandparents: whereas for the new parents concerned the birth may cause joy, for the new grandparents the birth may be yet another marker in the long road towards old age and may be resented as such.[9] Change in one member of the family inevitably involves the wider circle. Indeed, it has been said that 'so central is the role of family process in rites of passage that it is probably correct to say it is really the family that is making the transition to a new stage of life at such a time rather than any "identified member" focussed upon during the occasion.'[10] In other

---

[9] Sue Walrond-Skinner, *The Fulcrum And The Fire* (SPCK, London, 1993), p. 136.
[10] E. H. Friedman, quoted by Sue Walrond-Skinner, *The Fulcrum And The Fire*, pp. 121–2.

words, effective pastoral care must always have the wider horizon in view.

Stages within a rite of passage

It was Arnold van Gennep who coined the phrase 'rite of passage'.[11] He showed that all such rites include three phases: separation from the old status, transition, and incorporation into the new status. The old status is the old way of life; the new status is the new way of life; and transition is the moment when one crosses the threshold between the old order and the new. Within the context of Christian worship and pastoral care the Church, as the community of love, is able through an appropriate rite of passage to surround and support those experiencing the crisis of transition.

We would emphasise that every transition is a 'crisis' of one kind or another. At first sight such a term may seem strange to use of some of the more joyful transitions of life – and yet every new beginning involves some kind of 'death' or loss. This sense of loss must not be minimised. For some the transition involved may prove to be profoundly disturbing and may even seem to involve the loss of God.[12] And yet there is always a positive side to the transition. Every transition also involves a new opportunity, a new challenge.

Christian rites of passage give us an opportunity to acknowledge both the negative and positive sides of the transition involved. In the words of Wayne Price: 'Nearly every transition involves grief over what is being left behind; ritual in a community context says we are allowed to grieve and we have caring people to grieve with us. Nearly every transition involves exhilaration and excitement; who can bubble over alone! Nearly every transition involves fear of the unknown . . . Who better than the church to stand with us at such times?'[13]

---

11 *The Rites of Passage* (The University of Chicago Press, 1960). Originally published as *Les Rites de Passage* (Paris, 1909).

12 See Sheldrake, *Befriending Our Desires*, p. 99: 'The spiritual dimension of letting go and of major transitions has sometimes been described in the Christian tradition in terms of a "dark night". Here there is real spiritual pain that engages the level of faith as well as that of the psyche.'

13 Wayne Price, *The Church And The Rites Of Passage* (Broadman, Nashville, 1989), p. 9; see also 'Rites of Passage and the Role of the Church', *Search* (Summer 1990), pp. 27–34. Used by permission.

To this we may add that the role of the Church is not only to enable those in transition to get through the crisis they are facing, but also to provide the necessary help to enable those in transition to emerge the stronger and the more mature in the faith. Indeed, hopefully as a result of the Church's 'turning-point ministries' people will in turn be able to help others.[14]

Worship and rites of passage

Although rites of passage are expressions of the Church's pastoral care, they take place within a liturgical framework and thus are expressions of the Church's worship life. Such an understanding of rites of passage rests upon a somewhat broader interpretation of worship than is commonly given. For on this interpretation worship is not simply an occasion for giving 'worth to God', it is also an occasion for 'the mutual giving and receiving of worth'.[15] Moments of change are inevitably moments of loss – at such a time many have need to be reassured of their own worth. These needs are met within worship, whether public or private. Worship is therefore 'a dimension of Christian pastoral care, and pastoral care is a dimension of Christian worship'.[16]

There is yet another strand to a Christian rite of passage. Not only is it an expression of pastoral care, it can also prove to be an expression of the Church's evangelism. Although in this chapter we are primarily focusing on rites of passage within the Church, inevitably there will be those who have not committed themselves to the covenanted community of believers but who will

[14] Similarly Loren Mead, *The Once And Future Church* (Alban, Washington, 1991), p. 52: 'Each life crisis . . . is also an opportunity for the community of faith to help a person go deeper into faith and into a new stage of ministry.'
[15] Robin Green, *Only Connect. Worship and liturgy from the perspective of pastoral care* (Darton, Longman & Todd, London, 1987), p. 18. See also Stephen Pattison, 'Pastoral care and worship' in *A New Dictionary of Liturgy and Worship*, edited by J. G. Davies (SCM, London, 1986), p. 427: 'While the primary aim of worship is to give praise and thanks to God, it also has pastoral effects in terms of building up human fellowship, creating personal wholeness and integrity and making the liberation of the gospel a contemporary reality.'
[16] Duncan Forrester, James I. H. McDonald & Gian Tellini, *Encounter With God* (T. & T. Clark, Edinburgh, 1983), p. 145.

also come within the scope of our pastoral care. Needless to say, where we are dealing with unbelievers our evangelism will not be highly pressurised. Rather, the Good News of God's unchanging love naturally comes to the surface as pastoral care in the context of worship is offered at the various turning-points of life. How precisely evangelism is linked to the rite of passage may vary. It could, for instance, be that the rite of passage would be followed up by an invitation to join an 'agnostics anonymous' group looking at Christian basics. In one way or another, rites of passage can prove a bridgehead for the Gospel. Interestingly, surveys have indicated that loving attention given to people at major turning-points in their lives has often proved more evangelistically effective than formal evangelism.[17]

Enabling transition at every stage of life

Transitions of childhood and youth

Starting school
Starting school is a major event in any child's life, although with the multiplicity of pre-school playgroups and nursery schools, it is not as traumatic an event as in the past. Indeed, with an increasing number of women going back to work within a matter of months after the birth, many children are used to being in all-day nurseries from very early on. Nonetheless, it is still a major transition when a child first attends school and begins to experience the rigours of full-time education. It can also be quite a transition for the parents – especially where it is either the first or last child. Surprisingly, this event has tended not to be recognised by churches. Within many

[17] Robin Green, *Only Connect*, p. 65, n. 9: 'Two surveys were undertaken in the Anglican deaneries of Wandsworth and Merton in South London to discover the routes by which new Christians had come to active faith. They both revealed that the largest group [in each case over 50%] had come to faith through ministry given at a major turning point, e.g. the birth of a child, bereavement, divorce etc. Events like evangelistic campaigns or special services were quite insignificant compared with that group.'

English churches, for instance, more attention seems to be focused on the relatively minor internal transition of children moving from one Sunday School class to another ('Promotion Sunday') rather than what is happening in the wider world outside.

A church might well mark this transition by introducing the children to the Sunday morning congregation on the Sunday before the schools go back and offering up prayer for them. To make the occasion more memorable as far as the children are concerned, maybe a small gift might be appropriate: e.g. a ruler with a Christian slogan such as 'Jesus is Lord' or even 'Church is fun'!

Moving up into a new school

Although patterns of education vary, few children remain in one school for the whole of their education. At seven, eleven or whenever, children will often change schools. Often such changes can be quite traumatic and disorientating as the child often moves from a relatively small school to a much larger school. Previously one had been important – a big fish in a small pool; but now one feels totally insignificant – a minnow in a massive lake. This change may be deemed significant enough for the children concerned to be publicly presented and prayed for in church. Clearly, any rite must take place within the context of pastoral care – experienced perhaps in a Sunday School class or through a home visit by the Sunday School teacher – where children are reassured that although at school they may feel lost in the crowd, God knows every hair of their head. It is not enough to teach children Bible stories. It is vital to relate the Christian faith to their lives.[18]

Leaving school

Leaving school is another major milestone in a person's life. New freedoms can now be entered into. Even if a young person continues into higher education, the style of learning has now changed: there is now far greater need for self-discipline. How is this change to be recognised? In American culture much is made of 'high school

---

[18] In all fairness, it should be noted that schools themselves are increasingly preparing children for this particular transition: e.g. there are often 'taster days' for children moving up into a senior school.

graduation'. In American churches, for instance, the names of graduating 'seniors' appear in the church news bulletin, and often there is a 'litany of recognition'. In a British context we tend to be less affirming – perhaps in part because of our divisive educational process, which accords varying worth to children depending on their scholastic attainments. Maybe there is all the greater need for the churches in Britain to devise a rite of transition within the context of Sunday worship in which all their young people – and not just the 'bright' ones – feel valued and affirmed. Such a rite can be supplemented by an after-church supper party at which one of the church leaders might speak about the challenges and pitfalls of life beyond school.

Transitions of adulthood

The transitions of adulthood, unlike the transitions of childhood and youth, tend to be less fixed and less universal.

Family transitions

Leaving home

Many – but not all – young adults leave home and live with a partner of their choosing. In the past marriage has been the appropriate rite of passage. However, increasingly in the secularised Western world couples live together without any ceremony, either secular or religious.[19] This refusal to go through a formal rite of passage creates problems for many parents. From a pastoral perspective, support often needs to be given to the parents involved, especially where the parents perceive their value-system to have been rejected. Perhaps in addition to devising new rites of passage for couples who have chosen to live together, it would be helpful if appropriate Scriptures and prayers could be devoted to parents of such couples. Indeed, along with private counselling, there is much to be said for bringing together parents in a similar position and giving them an opportunity to share their mutual pain and bewilderment.

[19] Statistics show that in Britain by 1987 50% of women had lived with their husbands prior to marriage: see *Social Trends* 22 (HMSO, London, 1992). It is suggested that by the year 2000 four out of five couples will live together before marriage: see Jeremy Collingwood, *Common Law Marriage* (Grove Books, Nottingham, 1994), p. 6.

Special birthdays

In any family birthdays are always an occasion for celebration. However, certain birthdays are an occasion for even greater festivity. An obvious 'special' is the day of 'coming of age' – in Britain it used to be 21, but now the 'key' is handed over at 18. Increasingly the beginning of a decade is marked with special celebrations – 30, 40, 50, 60, 70, 80, 90. Normally such celebrations are purely secular in mood. But is there not a place for Christian thanksgiving too? Whether in the public context of the party itself, or within the privacy of a pastoral visit, there is much to be said for, at the very least, marking the transition with prayer.[20]

Engagement

Although the subject of weddings is outside the scope of this chapter we would draw attention to the new Roman Catholic Marriage Rites proposed by the 1990 Roman Catholic Liturgical Conference for England and Wales, which has emphasised that marriage is a life-long and continual process which is not completed in one service. As part of the 'phased rites' they provide worship material for both the engagement and also the period of engagement. For example, the rite for celebrating engagement – which may take place in the home or in church – includes the lighting of family candles and the reading of Scripture verses; there is opportunity for the couple to pray, for the Peace to be exchanged, and for the engagement ring to be blessed.[21]

Pregnancy

Although rites of passage relating to birth itself are not part of the scope of this chapter, I wish to draw attention to the fact that a service of dedication by itself does not do total justice to the experience of birth. One possibility would be to mark the actual

[20] In respect to secular 'coming-of-age' parties, a fascinating contrast is found in the Jewish coming-of-age ceremonies. A boy, for instance, when he becomes a barmitzwah celebrates the occasion in the synagogue, where he reads publicly from the Torah for the first time.

[21] See Charles Read, *Revising Weddings* (Grove Books, Nottingham, 1994). The new Roman Catholic material contains prayers for every possible occasion. Read, *Revising Weddings*, p. 13, tells of how a group of nuns suggested to him that the one thing lacking in the Roman Catholic material was a set of prayers for the blessing of a ladder prior to elopement!

onset of pregnancy with an appropriate rite of passage: such a rite would give recognition to the fact that life does not begin with birth, but in the preceding months of gestation; such a rite, if held within the context of a public service of worship, would possibly prove more creative and would certainly be more positive than many an anti-abortion protest.

Wedding anniversaries

Long before the purveyors of greeting cards peddled their wares, it had been customary for special anniversaries to be observed – ranging from paper for the first, silver for the 25th, ruby for the 40th, gold for the 50th, and diamond for the 60th. Such special anniversaries deserve to be honoured within the Church. The first apart, where perhaps a card from the pastor will suffice, at the very least a pastoral visit is called for. Indeed, in many places it is customary for the occasion to be marked by a formal act of thanksgiving, either within the context of Sunday worship or at a service for friends and relatives, say on a Saturday afternoon.

Renewal of wedding vows

In many churches opportunities are given for wedding vows to be renewed. For the most part such a renewal of vows does not take place after any particular crisis, but is rather occasioned by the conclusion of a marriage enrichment course – or perhaps by a special church anniversary when the programme committee thinks it would be 'nice' if all those married in the church over the past 50 years return for a special service. On such occasions a number of couples renew their wedding vows.[22]

22 It clearly is important that preparation should precede any renewal of vows. In this respect Elaine Ramshaw, *Ritual and Pastoral Care* (Fortress Press, Philadelphia, 1987), p. 27, quotes an anonymous letter to *The Lutheran*: 'I inwardly recoil whenever I read or hear of a church service during which the pastor unexpectedly calls for all married couples to stand and publicly renew their wedding vows. If my former spouse and I had been placed in such an embarrassing position, we would have hated ourselves for our hypocrisy. Undoubtedly pastors who initiate these little rituals do so with the best of intentions. For those couples who are already lovingly committed to each other, this can be a beautiful reinforcement to their marriage. But it is unreasonable to expect a healing of a dying relationship through such one-shot, show-biz techniques.'

A renewal of wedding vows following a crisis in the marriage is different. There is a greater intensity where, for instance, a couple wish to recommit themselves to one another where one, if not both partners have been unfaithful. Normally it would not be appropriate for such a service to be public: rather, such a service might be conducted with just the immediate family (the children) and a few close friends present. It is good if such a renewal of wedding vows were to take place within the church sanctuary. Holding the ceremony in church adds strength to the vows, for in this symbolic way the couple concerned would be consciously calling upon God to be their witness.[23]

Divorce

Sadly, not all marriages survive the strains of modern life. Divorce, even among committed Christians, is an increasingly common phenomenon in many countries. How is the Church to react to this? Clearly the Church has to continue to affirm the ideal of life-long marriage. But such an affirmation does not help those whose marriages have irretrievably broken down. Nor does it help the Church if divorce is pushed under the carpet and a blind eye is turned to what is going on. For the sake of the couple, for the sake of their children, and indeed for the sake of the Church itself, some kind of rite of transition is helpful – if not necessary – where people are helped to face up to what has happened and

[23] The prayers on such an occasion inevitably have to include confession of sin. For example, following readings from John 15:9–11 and 1 Cor. 13:4–8a and before the vows are taken, the following prayer might be said together by the couple:

'Our Father God, confronted with your Word, we have to confess our sins against you and against one another. We have not loved as you would have us love. Father, forgive us for the times when we have hurt one another; when we have shown lack of respect and lack of understanding for one another; when we have fought with one another rather than prayed for one another. Forgive us for the many ways in which we have spoiled the perfect relationship you have planned for us together.

'Yes, Father, at this moment we are very conscious of our failings and mistakes. And yet we thank you too for all the good times we have had in the past – for all the happiness we have experienced together. Help us now as we make our vows afresh to rediscover that happiness, to know again your richest blessing upon our life together.'

to discover that even in the midst of the pain and the failure, God is there.[24]

As with the renewal of wedding vows where relationships have gone wrong, so with this ceremony of the parting of the ways it may well be wise to hold a private service, with invitations limited to the immediate family and friends. Such a ceremony would include the couple acknowledging before God their failure and their need of forgiveness, both from him and from one another; it might also include confession on the part of friends and family for failing to give the couple the support they needed. It would also include a prayer for the healing of all the hurt and brokenness which the couple – and also their family and friends – have experienced. It would be good to also include an opportunity for the couple to thank God for the good times they have had together – part of the sadness of most divorces is that the marriage has not been all bad. The assembled company would move on to ask God's blessing on the couple as they went their separate ways, and to pledge their support for them as individuals.[25]

It is important to emphasise that such a service would in no way be blessing the practice of divorce; rather it would be helping the couple – and also family and friends – to face up to the reality involved.[26]

[24] The situation here envisaged is where both husband and wife are members of the church and where both are desirous of going through such a ceremony. A different rite of transition might be necessary where only one of the partners wishes such a rite of passage.

[25] For a very useful discussion of the pastoral needs which such a service might address, see Elaine Ramshaw, *Ritual and Pastoral Care*, p. 53.

[26] Wayne Price, *The Church And The Rites Of Passage*, p. 119, gives an example of such a 'ritual of dissolution':

'The couple reading from printed copies of the rite, may affirm in unison:

"I John/Mary, give thanks to God for the love and the joy which have been present in this marriage. I pledge to keep sacred the memory of everything good and lovely we have experienced together. I further acknowledge my own sins of word, thought, and deed, which have contributed to this failure. I ask forgiveness of God, of you (John/Mary), of our children, and family and friends. Finally, I promise in both attitude and in word to refrain from anything which may be hurtful to you, our families, and our friends. I pray God's leadership in our separate lives."'

Needless to say, such a rite of passage should never precede the actual legal divorce itself. It is only appropriate where the marriage has irretrievably broken down. In so far as all too often divorce is surrounded by much anger and bitterness, such a rite of passage would only be possible after a good deal of private counselling and help. As with a wedding, so too with the dissolution of a marriage, much preparation is needed if the rite is to have meaning.

Furthermore, such a rite of passage would also enable the divorcing couple to know that, in spite of their failure, neither God nor his people had written them off. Experience shows that all too often the divorcing couple feel totally isolated from others. As with a death, many people do not seem to know what to say: the upshot is that they pass by 'on the other side' and say nothing, with the result that the individuals concerned feel even more lonely.

Singleness

To speak of singleness requiring a rite of passage may at first sight appear strange. Certainly, we do not envisage a ceremony akin to the monastic vow of celibacy. And yet there is surely a place for an acknowledgement – indeed, a celebration – of the freedoms to be found within the single state. Sadly, the significance of singleness has been undermined by the pro-family movements of North America and Europe. The fact is that whereas the Jewish religion is 'the religion of the family', the Christian faith emphasises the kingdom rather than the family. As it is, our Christian singles often feel marginalised.

It may be that what is required is an annual occasion when singles are enabled to affirm their singleness. Such an affirmation would involve not so much a rite of transition, as rather a recognition that, whether willingly or unwillingly, a transition has been made. Along with Mothers' Day and Fathers' Day, we might use the Sunday nearest 25 January (the day when the Church traditionally celebrates the Conversion of St Paul) to celebrate that great body of men and women who are freer than most to serve the Lord.

Work transitions

Elaine Ramshaw has highlighted the dangers of centring ritual around jobs and vocation. She is particularly mindful of the hurt that could be caused to those who are unable to work, whether they be the unemployed or the severely handicapped.[27] Yet this does not rule out recognising work transitions. Otherwise, using a similar argument, we would have to rule out recognising certain family transitions for the sake of singles present. Elaine Ramshaw's warning is helpful, however, in that it reminds us of the need for sensitivity. Work transitions are many and varied:

Unemployment

There was a time when a job was for life. Today technological advances and economic factors have changed all that. In certain countries redundancy and unemployment have reached alarming heights. The day of full employment is said to be over. Redundancy puts tremendous strain upon individuals and their families. Such strain is not simply financial; it also involves issues of human dignity and self-worth.

Career change

Then there is the increasing tendency to change careers. It is said that today most people will end up having two if not three separate careers. Sometimes this is linked with advances in technology and with modern economic patterns. At other times change comes about as a result of such diverse factors as pressure, boredom or altruism. Career change produces strain upon individuals and their families: retraining may involve extra expense, and almost certainly extra time and effort. It will also involve self-questioning: Have I made the right decision? Will I succeed in this new sphere of work?

Returning to work

Another transition involves married women with children returning to work. Of those who return immediately after maternity leave, some return reluctantly – they are working only because they need the money; others, however, return enthusiastically – they enjoy their chosen career. In both groups feelings of guilt may be present: Am I neglecting my family? Then there are women who return to

27 Ramshaw, *Ritual and Pastoral Care*, p. 50.

work because their children are older or are off their hands and their lives otherwise feel empty.

Mid-life crisis

Yet another transition takes place when people discover that they are no longer making transitions from one position to another at work, but rather are stuck in the one position. This transition from youthful ambition to mid-life realism can be painful. It is the time when most of us come to recognise that we will never make it to the 'top' – the chairmanship of ICI or the presidency of Exxon will never be ours![28] Inevitably issues of self-identity arise. The mid-life crisis is in fact a religious quest, for it is a search for renewed identity.[29] It is therefore not enough to give an opportunity for such individuals to 'grieve' those things which will never be. At the same time people need to be helped to gain a sense of self-worth which is independent of worldly ambition.[30] Handled aright, the mid-life crisis can prove a catalyst for achieving a new degree of maturity.

It is difficult to see how these important life-transitions can be properly marked by the worshipping community of God's people – as distinct from becoming the focus of a private pastoral call. And yet this does not mean that such transitions are not given any public

[28] Traditionally the mid-life crisis is viewed as a peculiarly male problem. Yet the reality is that it is experienced by women too. Here we have in mind not just the career woman, but also the woman coming to terms with the 'empty nest'. A peculiarly feminine expression of the mid-life crisis is, of course, the menopause: for that too raises questions of self-identity.

[29] It is in the context of the mid-life crisis that we can make sense of the well-known statement of C. J. Jung, *Modern Man In Search Of A Soul* (Kegan Paul, London, 1933), p. 264: 'Among all my patients in the second half of life – that is to say over thirty-five – there has not been one whose problem in the last resort was not that of finding a religious outlook on life.'

[30] See Robin Green, *Only Connect*, p. 90: 'In worship we can examine the distorted maps of our own cosmos and make honest choices about our future. Those honest choices are made in recognition that through worship my worth is restored to me by God. That begins to free me to let go of everything, including the dreams that can never be.'

recognition. Pastors can ensure that their preaching and teaching relate to issues both of work and of personal worth. The prayers of the church can relate not only in a general way to the world of work, but in a specific way too: for example, individuals can be interviewed about their work and prayed for; members made redundant can be mentioned by name in the church's intercessory prayers. Whatever else such praying achieves, it affirms the worth of the individuals concerned!

Transitions in older years

There is a danger that we sometimes underestimate the number of transitions through which older people go. In fact the years between 65 and 90 are probably the most dynamic period of life, excepting childhood. Change follows change. The period following statutory retirement is made up not of one stage but of a series of stages. The World Health Organization has suggested that the retired can be divided between 'the elderly' (60–74 years) and 'the aged' (over 75 years). In reality old age is much more complex. An imaginative approach to the life-cycle of older people has been developed by Tim Stafford, who breaks the years beyond 65 into seven stages – or, as he expresses it – into seven 'days of the week of old age'.[31]

Retirement

Retirement marks the entry point into old age. In Western societies, where so often people are what they do, retirement can prove a most

---

31 Tim Stafford, *As Our Years Increase* (IVP, Leicester, 1992), pp. 26–8:
　　'*The First Day* – Freedom Day – begins with retirement which introduces the life of leisure.
　　'*The Second Day* – the Day of Reflection – leads an elderly person to begin meditating on their life.
　　'*The Third Day* – Widow's Day – comes with the loss of a spouse.
　　'*The Fourth Day* – the Role-Reversal Day – begins when an older person needs frequent help to manage.
　　'*The Fifth Day* – the Dependence Day – comes when a person must lean on others for basic needs.
　　'*The Sixth Day* – the Farewell Day – is the period of preparing for death.
　　'*The Seventh Day* – the Sabbath Day – is the day of worship, the day of rest.'

difficult transition, for in ceasing to work they feel they are in danger of losing their worth, if not their identity. Yet, as with death, this 'loss' is often denied. The newly retired talk of being 'busier than ever' and delight to rehearse the advantages of a new life where they are now in charge – they are now enjoying the freedom of being 'self-employed'.

From a pastoral perspective it is important to get the balance right: retirement is not only an occasion of blessing, it is also a moment of loss. Indeed, for the unmarried the sense of loss may be even more acute.[32] The wise pastor will ensure that both the losses and the gains of this new stage of life are recognised.

In the first place these losses and gains will be articulated in pastoral conversation. In terms of the gains, hopefully such conversation concerning the 'second life of retirement' will highlight not so much the opportunities of further service for the church, but rather the opportunity for further growth and self-development.[33]

But these losses and gains also need to be recognised before God, with a view to giving thanks for the past and asking God's blessing for the future. Such recognition could take the form of an appropriate Scripture reading and prayer with the newly retired on a one-to-one basis. However, where the newly retired person is married, then clearly there would be advantages in involving the partner too, for here retirement has consequences beyond the individual. Better still would be if at the conclusion of a retirement party the pastor were given the opportunity – with the support of

---

[32] Michael Butler and Ann Orbach, *Being Your Age: Pastoral Care For Older People* (SPCK, London, 1993), p. 48, draw particular attention to the sense of loss experienced by the single woman: 'The decisive break at 60, with only a perfunctory party as a rite of passage, followed by that return to an emply flat, can feel like the beginning of dying.' However, newly retired single men can feel equally lonely.

[33] See T. S. Eliot, 'East Coker' from *Four Quartets* (Faber & Faber, London, 1944):

Old men ought to be explorers
Here and there does not matter
We must be still and still moving
Into another intensity
For a further union, a deeper communion
Through the dark cold and empty desolation.

friends, colleagues and family – to 'send out' the newly retired to encounter the new adventures and challenges of the future.

The second retirement

The transition from active retirement to a more passive form of retirement can prove difficult, accompanied as it is not simply by a loss of role, but also by a gradual loss of physical ability. This transition can be particularly difficult for church members, whose spirituality over past decades has been primarily expressed in terms of activity. The pastoral challenge is to help ageing members to let go of their responsibilities and discover that God is far more interested in who we are and who we are becoming, rather than in what we have done or are doing. With Simeon, older members need to be able to pray the 'Nunc Dimittis'; indeed, maybe they need to be helped to write their own version of the 'Nunc Dimittis'. Would it be beyond the bounds of possibility for such new liturgical creations to be read out within the context of public worship?

Final transitions

Preparing for one's funeral

'My bags are packed. I am ready to leave,' declared Pope John Paul. Would that were true of all Christians! Sadly, many Christians die without even making a will, let alone preparing for their funeral. And yet there is much to be said for the latter. When the hymns and Scripture readings have been chosen beforehand, it not only makes the eventual funeral service so much more personal, but more importantly it enables the person concerned to face up to the difference which Christ makes to death. As James White helpfully comments: 'Making plans for one's funeral is not necessarily a morbid preoccupation; it can be a witness to one's faith and a splendid way to advance in understanding of life.'[34]

Ritual with the dying

The traditional form of the last rites is the practice of 'extreme unction', where the dying person is anointed, not for healing,

---

[34] James F. White, *Introduction to Christian Worship*, p. 270. He adds: 'Members of one retirement home weave their own funeral palls, a magnificent final affirmation.'

but rather as a form of 'consecration for death'. In so far as death may be regarded as ultimate healing, maybe the practice advocated in James 5:16 could be applied in this way. Certainly, when the dying person is too sick to converse, physical actions such as anointing and laying on of hands can be a very meaningful form of communication.

At an earlier stage, there is much to be said for a last Communion, whether at home or in hospital, in which the pastor helps the dying person – together ideally with a few family members and/or friends – not only to look backward to the Saviour who died that we might be forgiven, but also to look forward to the feast that is to come. Within the context of such a rite of transition it might be possible for the dying person to make their peace with any family members where there has been a rift. Along with an assurance of sins forgiven, there will also be confirmation of the hope of the life to come.

Where the dying person is unconscious, the pastor can help family and friends to say their goodbyes by formally commending their loved one to Jesus. Similarly, where life-support is to be removed, it should not just be left to the medics to pull the plug – but an opportunity should be given for the pastor to release the loved one in the name of Jesus and to entrust the loved one to the Saviour as they go on their journey to the world beyond.

Untimely terminations

These days stillborn children are increasingly honoured with a funeral, but not miscarriages.[35] And yet for the mothers – and

---

[35] See Robin Lapwood, *When Babies Die* (Grove Books, Nottingham, 1988), pp. 5–8: 'Under British Law any baby who dies in the womb through natural causes less than 28 weeks after conception is termed a *Miscarriage*. Such a baby has no legal status. Its birth or death does not have to be registered; it has no name; and it may be disposed of in any way suitable to the hospital – frequently in the hospital incinerator. From 28 weeks and after this situation changes. A baby who dies during this period is deemed to have been a *Stillbirth*. Her birth and death must be registered, she may be given a name, and her body must be disposed of decently, usually in an unmarked common grave in the public cemetery.'

fathers (and even grandparents) – concerned there is a very real sense of loss. This sense of loss also applies to induced abortions, and there, feelings of loss are compounded with feelings of guilt. The estimated day of delivery is remembered, not only on the day itself, but often also on subsequent anniversaries.

Here surely there is a place for a private rite of transition, in which the loss – and in the case of an induced abortion, the guilt – is recognised and the help of God sought. Such a rite could include the celebration of the Lord's Supper, where the emphases of forgiveness of sin and of the communion of saints would be relevant.

The bereaved

Liturgical ministry to the bereaved is not simply limited to the funeral or thanksgiving service. David Howell in his autobiographical account of the grief journey tells of the difference which participating in the Lord's Supper makes to the bereaved, as 'with angels, archangels and all the company of heaven we proclaim his great and glorious name'. In the context of 'the communion of saints' he records how he dealt with some of his inevitable regrets for the past by writing a letter to his former wife and placing it in a sealed letter on the Communion Table at a special celebration of the Lord's Supper just three days after her death, 'reckoning that our Lord would know what to do with its contents. I can only say that the service was a truly healing experience for me and through it I felt deeply reassured'.[36] Whether or not people write letters in this way, there is no doubt that Communion services can prove unusually helpful and reassuring to the bereaved as they become aware of the wider 'communion of the saints'.

Other times for special prayer with the bereaved include the first anniversaries of a death.[37] In cases where both parents are

[36] David Howell, *The Pain of Parting* (Grove Books, Nottingham, 1993), p. 19.
[37] See Ramshaw, *Ritual and Pastoral Care*, p. 72: 'It should be remembered that the ritual occasions of the first year following death are particularly important milestones in grieving: the first Christmas without Dad, the first Easter, the first wedding anniversary.'

gone, the clearing of the family home can prove fairly traumatic: here too there may be a place for special prayer. Needless to say, praying does not do away with the need for grieving. It may, however, helpfully mark the end of a particular phase of the grief-process.

Transitions of residency

Transitions of residency come at any stage of life, and can prove traumatic at any stage. Older children and young people, for instance, can find the move to a new area particularly difficult – and all the more so because the move has not been chosen by them, but imposed by their parents.

The setting up of a new home is always significant – even more so in the case of a couple newly married, for whom it is their first home. The moving into one's last home – be it a retirement apartment or a small room in sheltered accommodation for the elderly – is another major transition.

All such transitions can be enhanced by some rite of passage. Such a rite may take place within the privacy of a pastoral visit, where the pastor asks God's blessing upon the new home – maybe even going from room to room and pronouncing an appropriate prayer or Scripture.[38] Alternatively – or additionally – some Christian rite of passage could be included in a house-warming party. Indeed, in some parts of the world the house-warming party is used as an opportunity to invite friends and neighbours round for an evangelistic event!

---

[38] See for instance the 'Order for the Blessing of a House' drawn up in a private paper by Revd Frank Wells of Stoke-by-Nayland, Suffolk, which links the following areas with the following scriptures: the entrance hall (John 10:9); the dining room (John 4:34); the living room (John 15:5); the kitchen (John 21:9); the study (Is. 34:16); the bedrooms (Matt. 11:28); the bathroom (Ps. 51:2); and the house (John 14:23). See also Read, *Revising Weddings*, pp. 12–13. With reference to the blessing of an elderly person's room, Butler and Orbach, *Being Your Age*, pp. 104f., comment: 'To bless a small institutional room will not alter its size or shape, but its occupant may feel that it has been turned into a home – perhaps even that it has been given a soul.'

Facilitating transition within the community of faith

Transitions of faith

Renewal of baptismal vows

Not infrequently people say that they would love to be baptised again – baptism would have so much more meaning for them. And yet baptism by its very nature is unrepeatable: it is the entry rite into the Christian Church.[39]

Baptismal vows can be renewed in various ways. In the first place, they can be renewed on a regular basis whenever the Lord's Supper is celebrated. If the Lord's Supper is to be at all meaningful, then it must end in renewed dedication – it must spur us onwards in our service of Christ.[40]

In the second place, baptismal vows can be renewed by the whole congregation at a significant time of the year: e.g. the first Sunday of the New Year, or Easter Sunday. Needless to say, the wise pastor will ensure that nobody is taken by surprise, but rather that the church is properly prepared for such a service.

A third instance is the case where someone has backslidden and wandered away from the Christian faith: here there may be room for a special opportunity for the renewal of baptismal vows. Such a reaffirmation of vows could fittingly take place at a service of baptism. The individual concerned would not be baptised again,

---

[39] What if someone doubted whether they had ever truly believed in the first place? In such a case there might be room for 'conditional' baptism: i.e. the individual concerned would be baptised 'again', on the understanding that if they had been properly baptised the first time around, then this second baptism was in fact not baptism!

[40] See Paul Beasley-Murray, *Faith and Festivity* (Marc, Eastbourne, 1991), p. 73: 'Traditionally, Baptists have not used the term "sacrament" of the Lord's Supper – no doubt in reaction against some of the magical associations with the word found in certain church traditions. However, it is good to be aware that the Latin word *sacramentum* at one time meant a soldier's oath of loyalty to his emperor. In this sense the Lord's Supper can be sacramental: a moment when worshippers renew their commitment to the Lord who loved them and gave himself for them.'

but after the giving of a testimony could receive the laying on of hands together with prayer for a fresh infilling of the Spirit – somewhat along the lines of an Anglican confirmation.

Reaffirmation of faith after trauma

Christians are not immune from tragedy and disaster. To many of us there come times when things go wrong and our world collapses around us. In such times some find themselves wonderfully upheld by the Lord; others, however, go through a dreadful time of darkness, when God seems to be absent and faith seems almost impossible. Depending on the pain, this 'dark night of the soul' may go on for weeks, if not months. They may hold onto the truth of Romans 8:28 in their minds, but they cannot feel it in their hearts. But given pastoral support and care, the day eventually comes when they are able to look back and discover that even in the darkness God was there. From the alchemy of fire a purer and deeper faith has emerged. How helpful it would be if that experience could be shared with the wider family of God. Then, after having given testimony and received Communion, prayer with the laying on of hands could be made by the church, as the church in turn commits itself afresh to care for the individual concerned.

Relational transitions

Entering into church membership

Church membership is about relationships; it is about commitment to one another. 'In a Baptist church membership involves a dynamic covenant relationship with one another – a relationship in which we commit ourselves not only to work together to extend Christ's Kingdom, but also to love one another and stand by one another whatever the cost.'[41]

If this understanding of church membership is right, then it is insufficient to speak of 'welcoming' new members into fellowship.

---

[41] Taken from the rite used at Victoria Road South Baptist Church, Chelmsford, to 'receive' people into church membership. See Paul Beasley-Murray, *Radical Believers* (Baptist Union, Didcot, 1992), pp. 49–57.

Before giving the 'right hand of fellowship' and receiving new members, an opportunity could be given for the new members to commit themselves to the church, and for the church in turn to commit themselves to the new members.[42]

Leaving church membership

If membership is about commitment to one another, then it cannot be right for members just to slip out of the fellowship. If church members are moving away, then on their last Sunday the rest of the church should be given an opportunity to say farewell to them.[43]

Even if members are moving not out of town but simply to another church, they should be encouraged not to slip out, but to say their farewells. Christians need to learn to disagree gracefully, even if it means that, like Paul and Barnabas, they need to go their separate ways. Their earlier commitment to one another needs to be formally dissolved. Unfortunately, it is probably unrealistic to expect a public dissolution of such vows. At the very least, however, it could take place privately in the pastor's office.

Rites of reconciliation

In every church from time to time there are relationship difficulties. People fall out with one another. People hurt one another. People sin against one another. As a result, some people leave the church; others stay in the same church, but relationships are cool. If the church is to live up to its calling of a reconciled and reconciling community, then steps have to be taken to talk to the parties concerned and eventually bring them together.

In this context, as part of the reconciliation process, there is something to be said for a rite of reconciliation, where both sides

[42] E.g. the new member may be asked: 'Do you commit yourself to love and serve the Lord within this fellowship and also in the wider world?' And the church may be asked, 'Do you promise to love, encourage, pray for and care for X?'

[43] See Wayne Price, *The Church And The Rites Of Passage*, p. 123: 'We ask them ahead of time to allow us to call them to the altar area where I bid them farewell on behalf of the church. The benediction to worship includes a benediction upon them as well. The congregation then files by with their own personal "Godspeeds".'

are able to ask forgiveness of one another. Where the breach of fellowship has been known only to a few, then such a rite of reconciliation can be conducted privately. Where the breach of fellowship is known to many, the rite could be conducted within the context of the church meeting. Where the breach of fellowship is known throughout the wider community, then reconciliation should be demonstrated within the context of public worship.

In all three such scenarios the rite of reconciliation would best take place within a celebration of the Lord's Supper. There forgiveness can be received from the Lord and strength found to extend such forgiveness to one another. On such an occasion the 'Peace' would gain special significance.[44]

Needless to say, reconciliation involves a process. Major rifts in relationships tend to be complicated in origin. Time will almost certainly be needed to address the underlying issues before any meaningful act of reconciliation can take place. Furthermore, even after the eventual 'reconciliation', it may be unrealistic to expect fellowship to be immediately restored in depth. Indeed, fellowship

---

[44] In a private communication Malcolm Goodspeed gave an example of the following rite of reconciliation:

Scripture readings: Matt. 5:21–4 & 1 Cor. 13.

Meditation: 'Love lets the past die. It moves people to a new beginning without settling the past. Love does not have to clear up all misunderstandings. In its power, the details of the past become irrelevant; only the new beginning matters. Accounts may go unsettled; differences remain unresolved; ledgers stay unbalanced. Conflicts between people's memories of how things happened are not cleared up; the past stays muddled' (Lewis Smedes, *Love Within Limits*).

Recalling of wrongs before God: wrongs are written down by each person privately, sealed in an envelope, and placed in a receptacle to be shredded later.

Act of reconciliation with the two parties saying in turn: 'Although our perception of things is different from yours, we understand that you have experienced wrong and hurt because of our actions and attitudes. We have therefore come to ask for your forgiveness'; 'We think you have wronged us and we have been hurt by your actions and attitudes. We have thought that we have been in the right in these matters that have hurt us all. We understand that you do not share this perception. We know that you hold the opposite view. Here in the presence of witnesses we freely forgive you and ask that you receive our love.'

The Peace & the Lord's Supper.

may never be experienced in the same way again. But at least boundaries can be set in which love can be exercised.

Rites of forgiveness

By rites of forgiveness we refer not to the receiving of forgiveness, but the extending of forgiveness to those who either will not or cannot ask for forgiveness. In particular we have in mind those who have been abused by others and who for the sake of their own spiritual and emotional health need to be able to release their feelings of anger and pain over the undoubted wrong they have suffered before they can move on to a new, more positive stage where they forgive the wrongdoer. Indeed, the releasing of the anger and pain is part of the process of forgiveness. In this respect Gordon Sleight has perceptively pointed out that the fundamental meaning of the Greek word usually translated as 'forgive' (*aphiemi*) is 'to let go, let out, allow to depart, leave behind, dismiss – and the exact opposite of suppress and hold on to! – Many of the attempts of the Christians to whom I have listened to forgive their abusers, have been based on suppressing their bad feelings (anger, guilt, fear etc.) in the belief that this was what their faith called them to do, when in fact what the need to do was to let go of these feelings.'[45] In other words, rites need to be devised whereby people who have suffered abuse can tell their story and express their anger and pain, and then through supportive prayer – with laying on of hands? – be helped in Jesus' name to begin to release those feelings and discover healing for their past wounds.

We say to 'begin to release' feelings of anger and pain: it is important to emphasise that all this takes time. The reality often is that the pain may be so deep that sometimes many years elapse before full healing is accomplished – if indeed ever. In this regard the rite of passage may be seen as a help in an on-going process, giving fresh strength to face up to the pain of the past.

Needless to say, such a rite does not dissolve responsibility from the abuser – it does, however, enable the abused person

[45] Gordon Sleight, 'Can confession damage your health?', *Contact* 111 (1993), p. 22.

to move on ('a transition') and gain control over their lives again.[46]

Such a rite of forgiveness could prove a great help to a wide variety of people. We have in mind not only those who have been abused physically or sexually (e.g. battered wives, rape victims, those who suffered child abuse), but also those who in a wider sense have been abused by the institutional church (e.g. young people who suffered from 'heavy shepherding', women whose gifts were never recognised by a male-dominated hierarchy, pastors unfairly treated by their church).

Transitions galore

It is difficult to bring this chapter to a conclusion. The fact is that there are yet other transitions which may be marked. For instance, we have not dealt with helping those who have suffered some non-life-threatening disability: e.g. the onset of blindness, the loss of a limb, or the paralysing effect of a stroke. Nor have we looked at transitions of a specifically ministerial nature: here we have in mind, for example, not only the loss experienced by pastors and their families as they move on to another church, but also the loss experienced by the church.

Life is indeed a journey marked by many different stages. One of the joys and challenges of pastoral care is to come alongside fellow pilgrims and be, as it were, an agent of God's grace at times of change and transition.

[46] An example of such a rite is provided by Ruth Bottoms, 'Rite of Healing For A Woman Threatened With Rape', *Worship File* 4 (Baptist Publications, 1993), 013–016. Here the woman is given an opportunity to tell her story and then is affirmed and 'exorcised':

'We affirm our sister who has been hurt, we declare she is loved of God and created in the image of God. Though she has been abused she is not destroyed. Although she has been deceived and demeaned, she retains her integrity. Though she has been a victim, she is a survivor.

'In the name of Christ the wounded healer we pray: From violence to your feelings, be healed. From the echo of violent words, be healed. From violence to your mind and spirit, be healed.'

The abused woman is not, however, given an opportunity to move on and forgive her abuser, although the intercessions that follow include prayer 'for the perpetrators of these things'. See also Judy Hanson, *Rape As Bereavement* (Grove Books, Nottingham, 1992), pp. 21–5.

Providing rites of passage for the Church Year

Many of these individual rites of passage could be recognised in a corporate manner. Indeed, there is much to be said for fitting them into the Church Year. Certainly, from the perspective of pastors this could be helpful: it would help them in their planning to ensure that various groups within the church are not missed out. It would also be helpful to the church as a whole: members would be made more aware of their responsibilities to each other, and the fellowship of the church would be deepened as a result.

With this in mind, let me offer the following suggestions:

1st Sunday of the New Year (January): Renewal of membership vows.

Sunday after the Conversion of Saint Paul (25 January): Celebration of singleness.

Sunday before Valentine's Day (14 February): Renewal of wedding vows; Recognition of all those who in the past year celebrated special wedding anniversaries.

Mothers' Day & Fathers' Day (in the UK, March and June): Prayer for all those who have lost their parents over the past year.

Easter Day: Renewal of baptismal vows.

Sunday nearest May Day (1 May) or Labor Day (USA, September): Prayer for all those unemployed; Recognition of all who have retired since last year (their names and occupations could be listed in the church news bulletin).

Trinity Sunday: Prayer for right relationships in the church (that they might reflect the relationship between Father, Son and Holy Spirit).

Church Anniversary: Renewal of membership vows.

A June/July Sunday: Recognition of school leavers.

1st Sunday in September: Recognition of all those beginning or changing school.

UN International Day of the Elderly (1 October): A celebration of old age.

Sunday nearest All Saints Day (1 November): Recognition of all those who have died in the past year.

Chapter 5

The missionary strategist

The call to mission

Pastors are to excel as the Church's missionary strategists. This in turn involves defining the missionary task and then leading the Church out in mission.

This defining of the missionary task is rooted in the Great Commission. It is significant that, whatever the form of the Commission, whether it be found in Matthew (28:18–20) or Mark (16:15) or Luke (24:46–9; see also Acts 1:8) or John (20:21–3), the mandate is clear: the Good News of the Gospel is to be shared with people everywhere. Evangelism is no optional extra. It is the fundamental task of the Church. Indeed, 'a church not engaged in mission is guilty of apostasy'.[1] Evangelism is of the essence of the Church; for as Emil Brunner once said, 'a church exists by mission as a fire by burning'.[2]

However, evangelism, although an essential task of the Church, is not the sole task of the Church. Evangelism does not exhaust the Church's mission. Social action and service need to be seen as part of the Church's mission too. The incarnate Christ is the model for mission (see John 20:21), a model which displays the power of God transforming every aspect of human life. For Jesus not only proclaimed the coming of the kingdom (Mark 1:14), he demonstrated the kingdom in action as he drove out demons (Matt. 12:28: see 11:2–6). Kingdom action must therefore accompany

---

[1] A phrase attributed to John Stott.
[2] Emil Brunner, *The Word And The Church* (SCM, London, 1931), p. 108.

kingdom preaching. Evangelism must therefore always be part of a larger task of mission.

The twin tasks of evangelism and social action complement and support one another. This relationship is helpfully described by John Stott:

> Words remain abstract until they are made concrete in deeds of love, while works remain ambiguous until they are interpreted by the proclamation of the gospel. Words without works lack credibility; works without words lack clarity. So Jesus' works made his words visible; his words made his works intelligible.[3]

The Isaiah vision

One of the most imaginative approaches to mission is to be found in Raymond Fung's 'ecumenical strategy for congregational evangelism'.[4] There are three elements to the strategy:

1. *The local congregation, in partnership with other people pursues the 'Isaiah Agenda'*. This agenda is based on Isaiah 65:20–23, which speaks of children not dying, old people living in dignity, those who build houses living in them, and those who plant vineyards eating their fruit. Fung advocates churches going to their neighbours and saying: 'The God we believe in is One who protects the children, empowers the elderly, and walks with working men and women. As Christians, we wish to act accordingly. We believe you share in similar concerns. Let us join hands.'

2. *Invitation to worship*. This involves the Church saying to its neighbours who share in the Isaiah Agenda: 'Doing the Isaiah Agenda is hard work. There are so many needs, and so many problems. Once in a while, we need to pause. We need to get together, to share our concerns, to celebrate, to pray, to seek strength in order to go on. To worship our God. Would you join us? You know you are most welcome.'

3. *Invitation to discipleship*. Fung envisages that in the process of working and worshipping together, trust and friendship will

---

[3] John Stott, *The Contemporary Christian* (IVP, Leicester, 1992), p. 345.
[4] Raymond Fung, *The Isaiah Vision: an ecumenical strategy for congregational evangelism* (WCC Publications, Geneva, 1992), especially pp. 2–3.

develop. There will come occasions when it is appropriate for the Christian to invite others to consider the claims of Christ on their lives. 'You are invited to be a disciple of Jesus Christ. Whether you are somebody or nobody, rich or poor, powerful or powerless, you are invited to enter into friendship with Jesus and fellowship with the church. You are called to turn around. Take up your cross and follow Jesus, together with us. We are ordinary people called to do extraordinary things with God.'

There is much to commend Fung's strategy. The linking of social action, worship and evangelism in such an integral fashion is excellent. And yet, this approach is questionable. In the first place 'Isaiah's Vision' in Isaiah 65 is not so much of an 'agenda' to which God's people are called to commit themselves, as a picture of what happens when God brings in the kingdom. This is not to say that God does not want us in the here and now to be concerned for the rights of young and old, of the weak and the oppressed. But to base a call to action on Isaiah 65 is not, in fact, doing justice to the Scripture itself. In the second place, Fung's evangelistic strategy is limited to people of good will, to those who are already concerned for society and its needs. The fact is that the great mass of society is happily pursuing its own self-interest. People for the most part only become motivated to pursue Fung's Isaiah agenda once they have responded to the call of discipleship.

Going Christ's way and making disciples

My own preference is to go for an understanding of mission which is more central to the mission and message of Jesus. In this respect I believe that there is much to be said for basing the call to mission on the Great Commission as found in John 21 and Matthew 28. Here in an all-encompassing fashion we have the call to social action and the call to evangelism. The twin mandate of the Church is to 'go the Jesus way and make disciples'.

On the one hand, 'to go the Jesus way' is to model our mission on the mission of Jesus. Inevitably this means that our mission must be 'holistic', reflecting God's love and concern for every aspect of people's lives. Just as Jesus fed hungry mouths, washed dirty feet, and comforted the sad, so too must we. If our mission is to be patterned on the mission of Jesus, then our evangelism must always go hand in hand with costly compassionate service.

On the other hand, 'to make disciples' means that our mission includes winning people to Christ and to his Church. However, our evangelism goes far beyond calling men and women to decide for Christ. Discipleship is in view. As Jesus himself made clear (e.g. Mark 8:34), discipleship is costly and involves an on-going commitment to follow Jesus. Inevitably this means going 'against the stream' of world opinion – it means making Jesus Lord of every area of our lives.

What does this mean in practical terms? It is here that pastors need to be imaginative in their task of drawing up a missionary strategy. The fact is that 'going Christ's way and making disciples' will mean different things to different churches. What will be appropriate in one setting will not be appropriate in another. Furthermore, what may be right and proper at one period of a church's history may not be right and proper at another. No one missionary strategy can ever remain constant. However, the over-arching mission of the church will remain the same.

Creating a mission strategy
Let me give an example of the way in which in my present church we defined our overall mission, and then in the light of that mission statement began to devise a strategy.

We began by affirming that 'our purpose is to go Christ's way and make disciples'. This summary mission statement was then expanded:

> In other words, our chief task is to express God's love in the way we live and in the words we speak, and through our lives and through our words to help others to respond to his love through a lifelong commitment to Christ and his Church. Through our regular Sunday worship of God and through our fellowship with one another – as expressed not least through fellowship groups – we seek to find the strength and the resources for our mission.

After defining the task, we went on to take a long hard look at our present ministry. Although we were a strong church attracting a cross-section of people from all ages and all backgrounds, an analysis of our membership nonetheless revealed that our church's age profile did not reflect the general age spread of our town: we had, in fact, a preponderance of people over the age of 45. Furthermore, although as a church we were extremely active in running all kinds of activities and events, for the most part these activities and events were aimed towards the two ends of the age spectrum.

After looking at the opportunities presented to us in the local community, we realised that as a church we were faced with four possible strategies:

1. We could choose to take no fresh initiatives and continue to rely on our present activities to reach those in the community who were untouched by the Gospel. This would be the most comfortable option, for nothing would have to change. Almost certainly, however, it would be a path to decline!

2. We could seek to create a church for the under-25s. We are a town-centre church surrounded on three sides by the campus of a university. At night, the town is alive with young people looking for somewhere to go – many of these young people end up at two night clubs just up the road from the church. However, although a youth-oriented strategy might give us an opportunity to grow dramatically, it would certainly cause us to lose many of our older members, who would find it difficult to relate to a 'youth-culture' church.

3. We could seek to create a church for the over-55s. We recognised that the total number of people in the over-55 range will grow considerably in the next ten years. With 35% of our membership in this age group, one could argue that we would be well placed to target the older end of the age spectrum. On the other hand, such a strategy would undoubtedly cause us to lose not only our young people but also the under-55s, who would feel unwanted and alienated by the ministry they were being offered.

4. We could seek to create a family church for all ages by initially focusing our energies and resources on the 25–45 age group, with a view to redressing the present age imbalance in the church. We recognised that at a later stage it might be necessary to refocus our energies and resources into different areas of concern.

Perhaps not surprisingly, the church overwhelmingly adopted option 4. But this was not the end of the strategising – but simply the end of the beginning. For we had simply chosen to go a particular way in fulfilling our overall mission. The next stage was to draw up a detailed strategy for the next nine months in order to implement what we believed were the Spirit-inspired hopes and dreams present among us. This strategy involved drawing up measurable 'faith goals' in every area of the church's life with the 25–45 age group particularly in mind. In turn these 'faith goals' had to be presented to and adopted by the church as a whole. All this involved much time and effort – and yet it is only as a vision is truly communicated and owned by the church as a whole, that the church is truly motivated to go out and fulfil its mission. In other words, missionary strategising involves far more than dreaming dreams and seeing visions – it involves the hard work of thinking, sharing, persuading and motivating the people of God for mission.

Developing diverse mission strategies

A market-place of religious beliefs
A very different way of developing a mission strategy is to focus not so much on age, but rather on the distance people are from personal faith in Jesus Christ.[5] Thus, from the perspective of the Christian Church, society may be divided into five groups:

1. The 'near fringe'.
2. The 'far fringe'.
3. The 'neo-pagans'.
4. Followers of other main-line religions.
5. The 'secularists'.

The 'near fringe' range from those who attend church services

[5] For a somewhat different approach, see the Engel Scale developed by James F. Engel in *What's Gone Wrong With The Harvest?* (Zondervan, Grand Rapids, Michigan, 1975), by James F. Engel & Wilbert Norton.

regularly, but who have not committed themselves to Jesus, to those who have lapsed in their church attendance.

The 'far fringe', although not normally darkening the door of a church, will often still regard themselves as members of the Church – in an English context they would happily describe themselves as Church of England. David Edwards once referred to this 'far fringe' as the 'dispersed' Church, likening its members to the

> majority of Jews . . . dispersed in the Diaspora outside Israel . . . Although they are not regular churchgoers, they are also not convinced atheists. They like, rather than dislike, having their conduct called 'Christian'. Although they probably employ the words when swearing, they are made uncomfortable if people are seriously rude about 'God' or 'Christ' . . . when they watch television or listen to the radio they do not usually switch off or get indignant when the subject is religious. They are interested to read some religious news or articles in their papers or magazines, and some of them buy religious books. They want their children to get acquainted with the Bible. They like to have their children baptized, their marriages blessed, and their dead buried according to the rites of the Church – partly, no doubt, because the old habits have not completely died out, but also in order to assert a serious wish to see their lives at these turning points in a Christian context.[6]

The 'neo-pagans', to use a phrase coined by the Dutch ecumenist Visser t'Hooft,[7] are yet one step further away from the Christian faith. Unable to live happily in a truly secular world 'without windows', they pursue the 'sacred' under a variety of weird and

6 David Edwards, *A Reason To Hope* (Collins, London, 1978), p. 223.
7 W. Visser t'Hooft, 'Evangelism among Europe's Neo-Pagans', *International Review of Mission* LXVI (Oct. 1977), p. 355, distinguished between the 'pagan' who holds a non-Christian religious conviction and the atheist who (says he) does not believe in God: 'European culture had become a debate between three forces: Christianity, scientific rationalism and neo-pagan vitalism. For a long time it had seemed that scientific rationalism would take the lead. But recently the picture has changed. The atomic threat, the terrible pollution, the lack of meaningful perspective which the technocratic civilization had brought has led to the growth of a new irrationalism.'

wonderful guises. The Church may be in retreat, but belief in the supernatural is not. In the words of Ernest Renan, 'The gods only go away to make place for other gods.'[8] The fact is, as John Habgood has pointed out, 'The secularization of the mind has its limits . . . Science and technology can generate their own mythologies, and the growth of cults and other bizarre manifestations, including the various counter-culture movements, are signs that some limits of secularization have been reached.'[9] The present huge popularity of the 'New Age' movement is a clear sign of 'the inability of radically secularised worldview to satisfy deeply rooted human needs and aspirations'.[10]

The followers of other main-line religions are, of course, adherents of Islam, Hinduism, Judaism, Sikhism and the like. Although overall still a small percentage of the population, in some areas these folk form a highly significant minority. In the UK, for instance, there are some three million Hindus, Jews, Muslims and Sikhs.

Finally there are 'the secularists', those who have abandoned God and religion altogether. As T. S. Eliot once graphically put it:

> But it seems that something has happened that has never happened before: though we know not just when, or why, or how or where.
> Men have left GOD not for other gods, they say, but for no god; and this has never happened before.[11]

How many belong to this final category, it is difficult to say. What is clear, however, is that the extent of secularisation has been much exaggerated. *Homo religiosus* is very much alive. The truly secularist man or woman is still very much in the minority.

A plurality of strategies

In the light of the diversity of belief and unbelief, it is clear that no pastor can be satisfied with one strategy, for there is no one kind

---

8 Cited by Visser t'Hooft, *IRM* LXVI (Oct. 1977), p. 355.
9 John Habgood, *Church And Nation In A Secular Age* (Darton, Longman & Todd, London, 1983), p. 24.
10 David Smith, 'Secularisation: Changing Perceptions', *Church Growth Digest* IX.2 (Winter 1989/90), p. 8.
11 T. S. Eliot, Choruses from *The Rock*.

of people. People are at varying distances from the Christian faith. Unfortunately in the past all too much evangelism has assumed that people are nearer the kingdom than they actually are. As it is, a variety of approaches are necessary if we are to be effective in making disciples.

So what might be appropriate with these different groups? What possible evangelistic approaches might we adopt?

The 'near fringe'

For those on the near fringe of the Church the traditional forms of evangelism will probably continue to be effective: special services, evangelistic coffee mornings and dinner parties, visitation evangelism, mini-missions of one kind or another. All these activities and a thousand more may still be usefully used.

Unfortunately our evangelism often gets no further than this group. The Jesuit Thomas Stranksy has made the perceptive observation that in the USA up to 95% of those who swell church-growth statistics are '*de*churched' – former Methodists, Baptists, Episcopalians, Catholics etc.:

> Overall in the USA evangelism seems in fact to be the Christian exchange of pews, collection plates and parking lots, as well as 'the faith enhancement of the penitent returnees' who found it again but elsewhere. The truly *un*churched, those never before evangelized, the folk with no previous Christian experience or none of any religious tradition – alas, that far more difficult challenge is avoided.[12]

In my experience the situation in the UK is scarcely any better – in some areas it may be worse.

The 'far fringe'

The far fringe can be reached in two particular ways. First of all, by capitalising on the possibilities inherent in two of the main Christian festivals, viz. Christmas and Easter. Even in 'post-Christian' Britain

[12] Thomas F. Stransky, *WCC Letter On Evangelism*, no. 10 (Geneva, Oct. 1988).

these two festivals have an important place – not least because of their exploitation by commercial forces. Christmas and Easter are the two occasions of the year when people's attention is focused on the person of Jesus, the two times of the year when outsiders are more likely to attend church than at any other time. Here surely are occasions when pastors can cash in on the prevailing religious sentimentalism with a view to presenting the Gospel in a meaningful way.

In the second place, we need to take more seriously the opportunities that the traditional rites of passage afford. A Bible Society survey found that 81% of British adults (25 million) are in touch with churches for christenings, marriages and funerals. Large numbers still make their 'wedding vows' in the sight of God, and many still have their children 'done', while the overwhelming majority mark the death of a loved one with a religious service. Here surely there are opportunities for evangelism as, week by week, literally thousands upon thousands turn to the Church for help. True, such evangelistic opportunities must be sensitively used. In the words of Donald English, we are not 'to exploit vulnerability but . . . meet the real need at the heart of the occasion itself'.[13]

These rites of passage are often easier for state churches to exploit than for free churches. And yet opportunities abound for all. For example, in a Baptist setting, where the candidates for a service of believers' baptism are encouraged to 'fill the church' by inviting all their relatives, friends and acquaintances to see them baptised, the result is that on average each candidate is able to bring along 20 non-Christian friends. Somehow 'far-fringers' in particular realise that it is the done thing to turn up for such an event – and all the more if there is an invitation to a 'party' afterwards.

Another rite of passage which Baptists can exploit is the 'dedication service' – when parents bring their children to church to ask God's blessing on them and to dedicate themselves to the task of Christian parenthood. Frequently this service is an 'in-house' affair, with the guest list normally limited to the grandparents and a few other relatives. But with some imagination the situation can

[13] Donald English, *Evangelism Now* (Methodist Church, London, 1987), p. 17.

be transformed: neighbours, colleagues and acquaintances can be invited to the service – and for the party following – and the upshot is that the congregation is swelled by 30 or more guests, many of whom would perhaps not normally darken the door of a church. Handled with sensitivity, this could be a great occasion for preaching the Gospel!

The 'neo-pagans'

If the church is to reach this third group, then it will only be to the extent that Christians are prepared to go to them, as distinct from expecting them to come to church. In this area evangelistic programmes have little use. The costly business of bridge-building is called for. Friendship evangelism, lifestyle evangelism, incarnational evangelism – Christ must be seen in and through his people.

The trouble with the majority of Christians is that they have become so committed to Christ and his Church that they have lost all meaningful contact with the world. The sad truth is that the older most of us grow in the Christian faith, the more likely we are to move into a Christian ghetto. It is at this point that pastors have a responsibility for ensuring that their churches do not suck into their system all the time and energies of their people. Indeed, there might be something to be said for calling a moratorium on church activities for a while and encouraging people instead to enrol at the local centre for evening classes, with a view to making friends with some of the 'happy pagans' in the neighbourhood.

Evangelising 'neo-pagans' will also mean taking seriously the secular affairs of the world. The concerns of the world – whether they relate to ecology or to poverty, to educational curricula or to genetic engineering – must become the Church's concerns. What John Jonsson has called 'the secluded niceties of our internal church matters of faith' must be put on the backburner.[14] Alas, all too often the Church glibly sings 'Christ is the answer' without ever facing up to the problems that confront the world in which we live. It is as Christians wrestle with the world's concerns, whether in some political forum or simply around a table in the local bar,

---

[14] John Jonsson, *Facing The Third Millennium*, Baptist World Alliance Resource Book on Evangelism (McClean, Virginia, 1988), p. 2.

that those right outside the Church will begin to see that none of the world's great problems will ever be answered without reference to the crucified and risen Christ. To preach the Lordship of Christ without involvement in the world's political and social concerns is a meaningless exercise.

Followers of other main-line religions

There is no easy way to evangelise the Jew, the Muslim, the Hindu, or the Sikh – that surely is demonstrated by the story of the modern missionary movement. On the other hand, the task is far from hopeless – not least when understanding and sensitivity are combined with Christian proclamation.

With regard to the Muslims, Hindus and Sikhs, one obvious strategy which needs to be adopted in seeking to reach this particular group of people is to send a Macedonian call to our partner churches overseas: 'Come over and help us', we need to say to our African and Asian brothers and sisters. If we are to reach people for Christ in cultures so different from ours, we must use those who are familiar with these cultures.

As far as the Jews are concerned, a somewhat different strategy needs to be adopted – not least because of the unique relationship which the Christian faith has with Judaism. As the 1986 Lausanne Consultation on Jewish Evangelism pointed out:

> God's call to the Jewish people is irrevocable ... The salvation of 'all Israel' is also included in God's purposes for the world and will bring rich blessing to the nations ... The Jewish people and Jesus the Messiah are fundamentally bound to one another in God's purposes for the salvation of the world.

However, the members of the Consultation went on to make clear that this does not mean that the Church has no evangelistic obligation to the Jewish people. It was before the highest council of the Jewish people that the early Jewish apostles claimed, 'there is no other name under heaven given to men by which we must be saved' (Acts 4:12). On the other hand, as the 'Messianic' Jewish movement has rightly reminded the wider Christian Church, there is no reason why Jews have to become Gentiles in order to become Christians.

The secularists
The truly 'secularised' are the hardest of all to reach for the Gospel. Yet even the hardest of hearts can be melted by the love of Christ's people seen in action. The evangelistic potential of Christ-like lives must never be minimised. Thus Donald English has drawn attention to some research in North America which has shown that 80% of those who join churches do so because of the influence of family, neighbours, friends or colleagues at work, to which Donald English adds: 'The corollary is that an equal percentage of those who leave a church do so because at times of crisis they do not receive evidence of adequate care from fellowship members.'[15]

Our lives tell a story. This truism is surely particularly true in the area of Christian marriage. At a time when more than one in three English marriages are ending in the divorce courts, the witness of a happy Christian marriage can be incalculable. Here is a challenge to Christian living!

Leadership is the key
At the end of the day it is not sufficient to analyse society and to postulate possible responses. What is needed is missionary strategists, pastors who will not only be able to analyse and reflect upon the missionary challenge facing them and their churches, but who will also be able to mobilise the people of God for adventurous and imaginative mission. This is where the call to excellence is so necessary.

Going for growth
At the heart of mission is to be found the Church. It is in the worship of the Church that the people of God find motivation and energy for mission. It is through the teaching of the Church that the people of God gain their understanding of mission. It is through the fellowship of the Church that the people of God are sustained in mission. It is to a large extent through the life and witness of the Church that the people of God express their mission. It is into the Church as well as into Christ Jesus that converts are baptised. It is

[15] Donald English, *Evangelism Now*, p. 10.

through the teaching of the Church that these new Christians are nurtured and equipped for mission.

With the Church having such a key role to play in the purposes of God, it is not surprising that many have been concerned for 'that nature, function, structure, health and multiplication of churches as they relate to the effective implementation of Christ's commission to "Go therefore and make disciples of all nations" (Matt.28:19)'.[16] Yet surprisingly, in some circles at least, consciously 'going for growth' is deemed unacceptable and theologically 'naff'.

Church growth has indeed had a bad press. The American Methodist, William Abraham, for instance, criticises the church growth movement for its poor theology and for its corrupting pragmatism, and believes that it represents 'a conspicuous failure to face up to the demands of the Christian Gospel'.[17] In particular he singles out five aspects of the Church growth movement which call for condemnation:

1. The homogeneous unit principle rides roughshod over the radically inclusive character of the people of God.
2. The New Testament concept of discipleship is undercut.
3. The call to repentance is non-specific.
4. The primary horizon of the Kingdom of God is ignored.
5. The reality of injustice and oppression in the world is soft-pedalled.

Abraham really does take the church growth movement to the cleaners, and even suggests that it may be a form of 'bogus Christianity'!

Nor has British Methodism been any kinder. Richard Jones, for instance, argues that the church growth movement represents 'a narrow doctrine of God'. In terms of the church growth movement, God is only interested in the Church; he is not interested in hunger, racism, war, poverty, ecology and injustice.[18]

---

[16] Taken from the British Church Growth Association's definition of church growth.
[17] William Abraham, *The Logic Of Evangelism* (UK edition: Hodder & Stoughton, London, 1989), p. 81.
[18] Richard Jones, 'Church Growth Theory', *Epworth Review* XVI (May 1989), pp. 27–35.

Jones goes on to say that church growth theory avoids the four great crunch issues confronting Christian mission in Europe:

1. Dialogue with other faiths.
2. Criticism of Western culture.
3. Struggle for Christian unity.
4. A need for a Christian apologetic.

In conclusion Jones states: 'Church Growth takes us into a rather triumphalist world, where the Christian soldiers need only to organise and enthuse themselves better and then go over the top, advancing evermore. Too easy by half.'

It is not my intention to evaluate each of the individual criticisms made by Abraham and Jones. It must be freely acknowledged that there is much truth in the general thrust of their criticisms. Certainly, the way in which the church growth movement has developed in parts of North America has led to a trivialisation of the Gospel.[19] And yet the church growth movement has made a very valid contribution to 20th-century mission thinking.

Let me highlight just three such contributions: the church growth movement has

1. put the Great Commission back on the map;
2. put the Church centre-stage;
3. distinguished between various kinds of growth.

Firstly, the church growth movement has put the Great Commission (Matt. 28:18–20) back on the map, in the sense that it has pointed the churches afresh to their task of making disciples. Yes, mission is broader than simply making disciples – but it certainly includes making disciples. A church that is 'gung ho' on social action but has no concern for evangelism is as unbalanced as a church which puts

[19] See, for instance, Eugene Peterson, *Under the Unpredictable Plant: an exploration into vocational holiness* (Eerdmans, Grand Rapids, Michigan, 1992), p. 37: 'It is interesting to listen to the comments that outsiders, particularly those from Third World countries, make on the religion they observe in North America. What they notice mostly is the greed, the silliness, the narcissism. They appreciate the size and prosperity of our churches, the energy and the technology, but they wonder at the conspicuous absence of the cross, the phobic avoidance of suffering, the puzzling indifference to community and relationships of intimacy.'

all its efforts into evangelism but is totally oblivious to the needs of the poor and the oppressed.

In the light of the Great Commission, a church that fails to make disciples is a church that fails. Alas, not all churches have taken this on board. In the colourful words of two Southern Baptists: 'Thousands of evangelical churches in America today are on the pill. They do not want to grow. Consciously or unconsciously they have repudiated reproduction.'[20] The fact is that growth, as parents of teenage children often know to their cost, can be uncomfortable! A price has to be paid for growth, and sadly far too many churches are not prepared to pay that price. This point is well made by Lyle Schaller:

> The majority of members in the vast majority of Protestant churches on the North American continent are more comfortable with stability or decline than with the changes required to move up off a plateau in size. The status quo has more appeal than growth. Numerical growth simply is not a high priority in most churches! Taking care of today's members is a higher priority than reaching people beyond that fellowship.[21]

What is true of churches in the States is true too of churches in the UK. Otherwise, why is it that overall so many denominations are not growing? It only takes a net increase of one member per year to be a growing church. In other words, to be a growing church we do not need to experience revival – all we need to do is to begin to be obedient to the Great Commission!

Secondly, the church growth movement has put the Church centre-stage by its emphasis on 'body evangelism'. Evangelism that is true to the New Testament involves not only commitment to Christ but also commitment to his people. For many Christians there is nothing radical in such a statement. But as far as certain groups of modern evangelicals are concerned, such a statement is revolutionary. For instance, 'crusade' evangelism in its classic form has only been interested in 'decisions' – the success of Billy

---

[20] Charles L. Chaney and Ron S. Lewis, *Design For Church Growth* (Broadman, 1977), p. 184.
[21] Lyle Schaller, *44 Steps Off The Plateau* (Abingdon Press, Nashville, 1993), p. 23.

Graham's evangelistic preaching has been measured in the number of 'decisions made for Christ'. But a so-called decision for Christ is only the beginning of a process, which can often lead absolutely nowhere. American statistics in fact show that there is a mortality rate of 75%: i.e. only one in four make it to the point of church membership. It has been rightly said that 'A great deal of evangelism is ineffective, because it does not lead to incorporation into the church. It is like spending all one's effort in delivering a baby only to abandon it in the delivery room ... Conversion without nurture is infant genocide'![22] Where is that nurture to take place? Not in some para-church grouping, but in the local church itself.

Thirdly, the church growth movement has helpfully distinguished between various kinds of growth. On the one hand, from the start there has been the recognition that there is more to growth than numbers. Initially the distinction was made between 'numerical' growth and 'spiritual growth', and then later church growth theoreticians talked of 'incarnational growth' and 'organic growth'.

(a) 'Numerical' growth centres on the adding of new Christians to the community of the body of Christ.

(b) 'Spiritual' or 'conceptual' growth focuses on the deepening of individual understanding and enactment of the Christian faith.[23]

(c) 'Incarnational' growth relates to the costly, loving, self-giving involvement of the Church with all levels of society.

(d) 'Organic' growth leads to the building of deep, loving, interpersonal relationships within the body of Christ.[24]

---

[22] Robert J. Hillman, *The Church Growing Up And Growing Out* (Unichurch Publishing, Sydney, Australia, 1981), p. 41.

[23] Loren B. Mead, *More Than Numbers: The Ways Churches Grow* (Alban, Bethesda, 1993), pp. 44–6, gives particular emphasis to what he terms 'maturational growth'. He encourages congregations to view themselves as 'a new kind of seminary ... Members need to be challenged beyond religious dilettantism to serious long-term engagement with the stuff of the faith.' He imaginatively refers to life situations as 'field placements': 'members can present case material from daily experience and receive help in critically analyzing the theological and missional dimensions'.

[24] See further Orlando E. Costas, 'Church Growth As a Multidimensional Phenomenon', *International Bulletin Of Missionary Research* V (Jan. 1981), pp. 2–8; also *Christ Outside The Gate* (Orbis, Maryknoll, New York, 1982), pp. 43–57.

On the other hand, there has been the important distinction between biological growth, transfer growth, and conversion growth.

(a) Biological growth is the result of Christian parents coming to faith and active church membership. According to Peter Wagner, in the American context any church can grow by 25% per decade just by biological growth![25]

(b) Transfer growth represents the movement of Christians from one church to another. Such growth can result from people moving homes; it can also simply involve people moving churches. Needless to say, from the perspective of the church left behind, such transfers are not growth but loss! Somewhat controversially Arn and McGavran have said: 'Well fed sheep cannot be stolen – if they can be stolen, it is not sheepstealing!'[26] Transfer growth can be very helpful in getting a church moving again, but ultimately the Church is about making disciples, as distinct from receiving transfers.

(c) Conversion growth results when 'pagans', i.e. those outside any church, are brought to repentance and faith and join the Church. This is what evangelism is really about!

The church growth movement has done the wider Church a service in emphasising the importance of the Church's task in making disciples, in winning people for Christ and his Church. In such a context I believe that it is right and proper for missionary strategists to encourage their churches to 'go for growth'. Growth is healthy. Growth is a sign of life. Growth is what God intends for his Church.

But it is important to set the challenge to growth within the context of the Great Commission. The Risen Lord does not say 'Go and grow bigger and better churches', but rather 'Go and make disciples'. Growth may be the consequence of making disciples, but it is not actually the objective. It is important that we get our focus right.

An interesting parallel may be drawn with the profit motive in the world of business. Thus a one-time chairman of McKinseys, a

[25] See Paul Beasley-Murray, 'A Godly Upbringing? "Biological Growth", Baptism & Church Membership', Church Growth Digest XIII (1991/2), pp. 6–8.
[26] Win Arn and Donald A. McGavran, Church Growth Principles (Vital Publications, Bayswater, Victoria, Australia, 1976), p. 47.

large US management consultancy firm, once said: 'Profit is not an end in itself, but is merely the reward of good management.' Perhaps with reference to the Church we need to say: 'Growth is not an end in itself, but is merely the reward of good stewardship'! Of course businesses need to make money – of course churches need to grow. But just as a healthy business must not be dominated by making short-term profits, neither can a church – if it wants to remain healthy – be dominated by the numbers game.

There are in fact three very real dangers when church growth is pursued for its own sake:

First, it leads to an inevitable confusion between conversion growth and transfer growth. The pastor who aims at growth *per se* runs the risk of being as satisfied with drawing people from other churches as winning people from outright paganism.

Secondly, it leads to putting the expansion of the Church before the salvation of the world, whereas in fact the theological context of church growth is not the Church at all, but rather the world. In other words, the pursuit of church growth should be motivated by concern for those without the Word of life.[27]

Thirdly, it leads to the worship of the institution rather than to the worship of the Saviour. Thus David Wasdell wrote with some perspicuity when he said:

> Motivation for church growth which loses sight of the glory of God and pursues growth for its own sake, smacks of institutional aggrandisement and is a subtle form of idolatry. The church exists, serves, evangelises and grows to the glory of God, and it is in the light of that fundamental purpose that all secondary tasks and means are to be judged.[28]

Yet, with these important caveats, it surely still is right for

[27] *The Manila Manifesto* (Lausanne Committee for World Evangelization, Pasadena, 1989), Section 11, 'The Challenge of AD 2000 And Beyond': 'The world population today is approaching six billion. One third of them nominally confess Christ. Of the remaining four billion half have heard of him and the other half have not.'
[28] David Wasdell, *Tools for the Task: Growth In Context* (Urban Church Project, London, no date).

missionary strategists to 'go for growth'. How to achieve that growth is where the pursuit of excellence comes in!

Taking culture seriously

The Gospel has always been offensive. In the words of one Oxford philosopher, Professor Sir Alfred Ayer, 'Among religions of historical importance there is a strong case for considering Christianity the worst,' for it rests 'on the allied doctrines of original sin and vicarious atonement, which are intellectually contemptible and morally outrageous.'[29] Equally scathing was the German Joachim Kahl, a former Protestant pastor who then turned his back upon the Christian faith: 'What . . . is the cross of Jesus Christ? It is nothing but the sum total of a sadomasochistic glorification of pain.'[30] I am reminded of the Apostle Paul: 'We preach Christ crucified: a stumbling block to Jews and foolishness to Greeks' (1 Cor. 1:23).

My particular concern is that the Church has become offensive to many, in the sense that it has become inextricably linked with one particular dominant culture. The Gospel in many places has become culturally bound. For many, Christianity is perceived to be white, Western and middle-class. But what about those who are not white, not Western, not middle-class? Is the Gospel not for them?

Hitesh Dodhia, an East African convert from Jainism, who now works as an Anglican pastor in England, has written:

> Jesus Christ is often portrayed in European art, literature and song as an English-speaking gentleman with white skin, fair hair, and blue eyes; bearded and middle class. Thus becoming a Christian is often related with becoming white (though it is not possible!, i.e. for me), middle-class (which is anything but Jesus' background) and westernized (which is not eastern!). It also means having to give up or deny our own culture, heritage and background. An example of this is when people say to me that they do not even look at my skin colour . . . But think of

---

[29] Cited by John Stott, *The Cross of Christ* (IVP, London, 1986), p. 43.
[30] Joachim Kahl, *The Misery of Christianity* (English translation: Penguin Books, Harmondsworth, 1971), p. 30.

me as a person. Though they do not say it, what they often mean is that I have conformed to a white western Christianity which suits their framework and does not challenge or confront their assumptions about Christianity.[31]

These are sobering words. For they reveal that we have allowed our cultural accretions to be confused with the Gospel itself. Indeed, they suggest that we believe people have to become like one of us in order to become Christians. We white, Western, middle-class Christians are in danger of committing the sin of the Judaisers, who confused their cultural trimmings with the heart of the Christian faith (see Paul's Letter to the Galatians). The fact is that the Gospel cannot be contained within any one particular culture.

Birds of a feather flock together

If the Word of the cross is to be heard, then there must be churches that are culturally relevant. This in turn means that we need to take the 'homogeneous unit principle' of church growth seriously. In the words of Donald McGavran, the father of the 20th-century church growth movement, the homogeneous unit is 'a section of society whose common characteristic is a culture or a language'.[32] Or to put it more simply, 'birds of a feather flock together'. Like attracts like.

It is this principle which the church growth movement has used as an evangelistic tool. For McGavran observed that 'people like to become Christians without crossing racial, linguistic or class barriers'.[33] He went on: 'In most cases of arrested growth of the Church, men are deterred not so much by the offence of the cross as by nonbiblical offences.'[34] McGavran therefore argued for the deliberate creation of 'one-people churches'. He made it clear this is not 'segregation':

> Segregation is a sin because it is an exclusion enforced by one group on another. 'One-people' churches are not, since they are

[31] Hitesh Dodhia, *Crossing The Cultures* (Grove Books, Nottingham, 1989), p. 12.
[32] Donald McGavran, *Understanding Church Growth* (2nd edition, Eerdmans, Grand Rapids, 1973), p. 85.
[33] McGavran, *Understanding Church Growth*, p. 199.
[34] Ibid., p. 201.

the choice of a group as to language and customs and do not come about through a desire to exclude 'inferiors' – quite the contrary.[35]

McGavran's thinking was developed by Peter Wagner; according to him the homogeneous principle was one of the seven 'vital signs' of a healthy growing church. Wagner stated: 'The membership of a healthy growing church is composed basically of one kind of people'; 'Even in church, "birds of a feather flock together".'[36]

If McGavran and Wagner are right, and that the great obstacles to conversion are social and not theological, then clearly we must do something about it. The Church must cease to be unnecessarily offensive; it must become culturally relevant.

Using the homogeneous principle in evangelism

It must be admitted that not all Christians have welcomed the insights of the church growth movement with open arms. This homogeneous unit principle in particular has proved most controversial. It has been argued that the Christian Church should rise above cultural division and separateness. Does not the New Testament teach that 'There is neither Jew nor Greek, slave nor free, male nor female, for you are all one in Christ Jesus' (Gal. 3:28)? Juergen Moltmann, for instance, declared: 'National churches, racial churches, class churches, middle class churches, are in their practical life heathenish and heretical.' To reflect the will of God a community must consist of 'the unlike, of the educated and uneducated, of black and white, of the high and the low'.[37]

I confess that I have considerable sympathy with this point of view. But the fact is, the heterogeneous unit does not always work as an effective evangelistic principle. The distinguished American church consultant, Lyle E. Schaller, commented: 'Despite the dismay and objections of those who attack the use of the homogeneous unit principle as a foundation for any church growth strategy,

[35] Ibid., p. 211.
[36] C. Peter Wagner, *Your Church Can Grow: Seven Vital Signs Of a Healthy Church* (Regal Books, Glendale, California, 1976), p. 110.
[37] Juergen Moltmann, *The Gospel of Liberation* (English translation: Word, Waco, 1973), p. 91.

scores, perhaps even hundreds, of carefully designed research projects suggest it ranks behind only kinship ties as a facet in determining who joins which church – and . . . of course, some will argue that kinship ties represent the number-one extension of the homogeneous principle.'[38] Robert Plaisted made the interesting observation that people's reaction to McGavran's findings 'recalls the rage that medieval clergymen directed against Galileo because the universe he saw through his telescope obstinately refused to behave as their dogma said it should'.[39]

Some argue that there is a middle way, whereby one could use the homogeneous principle in evangelism, but refuse to build a one-class or one-culture church. On this basis one would set up evangelistic groups which would be targeted at particular groups – whether of age, class, or race – but once people are won to Christ, then they would be integrated into the heterogeneous fellowship of the Church. Peter Cotterell was clearly of this point of view, when he wrote:

> The homogeneous unit . . . is a reality. It is necessarily found in unredeemed society, and since evangelism must take place in unredeemed society, it is apparent that *evangelism* ought to take note of the role of the homogeneous unit . . . But when people become Christians, when they *join* a local congregation, they have to learn a new way of life. They must learn biblical ideas which are *not* exclusive. In the church *all* are welcome.[40]

But does this work? I confess it did not always work in the 13 years that I was pastor of the Baptist church in Altrincham. Yes, the church was mixed – there was a good deal of variety in terms of social class and educational background. And yet this undoubted variety was all within limits. I remember how, at one stage, we sought to use the homogeneous unit principle in evangelism with our youth group: in fact, we had two youth groups running – one

[38] Lyle E. Schaller, *Reflections Of A Contrarian* (Abingdon Press, Nashville, 1989), p. 16.
[39] Robert Plaisted, 'The homogeneous unit debate; its value orientations and changes', *Evangelical Quarterly* 69 (July 1987), pp. 217–18.
[40] Peter Cotterell, *Church Alive* (IVP, Leicester, 1981), p. 114.

for working-class kids, and one for middle-class kids. We sought to integrate the working-class kids into the church, but by and large it didn't work – the church was middle-class. We were expecting them to cross an unnecessary barrier in order for the church to become heterogeneous. It's amazing how much self-deception we employ to hide this fact from ourselves!

Certainly, in the task of reaching people from other racial groupings, I now think that the homogeneous unit principle must be brought into the Church itself. If we are to make disciples of all 'people groups',[41] then we must get into the business of cross-cultural church planting. If the Word of the cross is to be clearly heard and men and women are to be saved, then there need to be churches for whites and churches for blacks; churches for Arabs and churches for Filipinos; churches for Tamils and churches for Bengalis; churches for the Chinese and churches for the Japanese.

A biblical basis for such cross-cultural mission may be found in John 1:14: 'The Word became flesh and lived among us, and we have seen his glory, the glory as of a father's only son, full of grace and truth.' Normally when preachers expound this text, they speak of the way in which the Lord of glory emptied himself of all that was rightfully his and became one with us. But the logic of John 1:14 implies more than that: not only did Jesus take upon himself our humanity, he actually became a first-century Jew. Jesus not only entered our world, he entered into the world of one particular culture. So much so, that Paul could speak of Jesus as having 'become a servant of the circumcised on behalf of the truth of God' (Rom. 15:8). The Word became flesh – within one particular culture. We need to reflect upon the significance of this fact: Jesus, God's Son, was swarthy in appearance, probably hook-nosed, spoke Aramaic, and lived all his life within one very limited geographical area of the world.

A biblical basis for mono-cultural congregations – if not actual churches – can be found. However, for the body of Christ to have its full meaning, ways and means must be found of associating with

41 That is one possible paraphrase of Matt. 28:19: *ta ethne.*

the wider Church. In some way expression must be given to the oneness we all may experience in Jesus Christ.

Taking local cultures seriously

Here again there is work for the pastor as missionary strategist to do. For the sake of the kingdom it is important to take stock of the various cultures present in the locality, and to devise ways and means of reaching for Christ the differing groups present. In some areas these cultural groupings will be racial and/or linguistic in nature. In other areas these cultural groupings will be related to education or to class. Our task, as pastors in pursuit of excellence, is to ensure that the Gospel does not prove unnecessarily offensive to anyone.

Empowering God's people

A different approach to mission, but equally necessary, is to empower God's people for their ministry in the world of work. Christians have to be salt as well as light in the world. But how?

First, as pastors we need in our preaching and teaching to develop a more worldly concept of ministry. The doctrine of the priesthood of all believers needs to be lived out beyond the confines of the Church. In the graphic words of Edward Patey: 'All orders are holy. Plumbers are as much in holy orders as the clergy, serving God and their fellows . . . Electricians, park-keepers, doctors and typists are all working as much with the things of God as the priest with the sacrament.'[42]

Clearly, such a concept of ministry is very much bound up with a theology of work. How often do we preach sermons on work? How often does preaching relate to that which occupies most of the time of most of God's people? Is work just a way of earning money, or is it a way in which we contribute to the needs of others?

---

[42] Cited by Mark Gibbs & T. Ralph Morton, *God's Frozen People* (Collins, Fontana, London, 1964), p. 15. Gibbs and Morton, *God's Frozen People*, p. 14, themselves state: 'There is no fundamental difference in calling between an Archbishop and his chauffeur, between a prime minister and a parish minister – providing they are both in each case faithful and committed Christians.'

'If you can't say a deep "Yes" to the work by which you earn your living,' says Kenneth Adams, 'you cannot say a deep "Yes" to your life as a whole because work forms such an important part of life.'[43] Preachers have the task of enabling their people to come alive, and in the process discovering that their work can be a form of ministry.

A creative way of helping people discover that their work can be a form of Christian ministry is given by an American Baptist, Richard Broholm, who attempted to look at what people do in terms of the threefold office of Christ's ministry as 'priest', 'prophet', and 'king'. For example, in terms of the priestly or pastoral ministry of Christ's body, he wrote: 'What we have often failed to see is that the contractor who builds houses, the lab technician who tests for cancer, and the postal worker who bridges the gap between other distant friends are all engaged in a caring ministry even though it is unlikely they will ever intimately know the persons they serve.'[44]

Secondly, pastors leading public worship need to ensure that their praying goes beyond the needs of the church, and that it has the world in view – not least the worldly ministry of God's people in view. Kenneth Adams points out that in the Index of Prayers in the Anglican *Alternative Service Book* 'not one prayer, in that long list of things we should pray for, concerns our ordinary work'.[45] Needless to say, it is not only the Anglicans who are at fault!

In *Dynamic Leadership* I suggested that from time to time we need to interview within the context of public worship some of our members who are professionally involved in community service – social workers, teachers, policemen, prison officers, health visitors, doctors and nurses – and pray for them publicly.[46] On reflection, only to interview such people could signal to others

---

[43] 'The Workplace', pp. 218–19 in *Treasure In The Field*, edited by David Gillett and Michael Scott-Joynt (Fount, London, 1993).
[44] Richard Broholm, 'Towards Claiming And Identifying Our Ministry In The Work Place', pp. 151–2, in *The Laity In Ministry*, edited by George Peck and John S. Hoffmann (Judson, Valley Forge, Pennsylvania, 1984).
[45] Kenneth Adams, 'The Workplace', p. 218.
[46] Paul Beasley-Murray, *Dynamic Leadership*, pp. 88–9.

that their work is of little consequence to the kingdom.[47] We should rather make an effort to include people from all walks of life.

A sample interview could include three questions:

(1) What do you do for a living?
(2) What are the issues that you face in your faith in the context of your daily work?
(3) How would you like us to pray for you as a church in your ministry from Monday to Friday?

If this were done on a regular basis – whether weekly, fortnightly, or even monthly – such interviews could help a church make a substantial shift in its priorities in the course of one year.[48]

Thirdly, in our meetings we should ensure that our agendas are kingdom-centred rather than church-centred. If the focus of the church meeting or the meeting of the Parochial Church Council is the kingdom of God, then this means that there is no issue which lies outside the orbit of such meetings. All the major issues of life are of relevance – including those issues which face people at work as also in the local community. Sadly, there are too many churches where the focus is on the nuts and bolts of church life. The Baptist church meeting, for instance, is not a church 'business meeting' – or, if it is, then the business we are called to conduct is in the first place God's business, and not the trivia of church life. Issues of detail need to be delegated – and entrusted – to deacons. In the church meeting we need to be mindful of the injunction of Jesus: 'be concerned above everything else with the Kingdom of God and with what he requires of you' (Matt. 6:33, GNB).

Fourthly, instead of doing Bible study in a vacuum, home groups

---

[47] See David Field and Elspeth Stephenson, *Just The Job* (IVP, Leicester, 1978), p. 19: 'The tendency to catalogue jobs in some kind of spiritual football league is deeply engrained on the Christian mind. Way out at the top of the list come those who have "vocations" – including, no doubt, missionaries and clergy, followed at a short distance by RE teachers, doctors and nurses. Halfway down, we meet those with "ordinary jobs" (such as businessmen, electrical engineers and secretaries who do not work for Christian organizations). Then right at the bottom, and in serious danger of relegation, are those involved in much more dubious pursuits – pop musicians, perhaps . . . and barmaids.'

[48] See Stevens and Collins, *The Equipping Pastor*, pp. 137–8.

need to enable people to relate the world of work to their Christian faith. For example, a church might decide to put aside its traditional pattern of Bible study, and instead of beginning with the text begin with where people are. As a means of supporting one another's ministries it could encourage individuals to talk about their work. To do this at any depth it would probably have to devote an evening to each person.

Davida Crabtree suggests that the following questions might be asked of one another:

Describe how you spend your day.
What is satisfying for you in your work? What is stressful?
What is the impact of your work on your health, on your family, on your financial life?
How does your workplace need to change? How can you help, or not?
What are the ethical and justice or fairness issues you have to deal with at work?
Does it make any difference that you are a Christian in your workplace? How does your faith connect to your work?[49]

Home groups need to become genuinely supportive. Here is a way of upholding and encouraging God's people in their individual ministries in the world.

Fifthly, an alternative course of action, closely related to the previous idea, is to set up support groups for particular occupational groups. It could, for instance, prove more helpful for a group of teachers in the church to get together and talk about their work from a Christian perspective, than for an individual teacher to share his or her problems in a home group made up of people coming from a variety of occupations. Such mutual support groups can be on-going; on the other hand, they can be short-term or just one-offs.

Sixthly, run a stewardship campaign with a difference. Instead of approaching the theme of Christian stewardship with the church's needs in view, we could centre on the possibilities inherent in the

[49] Davida Foy Crabtree, *The Empowering Church: how one congregation supports lay people's ministries in the world* (Alban, Bethesda, 1992), p. 9.

individual. Thus, after appropriate teaching, we could pass out cards for members to write their names and the answer to a simple question such as: 'If time and talent and training were not obstacles (these three can all be found!) what would you really like to do for God in the church or the world?' Stevens and Collins, who advocate this approach, comment: 'The answers will be a pleasant surprise.'[50]

Seventhly, run church membership classes which encourage new members to see their ministry as primarily ministry in the world. Here I have in mind membership classes not just for new Christians, but also for older Christians transferring in from other churches. Both young and old in the faith would benefit from an opportunity to reflect on their mission and ministry in the world. In this context one could talk about gifts, and the way in which gifts could best be used in the service of Christ, whether in the church or beyond the church. Clearly, such membership classes would also include an introduction to the local church, the way it works, its ethos and understanding of itself. What a difference it would make if all the instruction were not simply church-centred![51]

Finally, give people time to live in the real world – as well as to live at home. I confess that this is something with which I am wrestling in my own church. There seem to be no natural breaks in our church year. I am sure that we need to take breaks, otherwise some of us will be consumed by the church. Indeed, I seriously wonder whether next Lent we should 'fast' from all church activity. Such a Lenten fasting might well benefit the kingdom – indeed, it might even benefit the church in the long run. We do well to pay attention to Robin Greenwood when he writes:

I have known people who are at church when they ought to be

50 See Stevens & Collins, *The Equipping Church*, p. 135.
51 Crabtree, *The Empowering Church*, describes a four-week-long series of membership classes with the following sequence of content:
   1. The church's way of work: 'how we are organised, history, understanding of membership and its meaning'.
   2. Gifts identification: 'When we do gifts identification now, it is done as a service to the person, not just as a self-serving talent hunt on the part of the church'!
   3. Introduction to the Ministry of the Laity.
   4. A frank talk about faith and money.

facing up to tasks at work or at home ... I fell into the trap of many clergy in small or precarious parishes, of working for the building up of the church, frequently at the expense of the development of the full life of its members ... We need to find strong ways of affirming all church members in their particular paths of discipleship, especially where these paths take them very far from the church's life and experience.[52]

Here then are a few ways in which we might encourage God's people to fulfil their role in the world. Let me end this section with a quotation from Hans Ruedi-Weber's *Salty Christians*:

In churches all over the world ... the majority of those who have made the *sacramentum* [baptismal vows] do not actually join Christ's struggle for the world. After taking 'the military oath', many of them become deserters, conforming themselves to the world, and not being transformed by the renewal of their minds (Rom. 12:2). Others go on permanent leave, only returning occasionally for a military inspection. They lead a double life, following two different sets of ethics – one for their private, Sunday life, and one for their life in the workaday world. Still others always remain recruits in the barracks, becoming more and more refined in the use of the spiritual armour of God, but never leaving their Christian camp in order to fight for reconciliation for the world. Under these circumstances, no wonder the battle soon begins in the barracks![53]

In conclusion

No true pastor can be unconcerned for the lost. Like the 'Great Shepherd of the sheep', pastors will seek the 'other sheep' who belong to the fold (John 10:16). They will want to go in search of the sheep who have gone astray (Matt. 18:12–14). Following Paul's injunction to Timothy, they will endeavour to 'do the work of an evangelist' and carry out their ministry 'fully' (2 Tim. 4:5).

[52] Robin Greenwood, *Reclaiming The Church* (Fount, London, 1988), pp. 138–9.
[53] Hans Ruedi-Weber, *Salty Christians* (Seabury Press, New York, 1963), p. 12.

However, pastors cannot win the world to Christ – nor should they even attempt it. Their prime task in this respect is to mobilise the people of God for mission. As leaders of the people of God, this in turn involves drawing up appropriate strategies for mission.

It is at this point that the call to excellence is so relevant. For excellence in mission is only achieved through constant creative thought and imaginative application. Excellence in mission rules out, for instance, the adopting of other people's ideas, however effective these ideas may have proved elsewhere; for each church is different. Effective strategies are strategies which are appropriate for the particular situation which an individual church faces. Hence, even the most brilliant of ideas from one church needs to be adapted in order to become truly relevant in another church setting. Indeed, even the ideas set out in this chapter are not to be taken over lock, stock and barrel. Tailor-made strategies for mission are needed.

The pursuit of excellence is far from easy. There are no short cuts to drawing up and implementing effective strategies for mission. Hard work at every stage is necessary. Yet where 'inspiration' and 'perspiration' come together, there much satisfaction is to be found.

Chapter 6

The senior care-giver

The call to care

Pastors as senior care-givers are called to care. They are called to be 'shepherds' to the flock.

The shepherd image

The shepherd imagery recalls Ezekiel's description of the divine shepherd: 'I myself will be the shepherd of my sheep, and I will make them lie down, says the Lord God. I will seek the lost, and I will bring back the strayed, and I will bind up the injured, and I will strengthen the weak, but the fat and the strong I will destroy. I will feed them with justice' (Ezek. 34:15–16). The translation of the penultimate sentence is in question. The somewhat harsh Hebrew version only makes sense if the meaning is that the divine shepherd will care for the needy by destroying the strong who would attack the helpless sheep, and therefore feed them with justice. On the other hand, from the perspective of pastoral care the rendering presented by the Septuagint, Syriac and Latin versions is more attractive: 'and the fat and the strong I will watch over' (so, for instance, the RSV).

On the basis of Ezekiel 34 the Strasbourg reformer Martin Buber defined the pastoral task as:

1. To draw to Christ those who are alienated.
2. To lead back those who have been drawn away.
3. To secure amendment of life for those who fall into sin.
4. To strengthen weak and silly Christians.
5. To preserve Christians who are whole and strong and urge them forward to the good.

In other words, on the model of the divine shepherd, the pastor's responsibilities are evangelism, restoration, teaching, encouraging and feeding.[1]

The multi-faceted nature of pastoral care as presented in the image of the shepherd is also seen in the Shepherd Psalm (Ps. 23). The good shepherd feeds, restores and guides his sheep. With his rod and staff he not only protects his sheep, but also 'disciplines his sheep and examines them for disease'.[2]

Paul's pastoral model

Pastoral care has many aspects. This comes out very clearly in the way in which Paul approached the pastoral task. Interestingly, in his letters Paul never described himself as a 'pastor' (but see Eph. 4:11; also Acts 20:28). Instead he used the imagery of the parent-child relationship. Tender and loving as a mother (1 Thes. 2:7–8), he was anxious to see his children grow in the faith (Gal. 4:19–20). As a father, Paul believed that both encouragement (1 Thes. 2:11–12) and correction (1 Cor. 4:14–21) were necessary for healthy development within the Christian family. For Paul discipline was not reserved as a final resort for gross moral error, but rather was perceived to be an essential part of Christian nurture, by which individuals and churches were built up in the faith (see Col. 1:28).

Significantly, Paul was concerned not just for the corporate health of the churches in his care, but also for the well-being of individuals. People counted for Paul: hence in Romans 16 Paul takes the trouble of greeting over 27 people by name. The personal character of Paul's pastoral work comes to the fore in 1 Thessalonians 2:11 and Colossians 1:28. All this is in line with Luke's account of Paul's speech to the Ephesian elders, which suggests that his normal practice was to combine preaching to the church at large together with the visiting of individual church members (Acts 20:20).

Although Paul was clearly a very dominant figure, he never operated as a solo pastor. Rather, he constantly surrounded himself with colleagues who could share in the pastoral task. It is reckoned

---

[1] See *Martini Bucer Opera Ominia Series 1: Deutsche Schriften VII*, pp. 67–245, cited by Derek Tidball, *Skilful Shepherds* (IVP, Leicester, 1986), p. 47.

[2] So Derek Tidball, *Skilful Shepherds*, p. 45.

that, if one adds all the names found in Acts and in Paul's letters, then at various times some 100 people were associated with the Apostle. What is more, Paul also encouraged his converts in general to be involved in pastoral care. Likening the church to a body, he spoke of the members having 'the same care for one another' (1 Cor. 12:25). Paul urged the Galatians to 'Bear each other's burdens', which in turn involved caring for those straying from the faith, restoring the backsliders (Gal. 6:1–2). Within the context of death and bereavement the Thessalonians were told to 'encourage one another and build up each other' (1 Thes. 5:11). Indeed, Paul expected the Thessalonians to share in every aspect of pastoral care: 'admonish the idlers, encourage the fainthearted, help the weak' (1 Thes. 5:14). Similarly, the Colossians were to 'teach and admonish one another in all wisdom' (Col. 3:16). Pastoral care was not exclusive to a particular cadre in the church: all were involved in 'the work of ministry' (see Eph. 4:12, 15–16).[3]

Modern definitions of pastoral care

From biblical images and patterns, which contain some very significant principles for contemporary pastoral care, we turn to pastoral care as it is understood today. By general consensus Clebsch and Jaekle's definition has for the most part been regarded as standard in North America and also in Britain. They say pastoral care

> consists of helping acts, done by representative Christian persons, directed towards healing, sustaining, guiding, and reconciling of troubled persons whose troubles arise in the context of ultimate meanings and concerns.[4]

There are, however, three distinct limitations to this definition. First, the underlying assumption is that pastoral care is exercised by professional pastors, i.e. 'representative Christian persons'. There is, however, no good reason why pastors should have the monopoly on pastoral care.

[3] See further Paul Beasley-Murray, 'Paul as Pastor', pp. 654–8 in *Dictionary of Paul and his Letters* (IVP, Leicester & Downers Grove, Illinois, 1993), edited by G. F. Hawthorne & R. P. Martin.
[4] William A. Clebsch & Charles R. Jaekle, *Pastoral Care In Historical Perspective* (Aronson, New York, 1975), p. 4.

Secondly, pastoral care is conceived in terms of what Martin Thornton called 'the ambulance syndrome'.[5] It has 'troubled persons' in view, as distinct from people in general. Pastoral care, however, needs to have a much broader base. Pastoral care, viewed from a Christian perspective, is not just helping the hurting, but also helping, encouraging and enabling people to grow and develop in the Christian faith.

Thirdly, to speak of care exercised 'in the context of ultimate meanings and concerns' is vague and ambiguous. Specifically, Christian pastoral care is rooted in the cross and resurrection of Jesus Christ. The Swiss Protestant pastor and theologian Eduard Thurneysen rightly said: 'True pastoral care does not rest until it has carried the forgiving Word into these depths in the strength of the Spirit and of prayer and has really ... brought [persons] again under the healing power of grace.'[6] In Jesus only is fulness of life to be found (John 10:10).

In the light of these criticisms, in 1988 Stephen Pattison offered a more welcome definition:

> Pastoral care is that activity, undertaken especially by representative Christian persons, directed towards the elimination and relief of sin and sorrow and the presentation of all people perfect in Christ to God.[7]

Interestingly, by 1993 Pattison was wanting to amend this definition. He now believes that 'the norm for thinking about care must now be that of the ordinary non-trained, non-professional person'.[8]

---

[5] Martin Thornton, *Spiritual Direction* (SPCK, London, 1984), p. 9: 'It is curious that what we ambiguously call pastoral care is seen as something entirely negative. It invariably suggests the dispensation of human benevolence with a sprinkling of Christian saccharin: helping those in trouble, counselling the disturbed, solving human problems. This is the ambulance syndrome, implying that Christianity might alleviate suffering but that it has nothing more positive to offer. The pastor is there to pick up the pieces after an accident, and barring accidents he is out of a job.'

[6] Eduard Thurneysen, *A Theology Of Pastoral Care* (English edition: John Knox Press, Richmond, 1962), p. 67.

[7] Stephen Pattison, *A Critique Of Pastoral Care* (SPCK, London, 2nd edition, 1993), p. 13.

[8] Ibid., p. 194.

In similar vein Alastair Campbell wants to 'prevent specialized counselling by clergy becoming normative for pastoral care'.[9] He is afraid lest in professionalising pastoral care we lose 'the spontaneity and simplicity of love'.[10] For 'pastoral care is, in essence, surprisingly simple. It has one fundamental aim: to help people to know love, both as something to be received and something to give'.[11]

The senior care-giver

It is against this background that I have entitled this chapter, 'The senior care-giver'. Pastors are not to be the only people in the church engaged in pastoral care. Although, as the senior care-giver, the pastor has general pastoral oversight of the church, the task of pastoral care must rightly be shared.

In one sense the task of pastoral care is to be shared with everybody. If pastoral care is primarily 'a kind of loving',[12] then clearly all can be involved. In these terms pastoral care is simply the fulfilling of the 'new commandment' to love one another (John 13:34). Pastoral care is the responsibility of every Christian.

Pastoral care in a deeper sense, however, is more than just loving. It is also a specialised form of loving, which involves the ability to listen and to discern, acting where appropriate as a channel of the grace and indeed of the discipline of Christ.[13] This in turn means that there are some more gifted than others to exercise pastoral care in the fellowship of the church. This being so, it makes sense for churches to recognise those with gifts of pastoral care and to encourage pastors to share the pastoral load with a team of 'care-givers'. In practical terms in my own church, this means

9 Alastair Campbell, *Paid To Care? The Limits Of Professionalism In Pastoral Care* (SPCK, London, 1985), p. 53.
10 Ibid., p. 4.
11 Ibid., p. 1.
12 The title of chapter 1 in Campbell's *Paid To Care?*
13 In the light of Jay Adams' strong commitment to 'nouthetic' counselling – see, for instance, J. E. Adams, *The Christian Counsellor's Manual* (Presbyterian & Reformed Publishing Company, Nutley, New Jersey, 1973) – where the emphasis is on counselling as directive and confrontational, it is interesting to discover that the Greek verb *noutheteo* ('to warn, to admonish') appears 13 times in the New Testament, whereas the Greek verb *parakaleo* ('to comfort, to draw alongside') is used well over 100 times.

that the ordained pastors work with a group of pastoral deacons, who together form the pastoral team of the church. Each pastoral deacon has responsibility for a geographical pastoral area, each of which is divided into 'care groups' led by 'carers' who work with the pastoral deacons to ensure that everybody in the church is meaningfully cared for. Clearly, this is only one way of expressing pastoral care within a fellowship. The important thing, however, is for the senior care-giver to share the pastoral care of the church in an effective manner.

Pastoral visiting

This leads on to the question of pastoral visiting. In times past one of the chief tasks of the pastor was to visit people in their homes. Some pastors still do, many do not. Nolan Harmon told of one energetic Baptist minister who used to get into every home in his church – he had over 2,000 members – once every year. Of course, his calls were necessarily short, about ten minutes each.[14] But Harmon was writing in 1928. Today things are different. According to George Barna, the average senior American pastor in 1992 was spending five hours a week doing visitation.[15] One gets the impression that if it were possible, American pastors would do even less, because only 10% listed pastoral care as 'the primary joy of pastoring'.[16]

Robin Greenwood is quite clear: pastoral visiting for the sake of pastoral visiting is to be avoided. Far from being helpful, it is actually harmful to the effective functioning of the church. 'It is a mistake regularly to visit the hale and hearty, because this reinforces in them the image of a priest who is there to look after them rather than as one to preside over their many and varied ministries.'[17]

Eugene Peterson is also far from enamoured with much of routine pastoral visiting, and suggests that it has little point. 'I want to be a pastor who listens. I want to have the energy and time to really listen to them so that when they are through, they know at least one

[14] Nolan B. Harmon, *Ministerial Ethics And Etiquette* (Abingdon, Nashville, revised edition, 1978), p. 83.
[15] George Barna, *Today's Pastors*, p. 130.
[16] Ibid., p. 65.
[17] Robin Greenwood, *Reclaiming The Church* (Collins/Fount, London, 1988), pp. 57–8.

other person has some inkling of what they're feeling and thinking
. . . Too much of pastoral visitation is punching the clock, assuring
people we're on the job, being busy, earning our pay.'[18]

A similar point is made by Stephen Pattison. Routine pastoral
visiting accomplishes very little, because there is no agreed understanding why a particular visit is taking place. Often the pastor has
no clear purpose, and even if the pastor does have a motive for
visiting, this motive is not normally communicated to the person
visited. Add to that the residual 'judgmental aspect' of the ministerial
role, and you end up with not only a pointless visit, but possibly an
unwelcome visit too![19]

However, the veteran Southern Baptist pastoral theologian,
C. W. Brister, still sees a role for pastoral calling, and on the grounds
of theological conviction and practical experience argues 'we just go
the distance'.[20] He rightly points out that at home a person generally
risks being real. True, there are people who even in the home put
up a facade, with the result that the visit – from the point of view of
the pastor at least – proves a frustrating experience. Nonetheless, it
is more difficult to put up a facade at home. Within the home setting
the discerning pastor can begin to understand the context from
which a person comes. There is no better way of getting to know
a person than actually visiting them in their home. In that respect
I believe it is a good thing for new pastors within the first year or
so of their call to a church, to aim to visit all the members in their
homes. Some pastors beginning their ministry in a new church feel
it is much more effective getting their secretaries to arrange people
to visit them in their church office – but while such a method may
be more effective in the use of time, in the long run it proves less
effective in getting to know and understand those in our charge.

This is not the same, however, as routine visiting. Routine visiting
must be delegated. Pastors are not the only care-givers. The front line
of pastoral care is formed by carers within the fellowship. As senior
care-givers pastors cannot afford the luxury of the traditional role

[18] Eugene Peterson, 'The Unbusy Pastor', *Leadership* II (Summer 1981),
p. 72.
[19] Stephen Pattison, *A Critique Of Pastoral Care*, pp. 75–6.
[20] C. W. Brister, *Pastoral Care In The Church* (Harper, San Francisco, 3rd
edition, 1992), p. 159.

of visiting every member on an annual basis. To do so inevitably entails missing out on the general priorities of ministry.

This, however, is not to say that pastors need not visit. It is a matter of pastors getting their priorities right in pastoral care. Clearly, where there is a crisis – whether it relates to birth, marriage, death or whatever – pastors will want to be involved. Hospital visiting is part of most ministers' brief. I, for one, am keen to visit prospective members – particularly if they are wrestling with the Christian faith. I also believe it to be important to care in particular for the leaders of the church, listening to their concerns and sharing with them my dreams.

As ministers know to their cost, there is no end to pastoral care. The possibilities are limitless. We could spend every minute of our lives engaging in pastoral care. So the question arises: is there a yardstick by which we can measure our activity? The only yardstick I have come across is Kennon Callahan's principle of visitation: 'Spend one hour in pastoral visitation each week for every minute you preach on a Sunday morning.'[21] In other words, if we preach for 20 minutes on a Sunday morning, then during the week we should visit 20 people. In actual fact that is quite a challenging task. Hard lines on the pastor who preaches for 40 minutes!

Pastoral surgery
A variation on pastoral visiting is for pastors to be available to see people in their studies or offices.

For instance, Richard Baxter, the celebrated 17th-century pastor of Kidderminster, used to devote Mondays and Tuesdays to catechising families within the parish. Since he was not in the best of health, he arranged for them on a systematic basis to come and see him for an hour. In this way he saw about 15 or 16 families a week and covered the whole parish in a year.[22]

Whereas Baxter adopted this custom on grounds of health, there is a lot to be said for adopting it today on grounds of accessibility. For example, at Chelmsford we hold a pastoral surgery on Wednesday

[21] Kennon L. Callahan, *Twelve Keys To An Effective Church* (Harper, San Francisco, 1983), p. 12.
[22] See Richard Baxter, *The Reformed Pastor*, pp. 172–256.

evenings. As with a doctor's surgery, people book ahead for appointments, albeit through the church administrator. Unlike a doctor's surgery, appointments are not for a brief ten minutes or so, but are none the less limited to half an hour: if more time is needed, then another appointment can be made for some other day. One advantage of this system is that it enables people after work to drop into the church and see the pastor before going home.

Caring or counselling?

The distinguished American pioneer in pastoral counselling, Howard J. Clinebell, defines pastoral counselling as 'the utilization by clergy of counselling and psychotherapeutic methods to enable individuals, couples and families to handle their personal crises and problems in living constructively'. He sees contemporary pastoral counselling expressing the five traditional functions of pastoral care:

1. The *healing* function is expressed in depth pastoral counselling (also called pastoral psychotherapy) aimed at helping those with major psychological and spiritual problems.
2. The *sustaining* function is expressed in supportive, crisis and bereavement counselling.
3. The *guiding* function is expressed in educative counselling (such as preparation for marriage), ethical guidance and spiritual direction.
4. The *reconciling* function is expressed in approaches such as marriage and family counselling designed to help people resolve interpersonal conflicts and increase the quality of their relationship.
5. The growth *nurturing* function is expressed in a variety of individual and small-group methods aimed at helping people enhance their lives and deal creatively with their developmental crises.[23]

At a very basic level, every pastor is involved in pastoral counselling. Pastoral care will inevitably include the ingredient of

[23] Howard J. Clinebell, 'Pastoral Counselling', pp. 198–9 in *A Dictionary Of Pastoral Care* (SPCK, London, 1987), edited by Alastair V. Campbell.

pastoral counselling, in which a pastor will seek to help people to work through their concerns to a constructive end. However, where pastoral counselling is linked with the insights and techniques of the modern schools of psychotherapy, it becomes a very distinctive discipline.

As ministers of the Gospel pastors are called in the first place to function within a specifically Christian context. While secular therapists look primarily to the 'healing forces of life' within their patients for recovery, pastoral counsellors rely upon the character and power of God to effect constructive changes in those whom they are counselling. In this respect C. W. Brister helpfully quotes the theologian John B. Cobbe:

> For pastoral counseling to carry forward genuinely the ancient tradition of the care of souls, it must separate itself further from secular therapy. Therapy can too easily be based on a model of restoring people to the capacity to function in society as it now exists. That can be a proper moment in pastoral counseling, certainly, but it cannot provide the basic model. The goal of pastoral counseling needs to be something like growth in grace, the strengthening of Christian existence, enabling Christians to be more effective disciples, of salvation. Such a goal will enable pastoral counseling to be spiritual direction as much as it is therapy.[24]

There is a very real difference between this kind of specific Christian counselling and what is offered by the modern pastoral counselling movement. Morgan Derham argues that ministers should not be involved in the latter – or at least not in their role as ministers. 'His ministry as a Christian pastor is a distinctive one, with spiritual concerns controlling the way he deals with people . . . The secular counsellor aims at wholeness . . .; but the Christian pastor is concerned for holiness, which is a very different objective, though it may well include wholeness.'[25]

This is not to say that there is not a place for the insights and

---

[24] See C. W. Brister, *Pastoral Care In The Church*, p. 189.
[25] A. Morgan Derham, 'Counselling or Christian Counselling', *Ministry Today* 2 (1994), pp. 14–19.

techniques of secular counselling. Morgan Derham, for instance, is happy at the thought of churches offering counselling services, provided it is made clear that they are counselling services in a Christian context, as distinct from 'Christian counselling'.

Pastoral care and pastoral counselling in its more technical sense are therefore quite distinct. The pastor seeks to encourage people to grow in Christ, while the counsellor seeks to enable people to reach self-understanding. The pastor may through prayer bring God and his grace into the situation, while the counsellor aims to release resources from within. The pastor is free to initiate a pastoral conversation, but the counsellor is only free to respond to a request for counselling. The pastor may be dealing with people on a one-off basis, while the counsellor rarely sees people for less than six sessions and often for very many more. The pastor, where necessary, can be directive, but the counsellor is always non-directive. The pastor relates to people primarily at conscious levels of experience, while the counsellor is concerned to relate to the unconscious dimensions of experience too. The pastor will often be dealing with people whom he sees in other church and social contexts, but the counsellor keeps at a distance and only sees clients.

As pastors, therefore, we are called to exercise pastoral care, but not to engage in the modern disciplines of pastoral counselling. Having said that, this is not to put down pastoral counselling. Far from it. It is simply to recognise that pastoral counselling is a distinct area of expertise calling for specific skills, which in turn call for specialised training and competent supervision. There are many times when the skills of pastoral counselling are required. In such situations, wise pastors will recognise their limitations in this area and happily pass the person concerned on to a recognised counsellor.[26] Not that this referral then brings the pastor's role of pastoral care to an end. The distinctive contribution of pastoral support and prayer still has a very real place.

[26] Needless to say, we do not agree that ordination is a guarantee of counselling skills – unlike Jay E. Adams, *The Christian Counsellor's Manual*, p. 20: 'We must insist upon the idea that every man who has been called of God into ministry has been given the basic gifts for . . . counselling'!

Caring for people young and old

Caring for children

Children are very much on the agenda of the Church. Much attention in recent years has, for instance, been given to the faith-development of children.[27] Similarly, much has been written about the admission of children to the Lord's Table.[28] But very little seems to have been written specifically about the pastoral care of children.[29]

This neglect of children is strange, because children have pastoral needs too. Yet for the most part we overlook those needs and assume that childhood is 'the golden age of innocence, a time of cookies and lemonade, all fun and play, with nothing to worry about'. However, the reality is, as Lester goes on to show, that 'for most children, childhood is filled with stresses and strains, doubts and fears, losses and separations – children go through all the experiences of death, moves, illness and accidents'.[30]

This being so, how might we address the needs of children? I believe that pastors need to formalise and develop the kind of work already being carried on by Sunday School teachers and leaders of other church activities for children. For probably in most churches, pastoral care is already being shown on an informal basis to children: thus if a child in the Sunday School is ill for any length of time, then in all likelihood a card will be sent and a visit will be made by the Sunday School teacher. This kind of care needs to be extended to cover not just all the children in the Sunday School or all the children who attend one activity or another of the church, but all children associated with the church, whether or not they attend a specific children's activity. This would therefore include children of mothers or fathers who have only a loose link with the church.

---

[27] See, for example, *Christian Perspectives on Faith Development* (Eerdmans, Grand Rapids & Gracewing, Leominster, 1992), edited by Jeff Astley & Leslie Francis.

[28] See, for example, Colin Buchanan, *Nurturing Children in Communion* (Grove, Nottingham, 1985).

[29] But see A. D. Lester, *Pastoral Care of Children In Crisis* (Westminster Press, Philadelphia, 1985).

[30] Ibid., p. 48.

I particularly like the suggestion which is being developed in New Zealand by Dr Lorna Jenkins of encouraging churches to appoint a children's pastor to work as part of the pastoral team of the church. Such an appointment, although normally only a voluntary position, recognises the importance and significance of children.

In a job description for a children's pastor Lorna Jenkins states:

> When a family has a crisis, such as a bereavement or marriage break-up, the children's pastor would make sure that there is someone who is caring for the child and talking with the child to help them through grief and misunderstanding. This may include situations in which a child is shifting into the district or is in trouble at school or with his peer group. Sometimes children are distressed about misfortunes which happen to their parents.

In my experience pastors are very good at showing pastoral care to adults at times of bereavement or marriage break-up. They are less good with the children – indeed, sometimes they seem to be totally oblivious to the needs of the children at the time.

In the New Zealand scheme the children's pastor would at once be alerted to the needs of the children. If counselling is required, the job description sets down that the parents should be made aware that such counselling is taking place. Significantly, the job description states that

> All matters which are shared by the children should be regarded as confidential. If there is a need to pass on information to parents or other people, it should be done with the child's permission, explaining carefully the need for further action.

It is important that in a church setting as much as anywhere else, the rights of children are observed. Other responsibilities of the children's pastor include the care of children's leaders, and where appropriate the care of families.

I have found this model of a children's pastor exceedingly challenging and useful. Biblically there are certainly many precedents for taking special care of children – not least the fact that Jesus himself on a number of occasions showed that children were important in their own right.[31] Indeed, the very shepherd model of pastoral care implies

31 See, for instance, Matt. 18:1–7; 19:13–15.

that special care needs to be given to the youngest sheep: 'The youngest lamb was also the recipient of the shepherd's guarding, guiding, nurturing, healing and seeking. In fact, since the young lambs were the most defenseless, and because they represented the future they probably received a disproportionate amount of the shepherd's attention.'[32]

Here then is a neglected area of pastoral care in urgent need of attention. For the sake of the children, let alone for the sake of excellence, proper care needs to be given to it.

Caring for older people

Another area where more creative care and attention might be given is at the other end of the age-spectrum. Statistically old age is the 'boom generation'. There are almost 10 million people over pensionable age in Great Britain, more than the number of children at school. Half the population is over 50. With life expectancy still on the upward trend, our society, like all other Western societies, is increasingly a society of middle-aged and older adults. And yet for the most part the Church has adopted the youth culture. For instance, while evangelistic efforts for young people abound, churches rarely include any special outreach events specifically for older people. Churches, it would appear, are guilty of ageism.[33] In the Church, as in the world, older people have become second-class

---

[32] Lester, *Pastoral Care of Children In Crisis*, p. 32.
[33] See the 'seven myths of old age' listed in the Search publication *Against Ageism*, quoted by Arthur Creber, *New Approaches To Ministry With Older People* (Grove, Nottingham, 1990), p. 7:
1. *The myth of chronology* – that people are 'old' simply by virtue of the length of their life.
2. *The myth of ill health* – that all older people are in need of medical treatment.
3. *The myth of senility* – that the intelligence of older people deteriorates with age and very many suffer from senile dementia. (In fact only 5% of people over pensionable age suffer from senile dementia.)
4. *The myth of isolation* – that all older people are lonely and isolated.
5. *The myth of misery* – that all older people are unhappy.
6. *The myth of unproductivity* – that older people are incapable of making a useful contribution to society, they lack creativity and are redundant to the real future.

citizens rather than senior citizens; their potential for growth and for service has been ignored. Instead they are seen as the weak and dependent who need to be helped and entertained.

In our care for older people we need to begin with the recognition that they are people of worth as much as those at any other stage of life. I suggest that one way in which we can recognise their worth is to stop using the phrase 'old people', which today tends to have derogatory associations. Instead let's use the term 'senior adults'. The very word 'adult' indicates that older people possess wisdom and maturity.

Secondly, in our care for senior adults we need to recognise that 'old age' is an exceedingly broad term, covering many stages of life. Far from being weak and feeble, many senior adults are fit and healthy, full of experience, and are keen to serve God and their fellows. Like 85-year-old Caleb, many feel as vigorous as ever (Josh. 14:11). We therefore need to ensure that this energy is constructively channelled.

Thirdly, in our care for senior adults we need to recognise that even those who are technically 'elderly' do not necessarily 'feel' any different from when they were young. 'On the contrary,' says American research anthropologist Sharon Kaufmann, 'when old people talk about themselves, they express a sense of self that's ageless – an identity that maintains continuity despite the physiological and social changes that come with age.'[34] No doubt as a result of such feelings, in a research survey of people over 80, although 53% admitted they were old, 36% reported that they considered themselves middle-aged, and 11% said they felt young![35]

Fourthly, in our care of senior adults we need to recognise that they still have enormous potential for growth. What is more, now that they are 'self-employed', senior adults may well have more opportunity for growth and development. For many the early retirement years are a time for learning new skills. One acquaintance

[34] Quoted by Michael Butler & Ann Orbach, *Being Your Age* (SPCK, London, 1993), p. 13.
[35] Tim Stafford, *As Our Years Increase* (British edition: IVP, Leicester, 1989), p. 12.

of mine taught himself classical Greek and read all of Homer in his retirement! From a specifically Christian point of view, old age 'is a tremendous opportunity for drawing nearer to God; indeed that may well be its main purpose; and each day becomes a day of opportunity, a day of spiritual growth, of radiating, albeit unconsciously, something of the peace and power of God to others'.[36]

Fifthly, in our care of senior adults we need to recognise that they are perhaps more open to the Gospel than any other group. The fact is that the older people become, the more frequently they experience life-changing events. These events provide 'windows of opportunity' in which people seem to move from resistance or indifference to the Gospel, on the one hand, to receptivity and openness, on the other hand.[37] Old age provides, therefore, an opportunity for sensitive evangelism.[38]

Old age is to be 'celebrated', declares Arthur Creber. Over against what he perceives to be the prevailing prejudice within the Church toward old age, he writes:

> It really cannot be satisfactory for us to present a gospel which encourages older people to withdraw from life and to prepare for death (although this may be wholly appropriate for a person suffering from a terminal illness). Neither is it satisfactory to

[36] H. P. Steer, *Caring For The Elderly* (SPCK, London, 1966), p. 32.

[37] See Win & Charles Arn, 'Catching the Age Wave', *Faith And Renewal* (Sept.–Oct. 1993), pp. 23–8. Also 'The Age Wave Is Here', *Church Growth Digest* 12 (Spring 1991), pp. 3–5.

[38] Within the context of a reminiscence programme the so-called 'Quaker Questions' lend themselves to sensitive evangelism:
1. The group are invited to share their memories of what kept them warm during the winters when they were about seven years old.
2. They are then asked to recall who they felt warm towards in their early life and why.
3. They are gently encouraged to share any experiences of God's warmth in their lives either as children or adults.
4. Friendly discussion is then encouraged about who or what makes them feel warm, now, where God's warmth is experienced in the present situation.

Arthur Creber, *New Approaches To Ministry With Older People*, p. 20, comments: 'the opportunities for sharing the gospel and helping people build their lives on their own declared experiences of God's love in their lives has been enormous'.

reduce our ministry to the patronizing provision of free handouts or cheap trips to the pantomime at Christmas. If the gospel has to do with new Life we should be encouraging older people to explore their potential for creative activity, for maintaining and improving their health, and for establishing or re-establishing loving relationships with other people and with God. We should be providing opportunities for the development of understanding, growth and experimentation. A positive approach to the potentialities of old age will motivate us as ministers and will ensure that the necessary resources are made available for the provision of creative opportunities.[39]

There is much to be said for consciously developing a 'senior adult ministry'. The fact is that while in most churches there are Women's Meetings or clubs for older people, in few churches is there any strategy toward helping senior adults to grow and develop.

Charles and Win Arn indeed suggest that churches develop a senior programme aiming to provide growth and development in the following areas:

Ministry. Encouraging the giving of time, insights, experience, energy for the benefit of others.

Spiritual Growth. Continuing to walk in the Christian life and faith.

Evangelistic Outreach. Sharing one's faith with non-churched friends, relatives and associates.

Small Group Involvement. Building meaningful interpersonal relationships.

Educational Development. Raising one's self-esteem and contributing to mental health.

Relaxing Activities. Recreational, social and physical.

They further suggest that churches look for a full-time (or part-time) senior adult pastor, and point out that 'while many congregations have youth directors, very few have senior adult directors. Yet in most churches there are twice as many adults over 55 as youth 13–20 years'![40]

---

[39] Creber, *New Approaches To Ministry With Older People*, p. 23.
[40] Win & Charles Arn, *Church Growth Digest* 12 (Spring 1991), p. 5.

Pastoral care of senior adults is therefore much more than keeping the 'old folk' happy. It is more than visiting the 'shut-ins' and taking them Communion. Pastoral care of senior adults lends itself to developing all kinds of innovative ministries.

Supporting church staff

One of the newer challenges of ministry is the managing of church staff. An increasing number of churches are appointing administrators, secretaries, associate or assistant ministers, pastoral assistants or associates, evangelists, music directors, youth workers, social workers, caretakers . . . The specialisations of church staff are many and various. In some large American churches, there are even church staff specialising in weddings.[41]

For busy pastors working on their own, the possibility of working together with a multiple staff team can sometimes seem like a wonderful dream. What a difference it would make to life if the work-load could be shared: the church could grow and develop and engage in all sorts of creative ministries. The truth of the matter is that the dream can sometimes turn to a nightmare. Personality clashes, misunderstandings and other relationship difficulties can arise.

'Multiple staff problems are so widespread that most pastors are leery about adding staff,' declared Kent Hunter.[42] In similar vein Calvin Miller wrote, 'Almost all head pastors I know agree that

---

[41] See Lyle E. Schaller, *Reflections Of A Contrarian: Second Thoughts On The Parish Ministry* (Abingdon, Nashville, 1989), pp. 158–9: 'When measured in terms of costs and productivity, the most expensive staff members often are the inexperienced full-time ministerial generalists. At the other end of the scale the biggest bargain on the program staff may be the mature laywoman who is a part-time specialist. Between these two are the associate pastor with 20 years' experience who sees this as a special vocation, the full-time administrative assistant to the senior minister who combines the roles of pastor's secretary – church mother – office manager – business administrator – alter ego of the minister – friend and cheerleader, the full-time lay program director, and the part-time person responsible for the assimilation of new members.'

[42] Kent R. Hunter, 'A Model For Multiple Staff Management', *Leadership* II (Summer 1981), pp. 99–100.

staff relationships are their greatest time consumer. They want to lead in a positive but gentle way, one that sets the direction of the church and yet accords to all team members a feeling of worth and dignity. And that is not easy.'[43]

Difficulties seem to surface particularly in the relationship between senior pastors and assistants or associates. But then, the latter role is difficult to fill, particularly where the assistant or associate is young and able. 'Bridesmaids dream of becoming brides. Runners-up want to win their next contest. Second bananas want to become the star of the show. One vice-president of the United States described his job "as worthless as a bucket of warm spit".'[44] There are not too many people who are happy to play 'second fiddle' for ever.

Should we be surprised or upset by these difficulties? I believe not. The fact is that difficulties are inevitable, for people are people. Relationship difficulties have been the order of the day since the beginning of the Church. 'Wherever two or three are gathered in Jesus' name,' said John Blattner, 'sooner or later there are going to be people problems. This is just as true among leaders as among other folks. We needn't be surprised. Galatians 5:20–21 makes it clear that discord, jealousy, ambition, dissension, factionalism, and all the rest are part of the fallen human nature that pastoral leaders share with everyone else. Occasional problems among leaders are inevitable, given what leaders are made of.'[45]

The question, however, is how we deal with such problems. Clearly, the pastor as the senior care-giver has a special responsibility. Indeed, the way in which pastors treat their staff members sets a pattern for relationships in the church as a whole. I wish to suggest that the key to relationships with other members of staff has to do less with line-management than with pastoral care. At the end of the day our task is not so much to 'manage' our staff as to give them opportunities for personal growth and development – and this is pastoral care. Particularly where an assistant minister is

---

[43] Calvin Miller, 'Fiddlin' With The Staff', *Leadership* VIII (Winter 1986), p. 105.

[44] Dale, *Pastoral Leadership*, p. 143.

[45] John C. Blattner, 'People Problems Among Leaders', *Pastoral Renewal* XI (February 1987), p. 3.

concerned, I see my task as one of training and enabling another to fulfil his God-given calling. I am not only in the business of serving my members; I am also in the business of serving my staff. They need my support and encouragement to become what God would have them be. Their ministry can be made or marred by my attitude toward them.

How does this all work out in practice? I wish to single out three lines of action:

Provide a meaningful job description

Job descriptions are vital for happy relationships. The job description needs to be meaningful in the sense that it is a full job description. Although this applies to all staff positions, this is particularly important for the assistant minister, where there can be so many opportunities for unclear demarcation of responsibilities.

Secondly, a job description needs to be meaningful in the sense that it delegates responsibility. For instance, treating an assistant like a dogsbody is degrading. The pastor should specify particular areas of responsibility, where the assistant can flourish and show initiative.

Thirdly, any job description needs to be reviewed at regular intervals. Such a review may well take place in the context of an annual appraisal. John Blattner points out that 'many misunderstandings and difficulties result from "structural problems", that is something about the way we have set up our decision-making process or aligned our working relationships. The problem lies not in the people but in the process.'[46] Job descriptions are not set in stone. They are to be written in pencil, so that they may be changed from time to time. Indeed, the longer an assistant remains at a church, the more responsibility may be given to him/her.

Communicate regularly

Most difficulties arise because of failures in communication. If more time were spent in face-to-face meetings, there would be fewer difficulties. Working together effectively requires lots of

---

[46] Blattner, 'People Problems Among Leaders', p. 6.

communication. This means, in the first place, that staff should work together on site. The traditional British model of the pastors working from their studies at home is not effective where there are other staff.[47] Staff members need to encounter one another daily, whether it be brewing up coffee together or dropping into one another's offices.

In the second place, this means regular staff meetings. Along with the informal socialising, there also needs to be a weekly meeting for all the staff in which news is shared and the needs of the church – and of individual staff members – are offered up to God.

In the third place, this means there must be opportunities for staff members to be open and honest with the senior pastor (and vice versa!) on a one-to-one basis. Problems don't go away by being pigeon-holed. Problems need to be faced up to and confronted. Otherwise those problems will only fester and become worse. 'Many of our staff problems come,' says Charles Bugg, 'because we are afraid of conflict and fearful to admit it.'[48] Dealing with problems may take time; it may be painful to all concerned (especially if we discover that we ourselves are part of the problem), but in the end facing up to problems not only is good for the church, it is also good for individuals, for if problems are rightly handled, personal growth often results.

In the fourth place, this means that there must be opportunities for staff to relax together and get to know one another better as persons – for this too helps the communication process. To quote Charles Bugg again: 'Our church staff plans two all day retreats away from the church each year. The emphasis is on the two "Ps", prayer and play. We do little of the third "P", plan, because we work on that in our weekly staff meetings. It is amazing how we come to understand some things about each other in those times free from the pressures of an agenda.'[49]

[47] Indeed, I see little point in pastors working from home even when they are on their own. Working from church makes for better time-management and encourages business-like attitudes. It also means that pastors are less likely to bring problems home.
[48] Charles Bugg, 'Professional Ethics Among Ministers', p. 567.
[49] Ibid., p. 567.

Support constantly

Publicly supporting staff members is vital. Public recognition needs to be given for their achievements. Thanks need to be expressed for effort made. Talking up one's staff in public is only fair and right.

Publicly supporting staff members also means that when things go wrong, the pastor shares the blame. 'Yes, we fouled it up' – never 'He or she fouled it up.' Criticism of staff members outside a staff meeting is taboo.

Privately too staff members need – and deserve – support. Encouragement should be a constant feature of the pastor's relationship with other staff members. There is much truth in the aphorism attributed to Goethe: 'If you treat people as they are, they will stay as they are. But if you treat them as they ought to be, they will become bigger and better persons.'

Constant support also means giving staff the freedom to fail and make mistakes. When an assistant minister, for instance comes up with a bright idea, unless it involves kamikaze, support it, however personally unconvinced you may be. Growth never develops in dependent relationships. People need to learn for themselves.

Encouraging personal growth

In pastoral care, it is very easy to major on the problems presented by individuals within the fellowship. And that is not surprising, because life is tough for so many people. Joey Faucette estimates that in a hypothetical American congregation of 500 people representing a cross-section of the population:

25 have been hospitalized in the past for a major mental illness.
24 are alcoholics.
50 are severely handicapped by neurotic conflicts.
100 are afflicted by moderate neurotic conflicts.
115 would answer 'yes' to the question, 'Have you ever felt you were going to have a nervous breakdown?'
70 have sought professional help for a personal or marital problem in the past.
1 will attempt suicide every other year.
8 will be involved in a serious crime.

Fewer than one-half of those persons married would rate their marriage as 'very happy'.[50]

Whether or not the situation is any better in the UK, I really don't know. What I do know, however, is that where the love of Christ is real, churches seem to attract all kinds of problem people. Many of these people need a good deal of help and support just to be able to cope with the pressures of day-to-day living. This kind of pastoral care is draining, it is costly, but nonetheless it is required if we are to truly go the Jesus way.

Yet pastoral care must not be restricted to helping people with problems. Pastoral care also involves enabling people to grow and develop in the Christian faith. As we have already seen, it is about the presentation of 'everyone perfect in Christ'. Or, to quote the Apostle Paul more fully: 'It is he whom we proclaim, warning everyone and teaching everyone in all wisdom so that we may present everyone mature in Christ.' To which he adds, 'For this I toil and struggle with all the energy that he powerfully inspires within me' (Col. 1:28–9).

Margaret Guenther likens the art of spiritual direction to spiritual midwifery. 'When in doubt,' she writes, 'I always assume that God is at work, that is, the person is pregnant.'[51] While there is truth in that metaphor (see Gal. 4:19), I think the alternative metaphor of children growing into maturity is preferable. The new life is already there and to be seen, but so many have yet to mature and to reflect the life and love of Jesus in their relationships one with the other (1 Cor. 3:1–3); they are still at the John 3:16 stage and have not really developed any further in their Christian lives. For various reasons they have got stuck in their walk with their Lord, and they need to be helped to get going and growing again. Others have even become stunted and twisted in their Christian development; they have been Christians for many years, but they have never received any real form of encouragement or discipline. Pastoral care is about helping people to grow, encouraging people to deal with those cancers that

---

[50] Joey Faucette, 'Pastoral Wholeness: Preaching And Teaching That Heals', *Congregations* (Nov./Dec. 1993), p. 10.
[51] Margaret Guenther, *Holy Listening* (Darton, Longman & Todd, London, 1992), p. 93.

threaten their spiritual lives, enabling them to deal with past hurts and gain the courage to forgive and move on.

But if pastoral care is to promote growth, then pastors must be prepared to take the bull by the horns and speak about spiritual things to their people on an individual basis. It always seems strange to me how so many of us shy away from our spiritual calling. We are happy enough to offer all kinds of practical help, where needed. But we back off when it comes to dealing with the 'cure of souls'.

We smile – and rightly so – at the way in which in earlier times young clergymen were advised to go about their pastoral visiting:

> At your first visit to the inferior families after the customary civilities, the following questions may be asked. What books have you? . . . Do you read some part of the Scripture daily? . . . Do you meditate on what you read? . . . Do you pray to God in secret? . . . Do you examine yourself as to the state of your soul? . . . Have you any family prayers? . . . Do you attend public worship? . . . Do you take your Bible to church with you? . . . Do you show the text to the absent? . . . Do you learn it by heart and frequently think on it in the following week? . . .[52]

Yet, for all the faults of such an approach, one has to admit that at least it was concerned with people's relationship to God, even if there were no questions about how they related to one another. If pastoral care is to have any depth, then it needs to go beyond passing the time of day with people. We need to confront people – in a gentle fashion – and ask them about their spiritual lives: where they have been, where they are now, and where by God's grace – and maybe with our help and the help of the church – they would now like to go.

Donald Bubna suggests that pastors should make a 'spiritual inventory call' and ask such questions as:

> What's one joy and one struggle you're experiencing in your life or ministry?
> How would you describe your walk with God this past year?
> Where do you feel you would most like to grow as a Christian?

---

[52] Quoted by Anthony Russell, *The Clerical Profession* (SPCK, London, 1980), p. 115.

Could you give me a thumbnail sketch of your spiritual history?
How did you first come to believe?
In your devotional life, what's one thing you've recently discovered?
How would you finish this sentence: 'I feel good about my walk with God when . . .'?
What have been some of the ups and downs of your spiritual life since you came to faith?
How has our church helped you in your spiritual development?
What do you need from me as a friend and fellow believer to go on to maturity in Christ Jesus?[53]

Pastoral care is not just about finding out how the children are doing, or how their parents are keeping, but how they are developing in their Christian life. As pastors we need to ask our people how they are getting on with the spiritual disciplines of Bible reading and prayer – not with a view to grading them, but rather with a view to seeing how we can help them. Likewise we should feel free to raise areas where we feel relationships might not be right, and to see how those relationships with God's help might be put right.

I like the idea that spiritual direction is the right of every Christian. Admittedly Thomas Merton felt that spiritual direction was not necessary 'for the ordinary Christian. Wherever there is *special mission or vocation* a certain minimum of direction is implied by the very nature of the vocation itself.'[54] But every Christian has a vocation – every Christian has a ministry to perform. Therefore Gordon Jeff is right when he says '*some kind* of spiritual direction is helpful for every Christian person'.[55] The question is, 'How? How can spiritual direction be made available to every Christian person?'

Gordon Jeff proposed that as many members of the church as possible be encouraged to go and talk with someone two, three or four times a year about their Christian journey, and especially

[53] Donald L. Bubna, 'The Spiritual Inventory', *Leadership* IX (Fall 1988), p. 69.
[54] Cited by Gordon H. Jeff, *Spiritual Direction For Every Christian* (SPCK, London, 1987), p. 3.
[55] Ibid., p. 3.

about how their prayer life is going on. He envisaged a church cutting down on its level of activity so that there would be more time 'for prayer, for real meeting, for talking about the things that really matter. Clergy may find themselves less in control, but acting far more as "enablers" who help to release the God-given potential already existing within their members.'[56]

All that sounds fine, but how can that become a practical reality? To whom would all these people be turning for spiritual direction, two, three or four times a year? Surely not to the pastor? In any but the smallest of churches that kind of pastoral care would not be possible.

The way forward is to be found in helping those with whom pastoral care is shared in the church to gain a vision for pastoral care as being about growth and development. I confess that here all too often we pastors fall down. For where pastoral care is shared with other 'carers' in the church, it tends to focus on helping the troubled, rather than prodding the comfortable. In my experience 'carers' see their task in primarily supportive terms – encouraging the bereaved, visiting the sick, helping the elderly. True, as a pastoral team we may be concerned for members who seem to be falling away and are no longer attending church services as regularly as they might. But what about all those people who sit in their pews Sunday by Sunday, who are fit and healthy, whose families are fit and healthy – what about their spiritual needs?

A way to enable those sharing pastoral care – as also other key leaders – to gain the vision is to let them experience this kind of pastoral care. Rather than in the first instance talking about the need for members generally to grow and develop, pastors need to speak to their leaders about their need to grow and develop. If pastors were to give basic spiritual direction to their leaders, there would be an appreciable 'spin-off' in the church. There would be a 'filter-down' effect. In theory at least, one could imagine spiritual direction spiralling downward in a pyramid-type shape.

Much as I would love to see spiritual direction on an individual basis becoming a reality for everybody, in practice I do not think it feasible. But there is another way forward. Life and growth do

56 Ibid., pp. 96–7.

not simply have to be promoted on an individual basis. They can be encouraged on a group basis too.

Here I have in mind using the home groups found in many churches with a view to developing Christian maturity. In such a group members can help one another by being open and honest with one another. Such groups are sometimes termed 'covenant' groups, where the members covenant with one another to help one another in their walk with the Lord.

Such a covenant might include the covenant of honesty, where the individual members of the group commit themselves to mirror back to one another what they are hearing others say and feel:

> If this means risking pain for either of us I will trust our relationship enough to take that risk, realizing it is in 'speaking the truth in love, that we grow up in every way into Christ who is the Head'.[57]

It could also include the covenant of accountability:

> I consider that the gifts God has given me for the common good should be liberated for your benefit. If I should discover areas of my life that are under bondage, 'hung up' or truncated by my own misdoings or by the scars inflicted by others, I will seek Christ's liberating power through my covenant partners, so that I might give you more of myself. I am accountable to you to 'become what God has designed me to be in His loving creation'.[58]

Then the dynamics of human potentials growth groups can come into play. For human potentials groups major on helping us 'discover and use more of our latent resources'.[59] In addition, however, Christian growth groups can help us discover and use

[57] Part of a covenant developed by Louis Evans at the National Presbyterian Church, Washington D.C., and cited by John Mallison, *Building Small Groups In The Christian Community* (British edition: Scripture Union, London, 1981), pp. 68–9.

[58] See again Louis Evans, quoted by John Mallison, *Building Small Groups In The Christian Community*, pp. 68–9.

[59] Howard Clinebell, *Growth Groups* (Abingdon, Nashville, 2nd edition, 1977), p. 3.

more of the resources that are available in Christ. Christian growth groups may become a corporate expression of spiritual direction.

The role of the pastor here is not to be present at such groups, but rather to give the vision for these groups to be set up and to see that appropriate training is available for the leaders. There is no 'magic' in groups *per se*; what counts is the purpose which causes people to come together in groups. In this case the purpose is that of spiritual growth.

In conclusion

Pastoral care may not be the unique province of the pastor. It is a task we need to share with others. On the other hand, it is not a task to give away. I am concerned by the number of pastors who no longer seem to be interested in caring for the flock. The role of being a charismatic preacher or an effective leader or a missionary strategist has captivated their minds instead. But pastoral care is of the essence of pastoral ministry. Furthermore, it is one of the great privileges of pastoral ministry. No other person in the fellowship has the entry that we do into the homes of our people. No other person is able to draw alongside people in their joys and in their sorrows as a pastor. Paul Cedar rightly declares: 'We give up an essential ministry when we give up pastoral care. Pastoral care is not only one of the greatest needs of our fast-growing impersonal society, it is also a unique privilege of the pastor.'[60]

In this chapter we have sought to reflect on some of the roles and skills a pastor needs to develop in order to pursue excellence in the role of pastoral care. In conclusion let us reflect for a moment on the key quality of pastoral care: love. Much as I am committed to encouraging pastors developing professional skills in ministry, it is undeniably true that what ultimately distinguishes a competent pastor from a great pastor is love for people.

Loving people can be a joy. It is a joy when people respond to our love. It is a joy to see those whom we love fulfil their

---

[60] Paul Cedar, 'The unique role of the pastor', p. 18, in *Mastering The Pastoral Role* (Multnomah, Portland, Oregon, 1991), by P. Cedar, K. Hughes & B. Patterson.

God-given potential in Christ. But loving people can be a pain too. It is painful when people do not respond to our love. It is painful when people wander away and fail to fulfil our hopes and aspirations for them. 'Good pastors have heart problems,' writes Kent Hughes.[61] He goes on:

> To have a pastor's heart it is necessary to have a heart problem – an enlarged heart. To be effective pastors, we must enlarge our love and make ourselves vulnerable. And when we do that it is inevitable that we will experience a godly angina, a deep and piercing pain of the heart.

But it is love which binds a people together. It is love which provides a climate conducive for spiritual growth. It is love which empowers preaching and motivates missionary endeavour. It is love which gives us pastors our authority and enables us to fulfil our calling. Pastors striving for excellence must ever be mindful that love is indeed 'the most excellent way' (1 Cor. 12:31).

[61] Kent Hunt, 'Maintaining a pastor's heart', p. 139, in *Mastering The Pastoral Role* (Multnomah, Portland, Oregon, 1991), by P. Cedar, K. Hughes & B. Patterson.

Chapter 7

The exemplary pilgrim

The call to become

There is in the Christian life an inherent dynamic of the Spirit. When by the Spirit of God we are born again into the family of God, we are born to grow. Conversion may be the end of one life, but it is also the beginning of another.

This dynamic may be in part expressed by one of the first descriptions of the Christian faith: 'the Way' (see Acts 9:2; 19:23; 22:4; 24:14). This new movement represented not just a way to salvation, but also a way of living. Men and women of the Way were by definition travellers.

Not surprisingly, with the paradigm of the Exodus, Christians came to see themselves as 'pilgrims' – as 'aliens and exiles' (1 Pet. 2:11; also Heb. 11:13); 'here we have no lasting city, but we are looking for the city that is to come' (Heb. 13:14). This picture of the Christian life as pilgrimage has been taken up by many Christian authors since: one thinks of John Bunyan's classic, *Pilgrim's Progress*; or more recently of Archbishop Hume's *A Pilgrim Way*.[1] Christians are on a journey, a journey which leads to God.

It goes almost without saying that pastors too share this general calling of the people of God to be pilgrims, to be travellers. They too have not arrived. Ordination is only a point on that journey. In the ordination ritual of the Early Church and indeed in some parts of the Church today there is a point in which the people cry out, '*Axios*' ('he is worthy') as they acknowledge the fitness of the

[1] Basil Hume, *A Pilgrim Way* (Fount/Collins, London, 1994).

person concerned to be ordained. Would that were true! As it is, no ministers worth their salt ever truly feel worthy in themselves – sanctification is a process in which they too must take part.

Yet, in that process, pastors are called to set an example. They are called to be 'exemplary pilgrims'. But in what sense? The fact is that although ordination does not of itself bring a person nearer to God, nonetheless the rite of ordination contains within it a call to live a life near to God. Pastors, like all God's people are called to be men and women of God; but, if they fail to live up to this calling, then the rest of their ministry is of little worth. What they do is dependent upon who they are. 'Being' and 'becoming' come before 'doing'.

The importance of a pastor 'being' in the first place God's 'man' or God's 'woman' has been expressed in various ways. The Christian mystic Evelyn Underhill, for instance, wrote:

> The very first requisite for a minister of religion is that his own inner life should be maintained in a healthy state.[2]

> The man whose life is coloured by prayer, whose loving communion with God comes first, will always win souls; because he shows them in his own life and person the attractiveness of reality, the demand, the transforming power of the spiritual life . . . The most persuasive preacher, the most devoted and untiring social worker, the most up-to-date theologian – unless loving devotion to God exceeds and enfolds these activities – will not win souls.[3]

In similar vein James Taylor declared:

> No higher reputation should, or can, be desired by a Christian minister than that possessed by the prophet Elisha in the mind of the Shunamite woman. 'I perceive', she said, 'that this is a holy man of God who is continually passing our way' [2 Kings 4:9]. No matter what other gifts a church fellowship may admire in their minister this is, in the final reckoning, what they most desire

[2] *Heaven A Dance: An Evelyn Underhill Anthology* (Triangle, SPCK, London, 1992), compiled by Brenda & Stuart Blanch, p. 85.
[3] *Ibid.*, p. 92.

him to be. All other virtues are virtually irrelevant and most other faults are forgivable if, to them and in their midst, he is a 'man of God'.[4]

The importance of this aspect of the pastoral calling to be a 'man' or 'woman' of God cannot be overemphasised. 'Vocational holiness', as Eugene Peterson calls it, is of the essence of ministry: 'Pastoring is not managing a religious business but a spiritual quest.'[5]

It is precisely because pastoring contains within it this call to vocational holiness that the apostle Paul could write to his churches and urge them to imitate him (1 Cor. 4:16; 11:1; Gal. 4:12; Phil. 3:17; 1 Thes. 1:6; 2 Thes. 3:7, 9). In the secular world of Paul's day sons were expected to imitate their fathers. Paul, as a 'father in God', expected his churches to imitate him. The call to imitation was not a mark of spiritual arrogance on the part of Paul, but rather a function of the pastoral relationship.

What was true for Paul remains true for pastors of today. We too are called to be exemplary pilgrims. At the best of times this has never been an easy calling. But today the multitudinous pressures of church life are such that this fundamental aspect of the pastoral call is constantly under threat. Pastors are so concerned for 'ministry' – i.e. relating to others in various forms of Christian service – that they do not always make time for 'spirituality' – i.e. relating to God, which is their prime form of Christian service.

Roy Oswald's description of his experience as a pastor is true of many pastors:

Pastors face unique problems, I believe, in keeping fresh spiritually. For one thing, the spiritual disciplines we learned as children and young adults are now the tools of our trade. For me, scripture, prayer and worship became overfamiliar and lost much of their mystery. It was difficult to read the Bible devotionally when I knew I had to prepare a sermon from those texts. I felt so much pressure to come up with something

---

[4] James Taylor, 'A Man Of God', *Fraternal* 156 (April 1970), p. 23.
[5] See Eugene H. Peterson, *Under The Unpredictable Plant: an exploration in vocational holiness* (Eerdmans, Grand Rapids, Michigan, 1992), p. 55.

meaningful to say that I read the Bible as though I were on a scavenger hunt! Everything I read was directed toward others' spiritual needs and not my own. I was doing so much praying with other people in hospitals, in homes and prior to meetings that I stopped praying on my own. I failed to recognize the essential difference between nurturing the spiritual journey of another and having a unique spiritual journey of my own.[6]

The only answer to this kind of dilemma is the establishing of regular spiritual disciplines. For as Henri Nouwen has rightly reminded us, 'A spiritual life without discipline is impossible. Discipline is the other side of discipleship.'[7]

As ever, Jesus is our model. Jesus knew what it was like to be under pressure. A day such as that described in Mark 1:16–32 would have exhausted even the fittest. And yet Jesus did not succumb to these pressures. Jesus retained his spiritual vitality and authority as a result of a disciplined life of prayer. 'In the morning, while it was still very dark, he got up and went out to a deserted place, and there he prayed' (Mark 1:35). The Gospels would seem to indicate that this was no exceptional occasion, but rather this retreating for prayer was a regular part of his devotional pattern (see Luke 6:12). Jesus lived a balanced life – a life of action and prayer.

Likewise, the followers of Jesus – and not least those of us who are pastors – need to live balanced lives. We need to live balanced lives to survive, for otherwise we will be crushed by the pressures of life, our spirits exhausted, our prayer life negligible, and our spiritual effectiveness nil. But we need too to live balanced lives in order to be all that God would have us to be.

The busier life is, the more need there is for a still centre; a place deep within us to which we can withdraw after the day-to-day buffeting and storms; a place where we can reflect on experience and try and make sense of life; a place where we can mull over events and savour them more fully; a place where, above all, we can listen . . . to what others are saying verbally or non-verbally, to what our feelings and fears are saying to us, and to what God is

6 Roy Oswald, *Clergy Self-Care*, p. 93.
7 Henri Nouwen, 'An Invitation To The Spiritual Life', *Leadership* XII (Summer 1981), p. 57.

saying through circumstances, through people, through creation, and his word spoken in the depths of our being.[8]

But if we are to listen, we must find a place to be alone, to be silent, to be still. And this means discipline. 'It is . . . essential,' wrote Kenneth Leech, 'that there should be in every pastor's rule, a built-in dimension of contemplative stillness and reflection. The "Sabbath principle", the law of rest and re-creation is vital, and its deliberate neglect is a grave sin whose results are all too apparent in broken lives and fragmented lives.'[9]

The precise shape of a disciplined life will vary from pastor to pastor. There is no one 'rule' of life. There is no one pattern of spirituality. What is vital is that each pastor has a rule.[10]

Such a rule needs almost certainly to extend beyond the traditional daily 'Quiet Time'. For many of us, at least, the pressures of daily life mean that it is not always easy to be truly 'still' at the beginning of each day and to 'centre down' on God. We may read God's Word, we may say our prayers, but we do so all too often conscious of the demands breaking in on our day. There is much to be said for carving out an additional chunk of time during the week – a morning, maybe, or perhaps more easily an afternoon – where we can more leisurely give ourselves to study, prayer and re-collection. To do so, however, it is essential to find a quiet place, away from the distractions of phone, visitors and family. The secret 'closet' of prayer may take the form of a room in a friend's house, the chapel of a local convent, a sunny spot out on the hills – anywhere we can be alone with God.

[8] Margaret Magdalen, *Jesus Man Of Prayer* (Hodder & Stoughton, London, 1987), p. 40.
[9] Kenneth Leech, 'The pastor and his devotional life', *Expository Times* 91 (Sept. 1980), p. 356. See also Thomas R. Swears, *The Approaching Sabbath: spiritual disciplines for pastors* (Abingdon, Nashville, 1991).
[10] See Harold Miller, *Finding A Personal Rule Of Life* (Grove Books, Nottingham, 1984), pp. 4–5: 'By embracing Rule, we make for ourselves a standard which we would like to attain, by the power of the Spirit, and we are enabled from time to time to do some appropriate assessment of where we have got to . . . Rule is merely a means to an end, and the end for me is that we might walk closely with God, and live more effectively for him.'

But our rule needs to contain more than a structured weekly discipline. A regular spiritual 'overhaul' needs also to be built in. Just as cars need major services, so too do we. An annual week's retreat, for instance, provides for me just such an overhaul, particularly where it is linked to fairly intensive spiritual direction. Such overhauls can prove to be painful affairs, as my spiritual director helps me to apply God's Word to some of the more secret parts of my heart. But 'no pain, no gain', as the slimmers say. Doing serious business with God can be painful, but it is also enormously cleansing, healing and freeing. For me, at least, the fact that I am accountable to my spiritual director for my walk with the Lord gives my ministry integrity. Spiritual direction means an end to ministerial 'play-acting'. It ensures that the inevitable discontinuity between the public expression and the private realities of my spirituality is kept to the minimum. It keeps me on the pilgrim way.

But all this involves the disciplined use of time – on a daily, weekly, annual basis. Now such time is not easily found – it has to be made. To make such time involves the disciplined setting aside of time in the diary. This in turn will mean that we will not be free to accept other engagements. We will have to say 'no' to people – we are not free; we have another appointment – with God!

Needless to say, such times of quiet with God are not to be regarded as personal time. This is church work. This is part of our calling. In this respect Evelyn Underhill helpfully draws attention to the words of Jesus found in John 17:19: 'For their sakes I sanctify myself' – 'That text has a most searching application to the priestly members of the Body of Christ. Cold perfunctory, negligent prayer in a minister of religion is not only a personal fault and personal loss. It is a sin against his people.'[11]

In other words, we do God's people a service by limiting our business in church things and spending time with God.

Pastors, first and foremost, are called to be exemplary pilgrims. As such they are not called to be perfect, but they are called to be seen as men and women who are making progress in the journey of faith. As the years go by, it can be somewhat sobering to ask ourselves: What progress in the life of faith have I made? How

[11] *Heaven a Dance*, p. 95.

far have I come since I was set aside with the laying on of hands for Christian ministry? How much closer am I now to Jesus, than when I first began? In the words of Henri Nouwen:

> The central question is, Are the leaders of the future truly men and women of God, people with an ardent desire to dwell in God's presence, to listen to God's voice, to look at God's beauty, to touch God's incarnate Word and to taste fully God's infinite goodness?[12]

Handling success and failure

Within the context of being an exemplary pilgrim, the themes of success and failure assume dimensions somewhat different from the norm.

In the context of pastoral ministry success is generally related to numbers. A successful pastor is generally a pastor of a bigger and better church. The larger the church, the more successful the pastor.

But is success in ministry necessarily about growing bigger and better churches? Certainly, in the world success is all about productivity – the successful businessman is the man who has extended his business and made his fortune. But what is success in ministerial terms? Is there a different yardstick?

Our ultimate measure in Christian terms is, of course, Jesus. It is at this point we run into difficulties. For in *institutional* terms Jesus was not much of a success. Although at times great crowds followed Jesus, at the end even his disciples left him. Accordingly Don Gilmore claims that Jesus was the world's greatest failure:

> He came to his own, and his own received him not. His family did not understand him; the religious authorities hated him; the political leadership was opposed to him; his friends deserted him; a disciple betrayed him; vocal supporters denied him; his

---

[12] Henri Nouwen, *In the Name of Jesus: Reflections on Christian Leadership* (Darton, Longman & Todd, London, 1989), pp. 29–30.

congregation spat on him – hurled stones at him; his enemies crucified him . . . He was a fantastic failure.[13]

Yet was Jesus 'a fantastic failure'? Gilmore has surely overstated his case. The cross was not some unfortunate accident. As the Gospels clearly indicate, long before his death Jesus saw himself as the Suffering Servant of the Lord and therefore accepted his death as part of God's plan and in accordance with Isaiah 52:13 – 53:12. For Jesus the cross was part of the divine strategy for establishing God's kingdom on earth. Indeed, Jesus himself said: 'And I, when I am lifted up from the earth, will draw all people to myself' (John 12: 32, which in turn echoes Is. 52:13). The very strength and size of the Church down through the centuries is an indication of Jesus' 'success'.

And yet it was precisely through a cross that God worked. The cross reminds us that ministry – even 'successful' ministry – is costly.

Jesus himself never mentioned the term 'success'. The nearest he came to the concept of success is in his use of the term 'harvest'. When Jesus spoke of the fields being 'ripe for harvesting' (John 4:35), he was speaking of a world rich in Gospel potential. This potential was also expressed in the parable of the sower (Mark 4). Yes, there was unreceptive soil, but there was receptive soil too, for the seed which fell into good soil 'brought forth grain, growing up and increasing and yielding thirty and sixty and a hundredfold' (Mark 4:8). This was indeed a bumper harvest. In today's terms, this was success.

Yet Jesus appears to have preferred to speak of faithfulness, rather than of success. On one occasion, for instance, he spoke of the faithful servant (Matt. 24:45–7; Luke 12:42–4); on another he picked up the theme of faithful stewards in a parable we know as the parable of the talents or of the pounds (Matt. 25:14–30; Luke 19:11–27). Elsewhere Luke records Jesus as having given a number of maxims on the theme of faithfulness (Luke 16:10–12).

Paul likewise spoke of faithfulness. In 1 Corinthians 4:1–2 we read: 'Think of us in this way, as servants of Christ and stewards

[13] G. Don Gilmore, *The Freedom to Fail* (Revell, Westwood, New Jersey, 1966), p. 21.

of God's mysteries. Moreover, it is required of stewards that they be found trustworthy.'

This emphasis on faithfulness turns our values upside down. For we are much more interested in success than in faithfulness. For example, I did a check on one major American seminary library and discovered that they had 217 books listed under success, but no book was listed under faithfulness!

What is faithfulness? According to the church growth pundit, Peter Wagner, who combines 1 Corinthians 4:2 with the parable of the talents in Matthew 25:14–30, a faithful steward is a fruitful steward: i.e. a faithful pastor is one who experiences church growth.[14]

But is it that simple? The fact, of course, is that Matthew 25:14–30 has nothing to do with church growth. Jesus was speaking about 'the need to "live up to our full potential" ... The opportunities open to a disciple may differ in character and magnitude, but they are to be faithfully exploited before the master returns.'[15] Yet even if the parable be interpreted within a church growth framework, the steward who failed to make a return on his master's investment is not described as unproductive, but as 'lazy'!

Peter Wagner's equation of faithfulness with fruitfulness was in fact somewhat crass. New Testament exegesis apart, church growth is a complex process, which is dependent not just upon the individual qualities of the people involved, but also upon all kinds of national and local factors.

Leith Anderson, who is also concerned for success in church life, is much more circumspect.[16] Numbers are important, but much more is needed to determine success or failure. On the other hand, the concept of 'faithfulness' is not always a helpful yardstick, because there are many churches which perpetuate extrabiblical traditions as faithfulness to God. He defines 'success' in ministry as 'reaching the right goal, using our resources according to a specified standard'.[17] Success in these terms is something to be sought and, by God's grace,

[14] Peter Wagner, *Your Church Can Grow* (Regal Books, Glendale, California, 1976), p. 37.
[15] R. T. France, *Matthew* (IVP, Leicester, 1985), p. 352.
[16] Leith Anderson, *A Church For The 21st Century*, pp. 81–99.
[17] Ibid., p. 89.

achieved. However, Leith Anderson does add this qualification: 'Success is as individually defined as eye-glasses are prescribed. It is fool-hardy, if not self-destructive, to use another's prescription.'[18]

This emphasis upon the individual nature of success is important. Churches are not to be measured against churches. Furthermore, as much as numbers are important, success cannot be measured on a purely external basis. Some years ago at the height of the Southern Baptist drive for numbers, the Southern Baptist strategist Ernest E. Mosley perceptively wrote:

> A minister can miss the mark in measuring success as easily as the rich fool about whom Jesus spoke missed the purpose of life. The danger is that the minister may measure up to success in terms of bigger membership, bigger budgets, bigger baptismal reports, bigger salaries, bigger houses, bigger denominational positions, and on and on, while the minister as the person becomes depleted and empty. Success can never be adequately measured without considering what the person is doing to the work and what the work is doing to the person. What does it profit a man to lead the whole association or state or convention in some statistical category and lose his own self, or wife, or children, or integrity?[19]

Mosley instead saw the fruits of the Spirit as the basic criteria for measuring successes in all areas of a minister's life and work:

> When love, joy, peace, patience, kindness, goodness, faithfulness, gentleness, and self-control are being expressed in any aspect of a minister's life, success is there. When any one of them is missing, success is limited.[20]

A sobering thought! Here, of course, we are back again at the idea of a journey, of a pilgrimage. There is far more to pastoral ministry than facts and figures, projections and statistics. Successful pastoral

---

[18] Ibid., p. 98.
[19] Ernest E. Mosley, *Priorities in Ministry* (Convention Press, Nashville, 1978), p. 129.
[20] Ibid., p. 129.

ministry also encompasses growth and development within the lives of individual people and within congregations, and also within the life of the pastor him(her)self!

A somewhat schizophrenic attitude to success is presented by Darius Salter, who wrote a book which initially seemed to equate pastoral success with flourishing churches.[21] From a survey of 100 men leading thriving churches with an average Sunday morning attendance of 1,650, he sought to profile 'successful pastors'. For example, 'Inducement is the honey that covers the dominant-steady person. Instead of repelling people he has an enticing attractive personality. He has a positive optimistic outlook on life, and when presented with a possibility, this pastor's first response is "Why not?".'[22] He discovered that such pastors 'weekly average 17 hours in sermon preparation and read 20 chapters in the Scriptures'.[23] 'Calling people by their first name is important. Compounded by a firm handshake, eyes that make direct contact with others, a warm inviting face, and a look of genuine concern are doubly important'![24]

However, in his final chapter he seeks to define success 'Biblically and Christologically', and immediately the book strikes a different note. For Salter rightly recognises that 'eschatology places the matters of this life within the perspective of quality rather than quantity'.[25] If the parable of the talents is a guide, then all we can say is that 'success is extremely relative: "to . . . each according to his ability" (Matt. 25:15)'. The fact is that 'any kind of objective, measurable, absolute standard is, at least in this life, both futile and false'.[26] Would that more such honesty were around! At the end of the day God, and God alone, will be the judge of our 'success'. And on that Day of Judgment we shall all be in for a number of surprises. For his values will be very different to our values. We only have

---

[21] Darius Salter, *What Really Matters In Ministry: Profiling Pastoral Success In Flourishing Churches* (Baker Book House, Grand Rapids, Michigan, 1990).
[22] Ibid., p. 26.
[23] Ibid., p. 51.
[24] Ibid., p. 70.
[25] Ibid., p. 165.
[26] Ibid., p. 165.

to look at the Risen Christ's evaluation of the seven churches in Asia Minor to see that. Jesus turns this world's values upside down: 'many who are first will be last, and the last will be first' (Matt. 19:30). This calls for humility, not least on the part of those who are pastors of larger churches. Ministry needs to be liberated from the 'success syndrome'.[27]

And yet, in the meantime, we have to live in the here and now, in a world where some pastors do appear to have successful ministries; and where many pastors do appear to fail. It is not easy living in a world where for some pastors everything they touch seems to turn to gold, whereas for others everything they touch seems to disintegrate. Even worse, perhaps, is experiencing a measure of success, and then experiencing that success turning to disaster. As many ministers know to their cost, pastoral ministry is not all sweetness and light. Church fights develop and forced termination – whether it be in the form of resignation or dismissal – is the result. How do we handle such failure – such apparently public failure – in the here and now?

In the first place, we handle 'failure' by going to the roots of our faith – by looking to Jesus rather than looking around at others. In spite of the advice of the unknown author of Hebrews to 'consider Jesus' (Heb. 3:1), to look 'to Jesus the pioneer and perfecter of our faith' (Heb. 12:2), when it comes to success in ministry it is all too easy to look to others and compare ourselves with them, rather than with him. When we look to others, the temptation is to believe that success is the norm; when we look to Jesus we realise that human approbation and acclamation are far from the norm. As pastors we often preach on the need for followers of Jesus to 'deny themselves, take up their cross and follow Jesus', but we do not always draw the consequence for ourselves and our ministry. The temptation is sometimes to think that by accepting a lower salary and working longer hours than we might otherwise receive and experience in a secular job, we are going the way of the cross, whereas in reality to go the way of the cross in any

27 See Kent & Barbara Hughes, *Liberating Ministry From The Success Syndrome* (Tyndale House, Wheaton, Illinois, 1987), who define success in terms of faithfulness, serving, loving, believing, prayer, holiness and attitude.

meaningful fashion is often to experience sacrifice, apparent failure and pain.[28]

Certainly the Apostle Paul knew what it was like to go the way of the cross. If our expectations of ministry were based on Paul's actual experience of ministry, 'failure' would not be a problem for us. He knew what it was like to be 'afflicted' and 'perplexed', 'persecuted' and 'struck down' (2 Cor. 4:8–9; see also 6:4–10).

In the light, therefore, of the experience of Jesus and Paul, Stephen Pattison goes on to comment: 'it would certainly put a question mark against the pastoral care of anyone who found that they never experienced the turmoil, anguish and failure which characterized the ministry of Jesus and the first Christians'.[29] And yet, we must be careful in attributing failure to Jesus and the first Christians. As we have already seen, in spite of the cross, the life of Jesus cannot be written off as a failure. Likewise, in spite of the sufferings of the first Christians, one can scarcely describe the Book of Acts as a record of failure of the Early Church! Although the first Christians suffered greatly, they were also greatly used. In no way can we therefore be justified in attributing 'failure' as a characteristic of apostolic ministry. Rather, the hallmark of the

---

[28] All this is well expressed in a devotional leaflet entitled *Brokenness*:

'Sometimes it is asked what we mean by Brokenness. Brokenness is not easy to define but can be clearly seen in the reactions of Jesus, especially as He approached the Cross and in His crucifixion. I think it can be applied personally in this way:

'When to do the will of God means that even my Christian Brethren will not understand, and I remember that "Neither did His brethren believe in Him" (John 7:5), and I bow my head to obey and accept the misunderstanding, this is Brokenness.

'When I am misrepresented or deliberately misinterpreted, and I remember that Jesus was falsely accused but He "held His peace" and I bow my head to accept the accusation without trying to justify myself, this is Brokenness . . .

'When my plans are brushed aside and I see the work of years brought to ruins by the ambitions of others and I remember that Jesus allowed them to lead "Him away to crucify Him" (Matt. 27:31) and He accepted that place of failure and I bow my head and accept the injustice without bitterness, this is Brokenness . . .'

[29] Stephen Pattison, *A Critique Of Pastoral Care* (SCM, London, 1986), p. 160.

ministry of both Jesus and of the Early Church is a readiness for willing sacrifice.[30]

In the second place, we handle 'failure' by trusting that in the providence of God good will come out of what at the time may appear to be unmitigated disaster (see Rom. 8:28). In the darkness and the pain it may be impossible to discern the hand of God at work. Indeed, much of the darkness and the pain may be anything but God at work – not all suffering is positive. And yet, the experience of God's people down through the ages is that where God has been trusted, good has emerged. They have been able to say along with Joseph: 'You intended to do harm to me. God intended it for good' (Gen. 50:20).

Certainly one of the benefits of apparent failure is often the deepening of the pastoral heart. It is precisely as a result of his failure, weakness, and grief that a wounded pastor is enabled to become a 'wounded healer'. Thus Henri Nouwen, who first used this image of the wounded healer, wrote: 'A deep understanding of his (i.e. minister's) pain makes it possible for him – with God's help – to convert his weakness into strength and to offer his own experience as a source of healing to those who are often lost in the darkness of their own misunderstood sufferings.'[31] Stephen Pattison comments:

> The hard, yet joyful lesson to be learnt is that good, and indeed successful, Christian ministry which follows in the steps of its founder is born not from skill, power and knowledge, but from the experience of inadequacy, rejection and sorrow transformed by the love of God and then offered to others.[32]

[30] Morgan Derham in a private communication helpfully wrote: 'The older "Keswick" spirituality made much of "dying to self"; Gal. 2:20 was its "text", just as 1 John 1:7 was the "text" of the Rwanda revival. Nowadays in the post-Frank Lake era, it is fashionable to talk of "self-worth", "self-affirmation", assertiveness training etc. But I suspect we have lost something. "Dying to self" can be overdone and produce masochistic Christianity. But unless some such major shift has taken place in our overall awareness of ourselves and God, we are not safe to be trusted with anything, particularly success. *Vide* Swaggart and Co!'

[31] Henri Nouwen, *The Wounded Healer: Ministry In Contemporary Society* (Doubleday, New York, 1972), p. 89. See also T. S. Eliot: 'The wounded surgeon plies the steel'.

[32] Pattison, *A Critique Of Pastoral Care*, p. 152.

In a very real sense, resurrection can only come out of death. Success may be born of failure. We are the better equipped for pastoral ministry precisely because we have experienced the dark side of pastoral ministry.

Another benefit of 'failure' may surely be an increased sense of dependency upon God. When all goes well, it is easy to succumb to the temptation of depending upon oneself and upon one's own natural gifts and abilities. But when disaster strikes, there is only one we can lean upon, and that is God. Certainly this was true of Paul: reflecting on one of his 'crushing' experiences, he wrote, 'We felt that we had received the sentence of death so that we would rely not on ourselves but on God who raises the dead' (2 Cor. 1:9). As he discovered on another occasion, it is precisely in weakness that God's strength can be revealed (2 Cor. 12:9–10). Indeed, our powerlessness and our humility seem to be a precondition for the life of Jesus being made visible in our lives (see 2 Cor. 4:7–12). It is sometimes only through failure that we learn the secret of successful ministry. As Oswald Sanders has written:

> All through history God has chosen and used nobodies, because their unusual dependence on him made possible the unique display of his power and grace. He chose and used somebodies only when they had renounced dependence on their natural abilities and resources.[33]

With God's help, what may appear to others to be failure can prove to be a tremendously liberating and growing experience.[34] However difficult the actual circumstances may have been, out of the crucible of pain and suffering a faith has been refined as never before. Christian leaders are the better equipped to serve God precisely because they have been through the fire. There is a depth and a maturity, a humility and a faithfulness, which otherwise might never be there. Failure in a very real sense can

---

[33] Oswald Sanders, *Spiritual Leadership* (Moody Press, Chicago, 1967), p. 141.
[34] On the other hand, there is nothing inevitable about failure issuing into a greater degree of wholeness and maturity. See Russ Parker, *Free To Fail* (Triangle/SPCK, London, 1992), pp. 102–8.

be an asset to the pastor in his or her journey as an exemplary pilgrim.

Yet failure is the last thing we wish to experience. As pastors we long to see 'a demonstration of the Spirit and of power' (1 Cor. 2:4) in our ministries, and so in our enthusiastic idealism we pray, 'Come, Holy Spirit, come.' We believe that when the Holy Spirit comes, he will bless our ministry with success, with all kinds of positive signs and wonders, whereas in fact the wind of God's Spirit may blow apart the structures we have so carefully built, bringing apparent failure rather than success. In this regard William Temple's comments on John 16:8–11 repay consideration:

> When we pray 'Come Holy Ghost, our souls inspire', we had better know what we are about. He will not carry us to easy triumphs and gratifying successes; more probably He will set us to some task for God in the full intention that we shall fail, so that others, learning wisdom by our failure, may carry the good cause forward. He may take us through loneliness, desertion by friends, apparent desertion even by God; that was the way Christ went to the Father ... For if we invoke Him, it must be to help us in doing God's will, not ours ... If we invoke Him, we must be ready for the glorious pain of being caught by His power out of our petty orbit into the eternal purposes of the Almighty, in whose onward seep our lives are as a speck of dust. The soul that is filled with the Spirit must have become purged of all pride or love of ease, all self-complacence and self-reliance; but that soul has found the only real dignity, the only lasting joy. Come then, Great Spirit, come. Convict the world; and convict my timid soul.[35]

On the other hand, we dare not attribute all failure to the Spirit! Failure may well be – altogether or in part – our own fault. Here perhaps is the need for a wise counsellor to enable us to face up to the ups and downs of ministry, and learn whatever may be the appropriate lessons.

[35] William Temple, *Readings In St John's Gospel*, Second Series (Macmillan, London, 1940), pp. 288–9.

Dealing with temptation

Ministers are human like everybody else. Ordination gives them no special immunity from the tempter's power. Indeed, the reverse is the case. They become all the more a target for the evil one. Their very position within the local church causes them to become the focus of the devil's attentions. For if a pastor falls from grace, the life of the church as a whole can be affected detrimentally.

Ministers need to take heed to the warnings of Richard Baxter of Kidderminster:

> The Enemy hath a special eye upon you. You shall have his most subtle insinuations and incessant solicitations and violent assaults. As wise and learned as you are, take heed to yourselves lest he overwit you. The Devil is a greater scholar than you are and a nimbler disputant. He can transform himself into an angel of light to deceive you. He will get within you and trip you up by the heels before you are aware. He will play the juggler with you undiscerned, and cheat you of your faith and innocence, and you shall not know that you have lost them. He will make you the very instruments of your own ruin.[36]

Are there particular temptations and sins peculiar to the Christian ministry? According to David Christie the temptations of ministers are three in particular: 'to recline, to shine and to whine'![37] For our purposes we shall look at the temptations and sins of ministry within the framework of the traditional seven deadly sins.[38]

Pride

Pride is probably *the* occupational hazard of ministry. While few ministers are likely to be tempted by all seven of the deadly sins, few are not tempted by the sin of pride. 'By way of quick and easy proof', challenges Andrew Blackwood, 'let any reader make a list

---

[36] Richard Baxter, *The Reformed Pastor*, pp. 74–5.
[37] David Christie, *The Service Of Christ* (Hodder & Stoughton, London, 1933), pp. 66–94.
[38] This list of the seven 'deadly' or 'cardinal' sins appears to go back to Pope Gregory the Great (AD 540–604). They are deadly in the sense that they lead to spiritual death.

of able ministers whom he knows to excel in humility. Then let him ask a group of honest friends if he can qualify.'[39]

Ministers, in a way which does not always seem to be true of others, seem to be obsessed with their ego. Often insecure in themselves, they tend to identify themselves with 'their' churches, and are easily threatened. They need to ponder afresh on the words of Jesus: 'Those who try to make their life secure will lose it, but those who lose their life will keep it' (Luke 17:33).

Michael Ramsey gives a wonderful description of the minister's frail ego:

If you do well, you can be pleased with yourself, and humility is in peril. If you do badly, you may worry about yourself, and humility is in peril. If people are nice to you and tell you what a good clergyman you are, humility is in peril. If people are nasty to you, you have a grievance and humility is in peril.[40]

As followers of the Servant King, we know there is no room for pride. For he who washed his disciples' feet said, 'I have set you an example, that you also should do as I have done to you' (John 13:15). And yet we so easily deceive ourselves. Like the Pharisees of old, we so often fool ourselves into believing that we are serving God and others, when in fact we are only serving self.

Sometimes the only way in which God can deal with our pride is to crush our spirits and in that way bring us to our senses. It is sometimes only through pain of grief and disappointment that God brings about the new creation, where fevered ambition and pushy pride are no more. Phoenix-like true humility can emerge out of the flames of crisis.

Envy
A close second to pride, envy is certainly a cardinal ministerial sin, along with its bed-fellows of rivalry, jealousy, ill will and what

[39] Blackwood, *The Growing Minister*, p. 104.
[40] Michael Ramsey, *The Christian Priest Today* (revised edition, SPCK, London, 1985), p. 78.

G. W. Byrt once called 'the-spirit-that-delights-in-the-downfall-of-others'.[41] Ministers seem to delight in making comparisons with other ministers. They delight in listening to gossip about other ministers and then passing it on. It is sad how ministers, who for the most part are good at keeping confidences entrusted to them by their flock, lack all discipline in keeping confidences about fellow ministers. Such gossip is for the most part ill-natured. It is part of the 'cutting-down-the-tall-poppies' syndrome. It is rooted in envy and jealousy.

A wonderful illustration of ministerial envy is found in the following story:

> The devil was once crossing the Libyan desert, and he came upon a spot where a number of small fiends were tormenting a holy hermit. The sainted man easily shook off their evil suggestions. The devil watched their failure, and then he stepped forward to give them a lesson. 'What you do is too crude', he said. 'Permit me for one moment'. With that he whispered to the holy man, 'Your brother has just been made Bishop of Alexandria'. A scowl of malignant jealousy at once clouded the serene face of the hermit. 'That', said the devil to his imps, 'is the sort of thing which I should recommend.'[42]

Jesus himself shows the way to dealing with envy. For when Peter said to him, 'Lord, what about him?' Jesus declared: 'If it is my will that he remain until I come, what is that to you? Follow me!' (John 21:21–2). Our business is to follow Jesus, and not to be concerned with anybody else. Jesus has a pattern and purpose for our lives, as indeed for our churches: there is therefore no point in casting envious eyes at other people and other churches; our concern is to follow Jesus, and him alone.

Covetousness

Improbable as it may sound, some years ago a pastor went to a small church in the South-West of the USA and made an agreement with

[41] G. W. Byrt, 'The Temptations of Ministry (1)', *Fraternal* 168 (Sept. 1973), p. 38.
[42] Gordon MacDonald, *Restoring Your Spiritual Passion* (UK edition: Highland Books, Crowborough, 1987), pp. 98–9.

the deacons at the start for 10% of the gross income. At the time I read the story the church had by then a Sunday congregation of more than 5,000. The pastor took home about $800,000 in the previous year. He was driving a Rolls-Royce Silver Cloud, wore a diamond the size of a pea and was living in a quarter-million-dollar home![43]

No British minister would ever covet such a lifestyle – it is beyond our wildest dreams. And yet this does not mean that covetousness is not around. In a situation where ministerial stipends are relatively low, it is not difficult for ministers to covet their neighbour's – deacon's? – house, car and bank account. At any ministerial gathering the conversation will get back to pay. Andrew Blackwood mentions a figure of at least 50% of ministers being dissatisfied with their lot, and usually because of a desire for more money.[44]

In times past the monks dealt with the sin of covetousness by taking a vow of poverty. Not that such a route is viable for those of us who are married with children! Richard Foster more helpfully writes of the desirability for Christians – and by extension, ministers – to adopt the vow of 'simplicity' so that we might be free of covetousness and no longer 'pant after the possessions of others'.[45]

Lust

Andrew Blackwood listed lust as one of the 'less common' ministerial sins. However, according to the North American magazine *Leadership*, many pastors struggle with this temptation.[46] Of the 300 pastors who responded to their confidential survey, 23% said that since they had been in local church ministry they had done something with someone (not their spouse) that they felt was sexually inappropriate. A further 12% acknowledged that they had had sexual intercourse with someone other than their spouse, and 18% admitted that they had participated in other forms of sexual contact with someone other than their spouse: e.g. passionate

[43] *Leadership* II (Fall 1982), p. 126.
[44] Andrew Blackwood, *The Growing Minister*, p. 108.
[45] Foster, *Money, Sex and Power*, p. 72.
[46] *Leadership* IX (Winter 1988), p. 12.

kissing, fondling, mutual masturbation. Of this total only 4% said they were found out.

There is, of course, nothing new in sexual immorality. One only has to think of the sexual misconduct of some of the medieval popes. On the other hand, these figures from *Leadership* are highly disturbing.

But are ministers particularly prone to sexual temptation? Of those responding to the *Leadership* survey, 70% expressed the belief that pastors are particularly vulnerable. Richard Exley has pointed out that for ministers sexual temptation is often rooted not in vice, but in virtue: 'What began as legitimate ministry – a shared project perhaps, compassionate listening, the giving of comfort – becomes an emotional bonding, which ultimately leads to an illicit affair.'[47]

One obvious way of dealing with this particular temptation is for ministers to establish clear guidelines in terms of their relationship with the opposite sex: e.g. establishing a set number of times one would see a person of the opposite sex before referring them on; ensuring that one always counselled a member of the opposite sex on church premises, at a time when other people were around.

Equally important as such guidelines is to ensure, in the case of a married minister, that one maintains a healthy relationship with one's spouse!

Anger

Anger is not necessarily wrong. Righteous anger, directed against some form of evil, may well be Christian love in operation. There is a rightful place for feeling angry, as Jesus in the Cleansing of the Temple clearly showed. But all too often our anger is unrighteous and egocentric, and has more to do with bruised self-esteem or a failure to get our own way.

But is anger an occupational hazard for ministers? Henri Nouwen perceptively points out that anger is very much

> a professional vice in the contemporary ministry. Pastors are angry at their leaders for not leading and at their followers for not following. They are angry at those who do not come to

---

[47] Richard Exley, *Perils of Power* (Honor/Harrison House, Tulsa, Oklahoma, no date), p. 11.

church, and angry at those who do come for coming without enthusiasm. They are angry at their families, who make them feel guilty, and angry at themselves for not being who they want to be. This is not an open, blatant, roaring anger, but an anger hidden behind the smooth word, the smiling face, and the polite handshake. It is a frozen anger, anger which settles into a biting resentment and slowly paralyzes a generous heart.[48]

The Psalmist urges us to 'ponder' our anger (Ps. 4:4). Why have we reacted in this way? What has been upset? Our own self-esteem? Our personal preferences? Has something unconsciously hooked into our past and gained a power which it ought never to have had? The first step in dealing with anger is recognising it for what it is. A second step then might be finding a 'safe' place with, for instance, a supervisor or counsellor, where the roots of the unresolved anger might be explored – for only as past anger is dealt with is true freedom gained.

Gluttony

As one who enjoys good food and who has constantly to fight the 'battle of the bulge', it gives me no joy to write about this particular deadly sin! Proverbs 23:2 with its advice to 'put a knife to your throat if you have a big appetite', is not exactly helpful. On the other hand, ballooning out to twice one's normal body weight is inexcusable, unless of course there are particular medical grounds.

Ministers are people constantly on show. Theorists claim that only 15% of what we communicate is verbal; the rest – 85% – comes through non-verbally. If our bodies communicate an eating disorder, what kind of witness is that to the Gospel?

On the whole I agree with Andrew Blackwood in listing this as one of the less common ministerial sins.[49] At least, I see no evidence to indicate that ministers are more obese than other members of their congregation. On the other hand, obesity is an occupational hazard of pastoral ministry. In the first place, ministry is for the

48 Nouwen, *Leadership* XIII (Summer 1982), p. 37.
49 Blackwood, *The Growing Minister*, p. 112.

most part a sedentary occupation – the only exercise some ministers get is sweating it out in the pulpit! Secondly, pastoral visiting almost inevitably entails kind people offering not only coffees and teas, but cakes and biscuits too. Thirdly, many church activities seem to centre around the act of eating. It takes discipline to survive such temptations!

Yet sometimes discipline is not the answer. For obesity is not always the product of gluttony. The temptation to over-eat can, for instance, be particularly strong when people feel unloved and uncared-for. As studies of anorexia show, 'food is love'. Over-eating may in fact be a means to find false comfort. Where this is the case, there is, of course, the need to find a proper sense of self-worth.

Sloth

To what extent ministers suffer from sloth is debatable. There are some lazy ministers – there are even more ill-disciplined ministers. But, as we have already seen, many ministers suffer from the very opposite of sloth, viz. activism. Activism, writes Richard Neuhaus, is a form of 'decadence': 'Decadence is the decay that hollows out the forms of life, leaving them devoid of meaning and even more fatally, flaunting such hollowness as virtue.'[50] Yet although opposites, both sloth and activism are related sins: for both are an escape from the pursuit of our God-given priorities. The answer to both sloth and activism is found in a meaningful spiritual walk with the Lord.

There are no easy answers to dealing with temptation. One thing is certain: before we begin to 'watch over all the flock' we must in the first instance watch over ourselves (Acts 20:28). Excellence, as Paul told the Philippians, is not least found in the way we live (Phil. 4:8–9).

Finding strength to forgive

If there is one aspect of the way of the pilgrim where the pastor is called to set an example, it is surely in the area of forgiveness. If a pastor can be seen to have the strength to forgive even the

---

[50] Neuhaus, *Freedom For Ministry*, p. 225.

apparently unforgivable, then others too in different areas of life will find the strength to forgive.

Forgiveness is a mark of a disciple of Jesus Christ. Jesus taught his disciples to pray: 'Forgive us our debts, as we also have forgiven our debtors' (Matt. 6:12). Augustine called this 'the terrible petition', terrible because of the condition attached – 'as we'. This is indeed the only petition with a condition: 'God forgives only the forgiving.'

This same need to forgive comes to expression on a number of occasions in the Gospels. 'Whenever you stand praying, forgive, if you have anything against anyone; so that your Father in heaven may also forgive you your trespasses' (Mark 11:25). Jesus also taught that the forgiveness of others was to be unlimited: even 'seventy times seven' (Matt. 18:22; see also Luke 17:3–4).

The teaching of Jesus is clear. Unfortunately the putting into practice of the teaching of Jesus is sometimes not so easy. In this particular section I have in mind not the general need to forgive when things go wrong in relationships, but rather the need to forgive even when everything cries out in us against the injustice of the situation. I refer here to the situation which many ministers may come across at some time in their lives, viz. the experience of enforced termination of ministry.

Let me quote again some statistics quoted at an earlier stage in this book:

> Within the first ten years of parish ministry roughly half will either be fired by their congregations or forced to move. Another fifteen percent will be forced out of their parishes during the last ten years of ministry.[51]

In other words, the majority of pastors in North America will at one time or another find themselves forced to move from a church. In Britain the figures are undoubtedly lower – not least because of the traditional freehold system in the Anglican Church. But in the Free Churches we seem to be moving the North American way.

Enforced termination is a shattering experience. Not only does the minister experience deep hurt and pain, but also his spouse and

[51] Roy Oswald in his Foreword to Gary Harbaugh's *Caring For The Caregiver*.

family.[52] In comparison with the trauma they are called to endure, the anger, grief, embarrassment or fear suffered by the church is negligible.

The reasons for enforced termination are many and various. Clearly churches are right to 'fire' their ministers when they are guilty of such matters as sexual immorality or financial transgression. However, often the issues are much more subjective and relate to things called 'incompetence' or 'ineffectiveness'. Speed Leas did a study of involuntary terminations of ministers within three American denominations: Episcopal, United Churches of Christ, and some Presbyterian churches and discovered that '40% of the Episcopal churches, 34% of the United Churches of Christ, and 45% of the Presbyterian churches had existing conflict or problems in the congregation before the terminated pastor started his or her job'.[53] In other words, in such situations the ministers concerned were the innocent 'lightning rods' who quite unjustly bore the brunt of their church's long-standing factionalism.

Not surprisingly, in situations where an injustice has been done – or has been perceived to be done – many ministers experience deep feelings of anger. The injunction of Jesus to 'forgive' is then far from easy – particularly where the offending party refuses to acknowledge that they have been at all in the wrong.

Many maintain that forgiveness is not only not easy, but actually impossible where the offending party refuses to face up to the wrong they have done. David Augsburger, for instance, writes:

Forgiveness includes, requires, follows repentance.

Forgiveness recognizes what has really happened, owns the hurt incurred, responds to the other person with integrity and affirms new behaviour for the future with genuine intentions.

Repentance is the central task of forgiving and being forgiven. Where there is no true repentance, there is no forgiveness.[54]

---

[52] See Myra Marshall with Dan McGee & Jennifer B. Owen, *Beyond Termination* (Broadman Press, Nashville, 1990).
[53] Speed Leas, *A Study Of Involuntary Terminations In Some Presbyterian, Episcopal, and United Church of Christ Congregations* (The Alban Institute, Bethesda, 1980), p. 11.
[54] David Augsburger, *Caring Enough To Forgive* (Herald Press, Scottdale, Pennsylvania, 1981), p. 66.

However, a failure on the part of the offending party to see their need for forgiveness does not lessen the need to forgive. It makes it much more difficult, but does not make it impossible. One can indeed have the willingness to forgive or the spirit of forgiveness regardless of the attitude of others. This willingness to forgive has sometimes been described as 'forgivingness' as over against forgiveness. Forgivingness, where it meets with repentance, brings about forgiveness; but forgivingness itself is not dependent on repentance.

The theologian Paul Fiddes, reflecting on the death of Christ, writes:

> Forgiveness must be completed in the repentance of the offender; the offer is unconditional, but the offer is itself a form of judgement awakening the wrongdoer to his offence. Forgiveness aims at reconciliation, and that requires the offender to come back into the relationship in sorrow and penitence.[55]

But to return to our scenario of enforced termination. Forgiveness in this situation is hard and, initially at least, may even feel impossible. However, some pastors, as they seek to be exemplary pilgrims, deny the range of negative emotions which such perceived injustice inevitably arouses.[56] Yet such denial actually makes true forgiveness impossible. For true forgiveness involves surfacing rather than suppressing all that has been wrong – and then by God's grace letting go of the anger and resentment. Such a letting go is far from easy, especially in situations where the other people involved refuse to acknowledge any responsibility for their part in the tragedy. This refusal not only adds to the pain, it also prolongs the resolution of it. Yet pastors must forgive. For as exemplary

---

55 Paul Fiddes, *The Christian Idea Of Atonement* (Darton, Longman & Todd, London, 1989), p. 185.
56 According to Paul Tournier, *A Place For You* (Highland Books, Crowborough, East Sussex, 2nd edition, 1984), p. 122, true forgiveness is rare: 'It is particularly so, perhaps, among religious people who wish to witness to their faith by their conduct. A committed Christian finds it more difficult than an unbeliever to express resentment and dislike . . . Then he makes an effort to forgive, and the need for an effort is the sign that he has not truly forgiven.'

pilgrims, they are called to go the way of Christ, even the way of him who cried out, 'Father, forgive them, for they do not know what they are doing' (Luke 23:34).

In such circumstances forgiveness takes time and tends to be a process. This process begins with a desire to forgive – but at least the desire to forgive is indicative of being on the right path. Forgiveness itself comes to completion only as a gift from God. It is, as Paul Tournier has rightfully observed, 'a grace, and not the result of an effort. It is a liberation, not a burden.'[57] This gift, however, is only received as people let go of their bitterness and allow room in their hearts for God to work.

Going the way of Christ is not easy. For any 'victim', the process of forgiveness is painful and costly, just as it was for Christ. Feelings of anger and pain must be 'released' before true forgiveness can ever be offered. But where such feelings of anger and pain are truly 'liberated', there the victim is liberated to live again.[58] Strange as it may seem, the victim may eventually prove freer than the oppressor, because the oppressor is still caught up in a web of deceit and denial. The victim is free to grow and develop and go the way of Christ; the oppressor remains stuck on the journey, and instead of growing becomes twisted and stunted. Paradoxically, it is then the oppressor rather than the victim who succumbs to the troubling 'root of bitterness' (Heb. 12:15).

All this is seen and observed by those who are without, so that even in a situation of pain and hurt, God is able through the example of the pilgrim-pastor to encourage others to find the strength to forgive too.

Growing into maturity

Pastors as exemplary pilgrims are on a constant journey. They have never arrived. They are always in the process of becoming. Not only as professionals are they developing, but also as sons and daughters

---

[57] Paul Tournier, *A Place For You*, p. 122.
[58] Dewey Bertolini, *Secret Wounds And Silent Cries* (Victor/Scripture Press, Wheaton, Illinois, 1993), p. 42, draws attention to Richard Nixon's remark: 'Always remember, others may hate you, but those who hate you don't win unless you hate them – and then you destroy yourself.'

of God they are hopefully growing in the faith. With the apostle Paul of old, they 'press on towards the goal for the prize of the heavenly call of God in Christ Jesus' (Phil. 3:14).

However, some models of ministerial development lead one to feeling not a little depressed. This sense of movement, this dynamic of pilgrimage, is not always present.

For example, the secular model of professional development described by Donald Super[59] and adopted by Charles Stewart as a model for 'career development in ministry',[60] divides the period of active ministry into three career stages:

1. Career Establishment (26–45)
2. Maintenance (45–60)
3. Decline (60-retirement).

With regard to stage three, Super says the mid-careerist 'feels no need to break new ground, either because the ground he is already cultivating gives him an adequate living and is such as to keep him fully occupied, or because he has not succeeded in a quarter century of effort to find or break good ground and has no hope of succeeding in renewed efforts'.[61] To which Stewart adds, 'the period of forty-five through sixty reveals either fruition or frustration',[62] as if there is an element of inevitability in life after the age of 45.

A little less depressing is the Southern Baptist *Minister's Personal Management Manual*, where the adult period of an individual's developmental process is divided into four stages:

1. Start-Up Stage (from about 15–25).
2. Stabilization Stage (from about 25–40).
3. Summit Stage (from about 40–55).
4. Sunset Stage (from about 55–).

Nonetheless, the fourth stage is perceived as having little 'career dynamic', and seems to be devoted to gaining 'meaning and

---

59 Donald Super, *Psychology Of Careers* (Harper & Brothers, New York, 1957).
60 Charles Stewart, *Person And Profession: Career Development In The Ministry* (Abingdon, Nashville, 1974).
61 Super, *Psychology Of Careers*, p. 148.
62 Charles Stewart, *Person And Profession*, p. 29.

mellowing'.[63] There is no real sense of development. Rather, the older minister is perceived as very much 'going over the hill'. This may be true physically, but certainly need not be true in other respects.

Far more encouraging is the scheme put forward by Andrew Blackwood in his aptly entitled book, *The Growing Minister*, who divides the period of active ministry into three stages:[64]

1. Years full of promise (25–40).
2. A period of transition (40–55).
3. A time of fruition (55–70).

It is true that Blackwood is cautious about the second stage. For although 'a man normally expects to keep maturing throughout middle age', he notes that 'in the ministry the reverse is often true . . . More ministers seem to make shipwreck, or get stranded, during middle age than at any other period. Much as we talk and think about the perils of a young clergyman, we ought to feel more concern about "the destruction that wasteth at noonday".'[65] Blackwood here refers to the 'double D.D.' of 'Disillusion and Discouragement, Despondency and Despair'.

However, according to Blackwood, even for the minister who goes through the mid-ministry crisis, there is hope: 'by the grace of God a minister past fifty can right himself and then keep going on to the most fruitful and blessed portion of his entire career'.[66]

Not surprisingly, this then leads him on to say that 'the closing years of a full-time ministry ought to be the most fruitful of all, and the most joyous'.[67] Indeed, he heads this section with the well-known lines from Browning's 'Rabbi Ben Ezra':

> *Grow old along with me!*
> *The best is yet to be,*

[63] Truman Brown (ed.), *Minister's Personal Management Manual* (Convention Press, Nashville, 1988), p. 58.
[64] Andrew W. Blackwood, *The Growing Minister: His Opportunities And Obstacles* (Abingdon, Nashville, 1960), pp. 152–66. See also Ray Ragsdale, *The Midlife Crises Of A Ministry*, p. 99, who speaks of the 'futile 50s'.
[65] Blackwood, *The Growing Minister*, p. 156.
[66] Ibid., p. 157.
[67] Ibid., p. 159.

> *The last of life, for which the first was made!*
> *Our times are in His hand*
> *Who saith, 'A whole I planned,*
> *Youth shows but half; trust God, see all,*
> *nor be afraid!'*

Is this just wishful thinking? I believe not. There is no reason why professionally, emotionally and spiritually ministers should not continue to grow and develop. What is more, such growth and development do not need to end with retirement.[68] Yet such development does not just happen by chance. It happens only as ministers give themselves to the pursuit of excellence throughout their ministry.

The Christian ministry is more than simply a career.[69] If it were merely a career, then ministers should regard churches as stepping-stones to success. Sadly, that is how some regard them: for some benighted ministers, ministry is the pursuit of the bigger and better church.[70] But if ultimately life is about a journey to God, then the size of the church one serves is – in the light of eternity, at least – irrelevant.

Church growth research has revealed the desirability of pastoral longevity: a church is more likely to experience numerical growth if its ministers stay awhile rather than hopping from call to call.[71] But ministers too benefit from pastoral longevity: for within the context of settled ministry, if a church is to grow and develop, the minister too must continue to grow and develop. Eugene Peterson is right

---

[68] Given basic good health, there is much to be said for pastors deliberately planning for a new stage in their Christian ministry.

[69] By 'career' I mean what the *Oxford English Dictionary* defines as 'a course of professional life of employment which affords opportunity for progress or advance in the world'.

[70] Michael Taylor, 'A Career In The Ministry', *Fraternal* 214 (April 1986), pp. 16–17, argued that a career structure for ministers should be created, but not involving the movement from smaller to larger churches, but rather 'from lesser to greater responsibilities . . . Most of us are far from perfect. We need a carrot or two in the form of prospects. We want opportunities to realise more of our potential. We look for the refreshment of new tasks instead of for too long trying to keep our approach to old tasks fresh.'

[71] See Paul Beasley-Murray & Alan Wilkinson, *Turning The Tide* (Bible Society, London, 1980), p. 34.

when he asserts that 'the *norm* for pastoral work is stability ... Far too many pastors change parishes out of adolescent boredom, not as a consequence of mature wisdom.'[72]

Whether or not he is right in urging that '20-30-40-year long pastorates should be typical among us' is perhaps more debatable! It certainly is a challenge for a minister to keep on developing and growing within one particular sphere of service over so many years.

To return to our theme. Pastors – like their people – are pilgrims on a journey. The settled life is therefore not for them. In terms of their own personal development and also of the development of their churches, one of the challenges of pastoral ministry is to find new and creative ways of continuing with that journey. It is here that pastors who pursue excellence can set an example.

[72] Eugene Peterson, *Under the Unpredictable Plant*, p. 29.

Conclusion

A Call to Excellence has addressed many issues pertaining to Christian ministry. Success and failure are concepts familiar to every church leader, and there is a tendency in society today to idolise the former and denigrate the latter. We do both to our detriment. It might even be felt by some that *A Call to Excellence* is aiming at 'success' in ministry. As I sought to set out in the Introduction, this was not my intention, but rather my hope is that the resources within this book will improve the quality of ministry and the quality of life for the Christian leader.

I am reminded again and again through my own experience, and also through the experience of others who have shared their stories with me, that 'survival' is a big word in ministry.[1] Surviving as prophets communicating the living Word; surviving as change-agents in a Church wedded to the past; surviving in situations where personal integrity is threatened; surviving against family pressures to opt for a more comfortable and less time-pressurised lifestyle; surviving as a Church in areas where little seems to be happening and numbers are dwindling. The possibilities are endless. Constantly there seems to be the pressure of the downward pull for those who are trying to live out their upward calling. However, *A Call to Excellence* is concerned for more than mere survival: rather, in attempting to address the issues that Christian ministry raises, it seeks to enable Christian leaders to thrive in their practice of ministry.

[1] 'Survival' in terms of 'endurance' is also a significant concept in the New Testament: see, for instance, Matt. 10:22; 24:13; Mark 13:13; 2 Tim. 2:10; Heb. 10:32; 12:3, 7; Jas. 5:11.

My mind goes to Jesus, who described his own ministry in terms of 'food' (John 4:32, 34). In other words, ministry was for him a satisfying, nourishing experience. Jesus was sure of his calling, confident of his self-worth in God's sight, and equipped through prayer and through his on-going relationship with God for every demand which ministry made upon him. It is my prayer that *A Call to Excellence* will have contributed to that goal.